INCOME MAINTENANCE
AND WORK INCENTIVES

INCOME MAINTENANCE AND WORK INCENTIVES

Toward a Synthesis

Martha N. Ozawa

PRAEGER SPECIAL STUDIES IN
SOCIAL WELFARE

GENERAL EDITORS

*Neil Gilbert and
Harry Specht*

PRAEGER

PRAEGER SPECIAL STUDIES • PRAEGER SCIENTIFIC

Library of Congress Cataloging in Publication Data

Ozawa, Martha N.
  Income maintenance and work incentives.

  (Praeger special studies in social welfare)
  Bibliography: p.
  Includes index.
  1. Income maintenance programs—United States.
2. Income distribution—United States. I. Title.
II. Series.
HC110.15097   362.5′82   82-434
ISBN 0-03-058647-X   AACR2

Published in 1982 by Praeger Publishers
CBS Educational and Professional Publishing
A Division of CBS, Inc.
521 Fifth Avenue, New York, New York 10175 U.S.A.

23456789   145   987654321

Printed in the United States of America

To my mother

PREFACE

In spite of the United States' increasing commitment to public income transfers, legislators, academics, and even recipients of income maintenance programs feel that the nation is losing its grip on what it is trying to do through income maintenance programs. Over the years many new income maintenance programs have been developed, and each one of them has expanded enormously. Government officials and experts in the field have attempted to improve and streamline the administration of programs. But in spite of this development—or maybe because of it—all parties concerned are somewhat puzzled and do not seem to know what to make of all these programs. Why is this happening? Why do they feel frustrated with income maintenance programs in America and wonder whether their efforts have too often been futile?

The author believes that one of the reasons for this frustration is that there has been no coherent vision or goals in developing and then tinkering with income maintenance programs. Policymakers and administrators are usually involved in one specific program. They do not normally pay attention to what is happening to the rest of the income maintenance system. Nor do they pay much attention to the question of how income maintenance programs fit into the larger context of the American economy and culture. The emphasis, rather, has been to provide income support through a particular program to the bottom layer of society, with the least cost to the taxpayer. The result has been that the government has created a number of uncoordinated welfare programs for the poor. Indeed, certain categories of poor families receive income support from several programs and find themselves above the poverty line. But, ironically, income maintenance programs, as they are administered, are making it extremely difficult for such families to improve their financial situation, through work, beyond what they receive from income maintenance programs.

Without anyone noticing what has happened, the society has ended up by creating dual norms: one applicable to income maintenance recipients and the other to the rest of the population. For the majority of American families, the traditional value of privately pursuing a way of life through work still is germane. But for the growing number of families who receive income support, society has created another set of expectations that pertain to the poor. The poor are told to apply for and receive income support from various programs if they want to improve their economic condition, but find that they cannot improve their living standards beyond that through privately pursuing a way of life that involves working.

In a basically unplanned society like that of the United States, people cannot be forced to behave in certain ways without causing strain. Nevertheless, despite the noncoercive nature of society—or perhaps because of it—the country needs a single unified, coherent incentive system so that the voluntary behavior of the citizen is in a direction that is conducive to societal survival and progress. Through its income maintenance programs society seems to prescribe one set of norms to one segment of society and another to another segment.

The effects of dual norms are expected to be adverse. Dual norms not only damage the opportunities for poor families to save and thus improve their living standards but they also erode the system of beliefs that the majority of American families hold dear to their hearts. Mutual understanding as to the way of life that people are supposed to pursue and even as to how they should contribute to social progress is becoming unclear. When society is in doubt about the basic tenets that bind the people together, the collective energy is dissipated, and, as a result, the nation cannot go forward with the full force of the collective energy. This author believes that this problem has been created in part because of the way income maintenance programs have been developed.

This book is an attempt to come to grips with a challenging question: How can this nation develop a system of income maintenance that is based on a coherent incentive system so as to preserve the work incentive and yet at the same time allow the nation to care and provide adequately for vulnerable groups of individuals—that is, children, the elderly, and the disabled? If the nation is successful in implementing such a policy thrust, the author believes, it can indeed ensure an adequate minimum floor of income to all families and yet preserve the incentive to work.

In envisioning future directions that this nation might take, one benefits greatly from past experience in the development of social policy in income maintenance. Only by knowing about the historical roots of the philosophy of current programs and knowing about attempts at welfare reform in recent years, can one conceptualize a system of income maintenance for the future.

Thus this book starts with the discussion of the ideological roots of income maintenance programs in the United States. Chapter 1 traces the origin and history of the two ideologies—classic liberalism and new liberalism—and indicates how they have influenced social policy in the development of income maintenance programs. Chapter 2 identifies and describes major income maintenance programs that are relevant to the purpose of this book. It draws a distinction between social insurance and welfare (or income-tested) programs. It also examines the public expenditures for these programs.

Analysis of policy in income maintenance is difficult without clarifying the indicators, or measurements, of poverty, because without the use of measurements the performance of income maintenance programs in reducing income poverty cannot be evaluated. Therefore Chapter 3 tells how the concept of poverty-line income was developed. It also discusses the policy issues involved in the official poverty-line income developed by the Department of Health and Human Services. Various studies that use alternative concepts of poverty-line income are reviewed. Also, the concepts of relative poverty and inequality are analyzed along with the concept of absolute poverty.

Chapter 4 evaluates the performance of current income maintenance programs in reducing income poverty. It presents a framework for studying the distributive impact of the various programs. Distributive impact is studied in dollar terms and with respect to its target efficiency, its antipoverty effects, and its feedback effects.

After dealing with the ideological roots of current income maintenance programs and their performance in reducing income poverty, it becomes appropriate to examine recent attempts at welfare reform. Thus, in Chapter 5, the welfare reforms attempted by Presidents Nixon and Carter are reviewed and discussed. Entangled policy goals in welfare reform that make it extremely difficult to improve current income maintenance programs are considered.

Because social security constitutes a major part of the income maintenance system in the United States, it is important to study policy issues involved in social security reform. It should be remembered too that the adoption of a new policy for social security would have a ripple effect on other income maintenance programs and their recipients. Therefore Chapter 6 discusses major policy issues confronting social security: the issue of income redistribution through social security, the earnings test, the emerging role of women in the labor market. For social security to be structurally reformed, these issues need to be dealt with in a coordinated fashion, because they are interrelated. The issues are discussed seriatim with the aim of arriving at a recommendation for the comprehensive reform of social security.

Development of a coherent and comprehensive system of income maintenance is difficult without adopting a new program that specifically deals with income security for children. As a matter of fact, the author argues in this book that the adoption of a program of children's allowances is an important key to developing such a system. Thus Chapter 7 is devoted to the delineation and discussion of policy issues in children's allowances. It highlights limitations of current income maintenance programs in dealing with income insecurity of children. It reviews and discusses arguments for and against a program of children's allowances, advanced in the past and currently implemented in other countries. Specific policy issues involved in the development of a program of children's allowances are raised and discussed, and a recommended plan of children's allowances for the United States is presented.

In the concluding chapter (Chapter 8), the author presents her own vision of a system of income maintenance for the United States. She develops such a system according to a hierarchical order of income maintenance provision for the adult population. The system provides adequate minimum wages as a first defense against poverty, followed by social insurance benefits, and then by public assistance payments. The author finds it possible to establish such a hierarchical order because the income insecurity of children is dealt with under a totally separate and independent program of children's allowances. In developing such a system, American values are recaptured and incorporated so that the system reflects diverse values and yet does not create conflict among them. Throughout the book the overriding concern is to come up with a system of income maintenance programs that can ensure an adequate minimum floor of income to all families and at the same time foster the incentive to work.

In developing a system of income maintenance, the author adopted two important schemes of income maintenance that have been advocated by Professor Eveline M. Burns: children's allowances and a double-decker system of social security. Like many other students of income maintenance, this author has benefited greatly from the writings of Professor Burns.

This book has dwelled heavily on past work by the author. Publishers' permissions for the author to use published articles are greatly appreciated. The author thanks the National Association of Social Workers for granting permission to use material from "Family Allowances for the United States: An Analysis and a Proposal" (1971) and "Who Receives Subsidy Through Social Security, and How Much?" (1982); The Child Welfare League of America for use of "Family Allowances and a National Minimum of Economic Security" (1971) and "Children's Right to Social Security" (1974); the University of Chicago Press for use of "Issues in Welfare Reform" (1978) and "An Analysis of HEW's Proposals on Social Security" (1980); the American Public Welfare Association for use of "SSI: Progress or Retreat?" (1974); The Family Service Association of America for use of "Anatomy of President Carter's Welfare Reform Proposal" (1977); the National Conference on Social Welfare for use of "The Earnings Test in Social Security," which appeared in The Social Welfare Forum, 1978; and Prentice-Hall for use of "Income Maintenance Programs," which appeared in Handbook of the Social Services, edited by Neil Gilbert and Harry Specht (1981).

In preparing this book the author has been helped by many people. She thanks William T. Alpert for commenting on Chapter 1, Sheldon

Danziger for commenting on Chapters 3 and 4, Morton Paglin for commenting on Chapter 4, Herman Grundmann for commenting on Chapter 6, and Robert J. Myers for commenting on Chapters 6 and 8. She has gained invaluable editorial assistance from Rosalie Hull. She thanks Kelly Clark and Elizabeth Doherty for typing the manuscript. The author alone is responsible for all expressions of opinion and for errors and omissions.

TABLE OF CONTENTS

LIST OF TABLES AND FIGURES

INCOME MAINTENANCE
AND WORK INCENTIVES

1

TWO IDEOLOGICAL ROOTS OF INCOME MAINTENANCE IN THE UNITED STATES

Among the industrialized societies of the world, the United States is one of the few that is ambivalent about aiding the poor through publicly supported income maintenance programs. Few industrialized societies spend more time and energy than the United States in debating about the poor: their motivation to work or not to work, their lifestyle as a possible threat to society, and their effect on the rest of society. Few countries other than the United States elect national presidents or state governors who are adept at arousing public passion against the poor and who seem to disapprove of public aid programs. The American public does extend a helping hand to the needy on special occasions such as Christmas and Thanksgiving, passing out baskets of food to poor families; but, for the most part, the public apparently wants to ignore the fact that poverty exists in the United States. That is, many people would rather not admit that poverty is a social and economic phenomenon in this country. To the majority of the public, poverty is an individual problem that the poor themselves should solve with the help of occasional and limited handouts from the government.

Despite the public's negative psychological disposition toward helping the poor, the government has spent more money every year in doing so. Public outlay aimed specifically at transferring income to the poor has increased enormously during the past four decades. If governmental actions reflect public sentiment, then one tends to surmise that, objectively at least, the public does support increasing governmental funds to help the poor, although it does not clearly know why.

Then, where does the public's ambivalence come from? In part, the public is ambivalent because it lacks an ideology in regard to why the government should help the poor to start with. This is quite in contrast to the fact that the public long ago established a coherent ideology in regard to why the government should not help the poor. Also, the public is not sure about how the government should help the poor. Uncertainty about these questions may be one reason why past attempts to reform welfare have focused primarily on making welfare programs more efficient and thus minimizing governmental expenditures for such programs.

Ambivalence about governmental intervention to help the poor also stems in part from conflicting ideological roots of income maintenance programs that have prevailed in the United States. One might be termed classic liberalism and the other new liberalism. Although individuals tend to subscribe consistently to one of these ideologies, society as a whole projects itself with two ideologies, thus creating an ideological confusion at the macrolevel.

CLASSIC LIBERALISM

The world view of classic liberalism still prevails strongly among Americans, and it not only dictates the way they theorize about why the poor became poor in the first place but also what should be done about them. Classic liberalism developed and flourished in the eighteenth and nineteenth centuries and is a view of society that is still prevalent today. Simply stated, this view upholds the virtues of individuals' freedom, free enterprise, minimum government, and the natural selection of the fittest. Those who adhere to this view assume that if these virtues are upheld and implemented, a society will not only be efficient in its use of limited resources but will also be a stronger society, with individuals maximizing their talents to their own best interests and ultimately to the best interests of society.

Several thinkers from different disciplines contributed to the development of classic liberalism. Adam Smith was one of them. Through his book An Inquiry into the Nature and Causes of the Wealth of Nations, he envisioned a natural order of the economy in which the factors of production—land, labor, and capital—would each receive a fair share of the rewards if nobody artificially intervened in transactions.[1] The economic behavior of individuals was to be controlled not by governmental regulations but by the invisible hand of supply and demand. Smith advocated abolition of the tariff, freedom in choosing the site of production and in the sale of produce, and elimination of controlled wages to laborers. Only under these conditions, he maintained, could individuals compete freely and fairly. To him, free competition was the cornerstone of economic growth and accumulation of national wealth.

Thomas Malthus, through his book An Essay on the Principle

of Population, also contributed to the development of classic liberalism. He stated that, while the amount of food would increase arithmetically, the population would increase geometrically. This imbalance was supposedly caused by excessive passion between the sexes among the lower classes. The only check against such imbalance would be the brutal processes of nature—pestilence, famine, war, and misery. There would be no other way to improve living conditions among working people.[2]

One economic consequence of Malthus's theory of population was the justification of low wages for workers. If artificially higher wages, such as minimum wages, were paid to workers, early marriages and therefore a higher birthrate would occur, with the result that the working population would increase until it was again checked by overcrowding, misery, and death.[3] Thus the reasoning went on to state that the absence of minimum wages might prevent the vicious circle of the rise and fall of the working population through misery and death.

Malthus's pessimistic view regarding population was reflected in the economic theories of Ricardo, Mill, and Pareto. David Ricardo developed the concept of the "iron law of wages," which stated that labor was bound to a wage that could never rise above subsistence.[4] John Stuart Mill argued that a fixed amount of funds was available for wages regardless of the number of workers. An individual worker's wage was determined by dividing the total available funds by the number of workers in the labor force. To improve the living standards of individual workers, the working population had to be decreased.[5] However, Mill thought that the United States presented an exception because it had an abundance of unoccupied land and thus there was no threat of diminishing returns for labor as the population increased.

Pareto asserted that the income distribution was dictated by natural law. Pareto's law regarding the constant shape of distribution of income also reflected Malthus's view of population. Pareto's law declared that income would be distributed with a constant degree of inequality regardless of place or time.[6] Thus, for example, the bottom fifth of the population would receive a constant proportion of the national income no matter which country or which point in time was investigated. The only way to help low-income families would be through economic growth; even then, their share of the national income would still be the same.

These economic theories are important ingredients of laissez-faire economics, which strongly influenced the course of social policy in regard to antipoverty legislation both in Britain and the United States. For example, a parliamentary committee in Britain argued against a minimum wage rate in 1808 as "wholly inadmissible in principle, incapable of being reduced to practice by any means which can possibly be devised, and, if practicable, would be productive of the most fatal

consequences."[7] Advocates of laissez-faire economics would argue
that the level of wages should be determined through a price mechanism
based on supply and demand. The goods and services thus produced at
the minimum cost would then be distributed to the highest bidder. The
highest bidder would be the one who would most value the commodity.
In this way the law of supply and demand would work to the best interests of the buyer and the seller—and ultimately to the best interest
of society.

Social and political thoughts are an important part of classic
liberalism, and these thoughts present much the same message as that
from laissez-faire economics. Among classic liberals, Herbert Spencer
was perhaps most influential in shaping social thought. Although his
writings were full of moralistic expressions, Spencer basically attempted to apply the model of natural science to his social philosophy;
that is, Darwin's theory of the evolution of species was the foundation
of Spencer's social philosophy. Darwin had theorized that plants and
animals developed from remote predecessors through gradual deviations and mutations.[8] Species that could adapt by mutation to changing
conditions in nature could survive and even evolve into higher orders
of species. Nature would select the fittest for survival. Spencer applied to social nature Darwin's theory of biological nature.

Spencer argued that in the ideal society individuals evolve into
a higher level of human being by acquiring a moral sense and hence a
respect for the natural rights of others as well as their own rights.
Individuals could have their desires fully satisfied as long as they did
not intrude upon the rights of other individuals to obtain like satisfac-
tion. He called the human ability to find the equilibrium between one's
rights and others' rights the "instinct of personal rights." When this
equilibrium was attained, then "equal freedom" was achieved.[9]

In any society going through the process of moral evolution to
attain such equilibrium, Spencer recognized that some individuals
would not come up to expectations. Just as the human body cannot
operate efficiently with a weak or malfunctioning organ, society, in
Spencer's view, cannot function with full efficiency as long as it has
weak segments made up of people incapable of evolving morally. (The
poor were often thought to be poor because they were weak and im-
moral. They were often considered criminal as well.) According to
Spencer, the situation could improve only if the weak segments died
out or changed. If the weak individuals died, natural selection of the
fittest was taking place. He gave much attention to explaining how
weak individuals in the population could change and come up to the
moral standards of society. But he insisted that each individual had
to acquire moral standards by struggling against the forces of nature.

To Spencer, superior human beings were not necessarily more
highly educated persons. Attaining knowledge from books was not

guaranteed to make individuals moral. To be moral, individuals had to feel rather than understand what was right and what was wrong. This natural, spontaneous, instinctive impulse to behave morally could not be acquired through study but through daily struggle with nature. [10]

The moral evolution of human beings should at best proceed naturally—not through governmental intervention. As a matter of fact, Spencer thought that governmental intervention would actually impede the evolutionary process of would lead to adverse consequences regardless of its initial intention. Governmental aid to a certain segment of the population would mean protecting and benefiting that group by moving against and depriving the rest of the population. When government habitually involved itself in economic activities, he warned, each generation would be less capable and willing to attain benefits for itself through individual effort. The ultimate result would be socialism. [11]

Classic liberalism is one of the pillars of conservatism in contemporary America. It helps individuals formulate a coherent view of how society ought to function. It assumes that each human being can be treated as an entity rather than as a member of a collectivity, that society is at its best when individuals can strive for their own interest, and that people should be left alone either to thrive or perish in nature.

Classic liberalism, on the one hand, imparts a sense of optimism, encouraging individuals to strive and succeed because their efforts would eventually bring about just rewards. But, on the other hand, it instills a sense of fatalism and near futility in regard to governmental intervention in the processes of human survival. Such intervention would impede natural forces from taking place, stifle economic growth, undermine the increased productivity of individual workers, and result in the misallocation of economic resources. Intervention would even offer misguided clues to working people, leading them to behave in ways opposed to those that nature might have directed. For example, providing minimum wages or public assistance to supplement earnings would encourage working people to procreate more than warranted by nature. The increase in the population of working-class people would make them worse off than before the government intervened. Also, governmental intervention in income maintenance, either by providing minimum wages or income transfers, might distort the real value of workers with the result that working people might stop improving their human capital. In the classic liberal view, all individuals are to be compensated according to their real value, no more and no less, if capitalist society is to function efficiently.

Much of the rationale and many of the principles involved in welfare programs, past and present, rest on classic liberalism. According to this ideology, the causes of poverty are to be sought in individuals. That is, the poor themselves bring about their own economic dependence. Thus poverty cannot be solved by having the government intervene in the economic system, as this will prevent the system from functioning efficiently. Rather, the solution is to help the poor help themselves with the least amount of public expenditures. If help for the poor is necessary, private helping networks should be mobilized first. If they fail, voluntary agencies should be called upon to aid families in need, before the government steps in. On the question of what type of assistance should be provided, direct provision—either in cash or in kind—is preferred to upgrading minimum wages or creating public works. Direct provision is preferable because the alternatives inevitably interfere with the economic system, which functions most efficiently when left alone.

A clear example of action in line with classic liberalism was seen in 1961, when the nation witnessed the welfare crisis in Newburgh, New York. Faced with the financial problems of paying families on welfare, City Manager Mitchell enforced the following rules: relief in kind, denial of aid to unfit mothers, a level of welfare payments lower than the lowest wages in the community, relief limited to three months a year for all except the aged or handicapped, and a "suitable-home" requirement for those receiving grants under Aid to Dependent Children.[12] These rules—which assumed that poverty is a personal problem for which the community does not need to take unlimited responsibility—were ostensibly made to eliminate "chiselers" and able-bodied men from relief. Besides claiming that Newburgh's financial problems were created because ineligible poor families abused the welfare program, Mitchell blamed the city's fiscal crisis on an influx of blacks from the South. Nelson Rockefeller, then governor of New York, appointed a special committee to investigate the charges made by Mitchell. The committee found the charges invalid.[13]

What is significant about the Newburgh crisis is that the city council not only believed that poverty was the poor's own making but also that the poor caused the community's decay. The special investigating committee, on the contrary, reported that Newburgh's crisis was due largely to the decay in the central part of the city, the decline in population, and the downfall of the needle industry.[14] The poor people were both misunderstood and mishandled in this instance.

But several functional aspects are involved in the way the poor have been handled in the United States. In the early stages of industrialization, new capital had to be raised and reinvested to accelerate economic growth. In those days, the economy typically could expand only if there were enough savings that could be used for reinvestment. It could not expand by the force of consumption as it has been able to do in later stages of industrialization. Thus few resources were available for helping families in need. As a matter of fact, too much comfort was thought to be bad for the motivation of poor people. The misery of poverty or the fear of becoming poor was thought to be necessary for motivating working people to work harder.

Furthermore, in the early days of industrialization, plenty of jobs were available. Even unskilled and uneducated workers could find such jobs as digging for construction or for railroads, shoveling snow from the streets, and so on. The economy, which did not depend on advanced technology, could produce countless odd jobs for the unskilled and the poor.

Welfare payments under the ideological umbrella of classic liberalism were never meant to be an entitlement. Therefore the government could arbitrarily choose the level of payments—however inadequate it might have been—and get away with it. It could also decide who was to be helped and who was not. All this made sense at a time when there were not enough surplus resources to spread around. If there were any, they had to be reinvested in the economy for its further growth.

Welfare oriented to classic liberalism does create some problems in postindustrial America. Many advocates of classic liberalism are well indoctrinated as to why government should not intervene, but they have a mental block about developing a positive rationale as to why government should intervene. In an affluent society with an economy of nearly $3 trillion, this poses a dilemma for the decision maker. Republican presidents especially tend to be placed in an awkward position. On the one hand, they constantly remind the public that public expenditures for welfare must be checked, abusers caught, and so on; on the other hand, they have to defend the growing welfare programs without having a coherent explanation for such growth. Nor can they explain positively and convincingly why government is becoming an important agent of transfer payments between taxpayers and recipients of welfare benefits.

Because welfare oriented to classic liberalism attempts to find the causes of dependence in individuals rather than in the economic system, the range of solutions for helping the poor is limited. As Robert Lampman theorized, there are three approaches to helping the poor: adapting the poor to the market, relieving the distress of the poor, and adapting the system to the needs of the poor.[15] Under welfare based on classic liberalism, the first approach could be used comfortably, the second approach used grudgingly, and the third possibly never used.

The problem of adhering to the classic liberal view of welfare in contemporary America is compounded by the fact that it is becoming increasingly difficult for unskilled workers to find jobs. Unlike the situation during the formative days of industrialization, even digging for construction and plowing land for farming are often done now by skilled workers with sophisticated machinery. Auto workers on the assembly line may soon have to be able to monitor robots and program robots by computers. Thus the welfare orientation under classic liberalism creates double jeopardy for the poor: continuous resistance to aiding the poor and not enough jobs to go around for the unskilled.

NEW LIBERALISM

New liberalism—the other root of income maintenance policy in the United States—projects a totally different view of how society can best function from that projected by classic liberalism. Advocates of new liberalism emphasize the importance of interdependence among individuals, cooperation in human endeavor, egalitarianism in allocation of resources, and willingness to accept a certain amount of governmental intervention for redistributing resources from one segment of society to another.

Many social thinkers have contributed to developing the ideology of new liberalism. Robert Owen, possibly one of the most important contributors, was himself an industrialist in the mid-1830s. Appalled by the adverse effects of economic recessions on working-class families, he believed that economic activities could be better pursued through cooperation rather than competition among individuals. He thought that working people themselves could own a factory, pool their resources, and share the fruits of their labor. Also, in his view, the objectives of economic activities were not only to earn a livelihood but also to develop human capital at the work place. He experimented with his scheme in New Lanark, Scotland, and later in the United States at New Harmony, Indiana.[16] His experiments failed in both countries, but his ideas for a new society influenced the labor legislation, the cooperative movement, and the trade union movement in Britain. What is important about Robert Owen's vision is that he stressed the interdependence of individuals. He believed that the welfare of each individual in society could be dealt with effectively if society recognized the dynamic relationships between individuals. No one person's well-being could be pursued in isolation. Only by pooling the risks of social and economic hazards and by pooling resources belonging to a group of people could each individual's well-being be ensured.

Advocates of new liberalism assume that the issue of the distribution of income can be investigated and subjected to governmental intervention that looks toward changing it. This view is quite a departure from that of the advocates of classic liberalism. To classic liberals, the idea of changing the pattern of distribution of income and wealth was taboo. Unchanging inequality was defended because concentration of wealth was thought to be necessary for economic growth. Classic liberals maintained that individuals could do whatever they wanted to do with accumulated wealth—including donating to charity; also that noninterference with the distribution of income and wealth should result eventually in less inequality. In contrast, new liberal thinkers believe that an excessive degree of inequality in income and wealth is undesirable and that such excessive inequality should be subject to governmental regulations—for instance, low-income families might be given preferential treatment under federal income tax laws.

An early argument for less inequality in income and wealth was Henry George's plea for the indirect confiscation of landownership through taxation. Distressed by mounting poverty amid prosperity after the Civil War, Henry George concluded that landowners were making unearned profits from God-given land. As land continued to become more scarce, an ever larger share of the national income would go to landowners. This would be to the detriment of persons involved in other factors of production, that is, those providing labor and capital. Working people who provided labor would inevitably become poorer as landowners became richer. George's proposed solution was to impose a land property tax of full rent value and abolish all other types of taxes.[17] Thus his tax scheme was called a "single tax." In this way, George thought, the poor could be helped to receive the adequate income justly due them.

A. C. Pigou, a British economist, using the theory of marginal utility, argued that the lesser the inequality in income and wealth the greater the economic welfare of a nation.[18] Another economist, R. H. Tawney, argued that more equal distribution of income and wealth would ensure more equal opportunities for all to develop their human capital to its full potential. He maintained that only when excessive inequality was absent from a society could human beings develop their unique capabilities, talents, and creativity.[19] Furthermore, he believed that equality under the law could be more effectively achieved if a fair amount of economic equality was also attained. He presented the same argument in regard to political equality. Thus, in Tawney's opinion, legal and political equality become reality only when economic equality is attained.

Against the contention by adherents of classic liberalism that concentration of income and wealth is needed for economic growth, new liberal economists argue that corporations nowadays seldom acquire capital from just a few rich people but from millions of shareholders; furthermore, the owners of corporations are not necessarily the persons who manage corporations.[20]

Once the issue of inequality in income and wealth became debatable, the distribution of income and wealth became a legitimate subject of academic inquiry. Simon Kuznets, in his classic study of distribution of income, found that the top 1 percent of families received 16 percent of the national income before taxes in 1913, 14 percent in

1920, 17 percent in 1929, 13 percent in 1939, and 9 percent in 1948.[21] Lampman, in his study of the distribution of wealth, found that between 1922 and 1953 the share of wealth for the top 2 percent fell from 33 to 29 percent. He also found, however, that the concentration of wealth had been increasing since 1949.[22]

Another important aspect of classic liberalism that adherents of new liberalism reacted to was the validity of the laissez-faire doctrine for explaining what was happening in the economy. To new liberals, the notion of free competition had increasingly become a myth. They saw monopolistic and oligopolistic competition emerging and concluded that fair competition among individuals was just a fiction. On the contrary, economic power was increasingly concentrated in new large-scale corporations. These corporations, they argued, came into being with the aid of the government through protective tariffs, export bounties, and indirect wage subsidies. If there was anything resembling competition, it was created by governmental intervention under the antitrust laws and the like. Free competition could not be achieved by merely allowing events to take their course.[23]

In recent years, the virtue of free competition itself has been questioned. Is it worth fighting to preserve fair competition by such means as antitrust laws? John Kenneth Galbraith contends that industrial monopoly is not undesirable, provided there is an equally powerful monopoly on the opposing side—for instance, on the side of labor or consumers. He termed such power "countervailing power."[24] When power is equalized between opposing sides, each finds limits in exploiting the other. When such equilibrium is found, the mechanism of self-regulation comes into play, making excessive governmental regulations unnecessary.[25]

The validity of laissez-faire economics has been questioned from another angle. Juliet Rhys-Williams, a British economist, argued that the classic economics of Adam Smith might have been valid in his time but is no longer valid in modern times because economic conditions today are very different. In her view, applying the classic economics of The Wealth of Nations to the current economy would be analogous to applying the principles of Plato's Republic to the governing of twentieth-century towns and cities.[26]

Some have carried out empirical studies that seem to invalidate the universal applicability of laissez-faire economics over time. Institutional economists such as John R. Commons, Thorstein Veblen, and Wesley C. Mitchell have sought to discover whether economic institutions—for instance, business enterprise, private property, or even capitalism itself—are products of universal, rational economic behavior, as classic liberals thought. Their studies indicate that these institutions are products of human habits and the social and economic climates of a given time. If human habits and social and economic climates change, economic institutions can and should also change. Mitchell observed that the business cycle was associated with the psychological expectations of businessmen at a given time. Hence, each generation should develop a theory of business to suit its own psychological expectations. In other words, these economists maintain that all economic theories, if functional at all, are transitory in nature.[27]

A general economic theory that is distinctly different from the classic economics of Adam Smith was presented by John Maynard Keynes in his book General Theory of Employment, Interest and Money.[28] He questioned the argument of the laissez-faire economists that unemployment is temporary because the economy has a self-regulating force: the invisible hand of supply and demand. Against this argument Keynes theorized that excessive savings and the lack of investment spending could cause a low level of demand. This could bring about economic equilibrium; in other words secular stagnation could develop within the economy. As a result, chronic unemployment could occur. This imbalance between savings and investment might come about typically in a highly advanced capitalistic society in which the persons who save are no longer those who take a chance and invest in the economy. Keynes's theory of secular stagnation also implied that there might not be enough jobs to go around for all who wanted to work. This view contradicts Say's law—set forth by the French economist Jean Baptiste Say—which holds that workers can always find jobs if they are willing to accept the wages that the market is willing to pay, no matter how low they may be.[29] At any rate, to correct such maladjustments in the economy, Keynes recommended governmental expenditures for transfer payments to those in need, governmental involvement in public works to stimulate the economy, and lower taxes to provide greater purchasing power to consumers—all through deficit financing.

Keynes's theory changed the public's attitudes toward governmental involvement in the economy, toward the value of personal savings, and toward drastic inequality in income and wealth. Thanks to Keynesian economics, many policymakers came to believe that governmental intervention would not be a villain, encouraging economic stagnation, as they had previously thought, but rather would provide an indispensable means of stabilizing the economy. They argued that excessive savings, although stemming from behavior virtuous for individuals, might impede economic growth. And finally, they felt that redistributing income to the poor through governmental transfers might be an effective way to stimulate the economy, as the poor tend to have a higher propensity to consume than do the nonpoor.[30] For the first time, moral justification for helping the poor through public income maintenance programs converged with economic justification for so doing. Before Keynes, the well-to-do could find an excuse for opposing income transfers to the poor on the grounds that distributing income would be bad for the economy, even though they might have felt morally guilty for not supporting these transfers.

New liberals increasingly came to recognize that people became poor mainly because of social and economic forces rather than because of individual faults. Many students of poverty launched systematic studies on it. Some, like Charles Booth and B. Seeborhm Rowntree, attempted to quantify the prevalence of poverty by finding the percentage of the population who fell below a subsistence level.[31] Booth found that 32 percent of the people living in London at the turn of the century were poor. Rowntree found that 38 percent of those living in York at that time were poor. William H. Beveridge—one of the founders of the British social security system—investigated the impact of the business cycle on family well-being. He found that during the 50-year period 1856-1907 the marriage rate rose and fell with the bank interest rate, the volume of foreign trade, and the rate of employment.[32] Other investigators found that poverty was perpetuated among many city dwellers in Britain because of the way the sweatshop system operated. Under that system, the worker was typically paid on a piecework basis. From these earnings, the worker had to pay for the use of equipment and such items as soap, hot water, and heat—expenses that often consumed more than 30 percent of the earnings.[33] Still other investigators found family size to be a structural cause of poverty. Eleanor Rathbone, an economist and a member of Parliament, found that 10 percent of all families were raising 40 percent of all children in 1920 because a large number of children were concentrated in a relatively few large-size families.[34]

Once students of poverty with a new liberal orientation found structural causes of poverty, they came to believe that poverty could be prevented for many if these causes were attacked. And if this could not be attempted, at least certain economic risks—such as old age, disability, death of the breadwinner, and unemployment—could be recognized as problems that would probably strike all. Society could pool economic resources to help individuals meet risks like these when they did occur. Everyone would contribute to a system of mutual help, and everyone would benefit sooner or later.

New liberal thinking appears to be behind the movement to develop various types of social insurance programs in both Britain and the United States. John R. Commons, a pioneering student of social insurance, defined insurance as "an arrangement for distribution among many of the loss of a few."[35] Social insurance incorporates into an insurance program social compulsion for all to participate—distinguishing it from private insurance, which operates on the basis of voluntary participation. Social insurance, then, provides a deliberate way for society to distribute income to individuals and families who experience specific social and economic hazards identified by law, such as unemployment, old age, disability, and death of the bread-winner. Although social insurance does not prevent such hazards, it helps individuals and families who encounter them to meet the conse-quences. It offers an organized way for all to contribute to the system and for all to benefit from it in case such events strike.

In many respects, social insurance reflects the spirit of new liberalism. Social insurance is predicated on the following ideas: The causes of economic dependence are largely due to economic forces; society can plan ahead to help individuals and families meet the vicis-situdes of life that are caused by economic forces; anyone may have to confront such vicissitudes sooner or later; everyone in society should cooperate in pooling risks and in pooling resources; and finally governmental intervention is indispensable for developing and imple-menting social insurance programs.

The United States has developed a variety of social insurance programs and is currently spending a larger amount of public funds to finance them than the amount spent to finance welfare programs. Many families who are not poor would have been poor in the absence of social insurance programs. The public, in general, seems positively oriented toward them. Nor does there seem to be an imbalance between the ideological base of social insurance programs and the degree of public commitment to finance them. However, there still is a great imbalance between the ideological base of welfare programs and the degree of public commitment to finance them. To compound the prob-lem, public expenditures for welfare programs have been on the rise, whereas the ideological base for such programs has changed little.

Unfortunately, social insurance programs, although popular, cannot deal with all life contingencies for all individuals and families. Families may be poor for reasons unrelated to the employment status of the head of the household. Families may be poor because there are too many dependents to support on the meager income that the head of the household earns even with year-round work. Welfare programs will still be required to meet the needs of many families.

The challenge is clear. The question confronting the nation is this: How can the United States develop a system of income mainten-ance that makes sense to the American public? That is,

- A system including both social insurance programs and welfare programs
- A system that is somehow congruent with fundamental American values
- A system that does not offend the basic expectations of the American people in regard to the role of individuals and the role of government in dealing with income needs

- A system that does not erode the incentive structure of the American economy
- A system that provides adequately for vulnerable groups of individuals—children, the elderly, and the disabled.

The challenge becomes even greater when one recognizes that such a system has to be developed despite the conflicting ideological roots of income maintenance programs in the American society.

NOTES

1. Adam Smith, An Inquiry into the Nature and Causes of the Wealth of Nations (London: Strahan and Cadell, 1776).

2. Thomas Robert Malthus, An Essay on the Principle of Population (London: Ward, Lock, 1890).

3. Amos Criswold Warner, Stuart A. Queen, and Earnest Bouldin Harper, American Charities and Social Work (New York: Crowell, 1930), p. 42.

4. E. A. J. Johnson and Herman E. Krooss, The American Economy: Its Origins, Development, and Transformation (Englewood Cliffs, N.J.: Prentice-Hall, 1960), p. 134.

5. John Stuart Mill, Principles of Political Economy (New York: Appleton, 1887), pp. 188-89.

6. Vilfredo Pareto, Cours d'economie politique professé a l'Université de Lausanne (Lausanne: I. Rouge, 1896), ii, pp. 306-07.

7. Sidney Webb and Beatrice Webb, The History of Trade Unionism (New York: Longmans, Green, 1920), p. 56.

8. Merle Curti, The Growth of American Thought (New York: Harper & Bros., 1943), p. 46.

9. Herbert Spencer, Social Statistics: Abridged and Revised Together with the Man Versus the State (New York: Appleton, 1892), pp. 56-57.

10. Ibid., pp. 175-76.

11. Ibid., p. 321.

12. Samuel Mencher, "Newburgh: The Recurrent Crisis of Public Assistance," Social Work 7 (January 1962): 3-11.

13. Eve Edstrom, "Newburgh Is a Mirror Reflection on Us All," Washington Post, August 6, 1961; and Meg Greenfield, "The Welfare Chiseler of Newburgh, N.Y.," The Reporter, August 1, 1961, pp. 37-38.

14. Greenfield, op. cit., p. 40.

15. Robert J. Lampman, Ends and Means of Reducing Income Poverty (Chicago: Markham, 1971), pp. 8-12.

16. Karl Polanyi, The Great Transformation (New York: Farrar

& Rinehart, 1944), p. 135; Curti, op. cit., p. 264; Sidney Webb and Beatric Webb, The Prevention of Destitution (New York: Longmans, Green, 1916), p. 223; and Webb and Webb, History of Trade Unionism, p. 134.

17. Louis M. Hacker et al., eds., The Shaping of the American Tradition (New York: Columbia University Press, 1947), p. 1125.

18. A. C. Pigou, Wealth and Welfare (London: Macmillan, 1912), p. 401.

19. R. H. Tawney, Equality (London: Allen & Unwin, 1964), p. 48.

20. Harry A. Millis and Royal E. Montgomery, Labor's Progress and Basic Problems (New York: McGraw-Hill, 1938), pp. 273-74.

21. Simon Kuznets, Share of Upper Income Groups in Income and Savings (New York: National Bureau of Economic Research, 1953).

22. Robert J. Lampman, The Share of Top Wealth-Holders in National Wealth (Princeton, N.J.: Princeton University Press, 1962).

23. Polanyi, op. cit., p. 139.

24. John Kenneth Galbraith, American Capitalism (Boston: Houghton Mifflin, 1952), p. 111.

25. Ibid., p. 151.

26. Juliet Rhys-Williams, A New Look at Britain's Economic Policy (Baltimore: Penguin, 1965), pp. 19-20.

27. Johnson and Krooss, op. cit., pp. 438-40.

28. John Maynard Keynes, General Theory of Employment, Interest and Money (New York: Macmillan, 1973).

29. Cited in Galbraith, op. cit., p. 69.

30. Ibid., pp. 80-82; and William H. Beveridge, Full Employment in a Free Society (London: Allen & Unwin, 1944), pp. 95-96.

31. Charles Booth, Life and Labour of the People of London (London: Williams and Norgate, 1891); B. Seeborhm Rowntree, Poverty: A Study of Town Life (London: Macmillan, 1903); and B. Seeborhm Rowntree, Poverty and Progress (New York: Longmans, Green, 1941).

32. William H. Beveridge, Unemployment: A Problem of Industry (New York: Longmans, Green, 1910).

33. Mrs. Sidney Webb and B. L. Hutchings, Socialism and National Minimum (London: Fifield, 1909), pp. 60-61.

34. Eleanor Rathbone, Family Allowances (London: Allen & Unwin, 1949), p. 13.

35. John R. Commons and John Andrews, Principles of Labor Legislation, 3rd ed. (New York: Harper & Bros., 1920), p. 382.

2

SCOPE OF
INCOME MAINTENANCE
PROGRAMS

In spite of the ideological confusion regarding its commitment to income maintenance, the United States has rapidly joined other Western industrialized countries in becoming a "welfare state." It currently spends nearly 20 percent of the gross national product (GNP) for publicly supported social welfare programs, compared with less than 9 percent in 1950, 11 percent in 1960, and 15 percent in 1970. This means that social welfare programs have expanded more rapidly than the general economy.

Broadly defined, publicly supported social welfare programs deal with five areas of public concern: income maintenance, health, education, veterans' programs, and other social services. For these purposes, $394 billion was spent in 1978 by all levels of government, constituting 60 percent of all governmental expenditures that year. Per capita public expenditures in 1978 for social welfare were $1,775 compared with $404 in 1950, $592 in 1960, and $1,142 in 1970.[1]

Among publicly supported social welfare programs, those for income maintenance constitute a major part. In 1978, over $227 billion, or 58 percent of all public expenditures for social welfare, was devoted to major income maintenance programs. More than 40 different governmental programs for income maintenance existed in 1978. The major ones are shown in Table 2.1. Programs are grouped into social insurance and welfare, each of which has two subgroups: cash-benefit programs and in-kind benefit programs. Because welfare programs provide only for those who can prove themselves to be in financial need, they are generally called "income-tested" or "income-conditioned" programs. They are also called "residual," as they supplement programs that are not income-tested, that is, social insurance programs.

TABLE 2.1

Major Income Maintenance Programs, 1978

Program	Expenditures (in $ billion)	Federal Share (in percentage)*
Total	227.7	
Social Insurance	175.1	
Cash Benefits		
Old-age, survivors, and disability insurance†	121.4	100.0
Unemployment insurance	12.5	100.0
Worker's compensation	9.8	0.0
Veterans' service-connected compensation	6.2	100.0
In-Kind Benefits		
Medicare	25.2	100.0
Welfare	52.6	
Cash Benefits		
Aid to Families with Dependent Children (AFDC)	11.9	55.3
Supplemental Security Income (SSI)	7.1	77.4
Veterans' pensions	3.3	100.0
General assistance	1.2	0.0
In-Kind Benefits		
Medicaid	20.0	56.4
Food stamps	5.5	100.0
Housing assistance	3.6	100.0

*The percentage is from 1977 expenditures. See George J. Carcagno and Walter S. Corson, "Welfare Reform," in Setting National Priorities: The 1978 Budget, ed. Joseph A. Pechman (Washington, D.C.:Brookings Institution, 1977), p. 253.

†Includes Railroad Retirement.

Source: Alma W. McMillan and Ann Kallman Bixby, "Social Welfare Expenditures, Fiscal Year 1978," Social Security Bulletin 43 (May 1980), Table 1, pp. 5-7; The Budget of the United States Government, Fiscal Year 1980 (Washington, D.C.: U.S. Government Printing Office, 1980), Appendix.

Several observations about the pattern of financing can be made from Table 2.1. The responsibility for financing income maintenance programs rests mainly with the federal government. Only two programs escape federal involvement in financing: worker's compensation and general assistance. The federal government is becoming increasingly responsible for financing even welfare programs. All in-kind welfare programs are financed solely by the federal government with the exception of Medicaid. Even Aid to Families with Dependent Children (AFDC)—for which the states traditionally claimed the prerogative in financing—is now financed to a large extent by the federal government, which in 1978 paid 55.3 percent of its costs. Since the Supplemental Security Income program was put into effect in 1974, the financing of income support for the aged, blind, and disabled has become mainly a responsibility of the federal government, which in 1978 paid 77.4 percent of the program's costs.

Another important observation from Table 2.1 is that income maintenance programs taking the social insurance approach are much more significant in terms of expenditures than income maintenance programs taking the welfare approach. Of the total $227 billion spent in 1978, 76.9 percent was for social insurance programs. Among the social insurance programs, the old-age, survivors, and disability insurance programs—nominally called social security—are by far the most important. Of $175 billion spent for social insurance more than two thirds was for cash payments under social security. Medicare, which is a part of social security but takes the form of in-kind benefits, cost another $25 billion.

AFDC, although the most controversial of the welfare programs, is not the largest one. The largest is Medicaid, which cost over $20 billion in 1978.

Over the years, publicly supported income maintenance programs have grown enormously in scope. The rates of growth in welfare programs and in social insurance programs are different, however. If one compares the patterns of growth since 1950, social insurance programs have grown faster than welfare programs; but if the period since 1960 is taken for comparison, the reverse is true.[2] The rapid acceleration in the growth of welfare programs during the 1960s and early 1970s reflects the sweeping advance of programs enacted or broadened after the beginning of the war on poverty declared by President Lyndon B. Johnson. During this period Medicaid for recipients of public assistance and for the medically indigent was introduced; adult public assistance programs for the aged, blind, and disabled poor were transformed into the federal program of Supplemental Security Income (SSI); Basic Educational Opportunity Grants (BEOG) were initiated; and the program of earned income tax credits was enacted. This period also saw an enormous growth in AFDC payments and an expansion of work and training programs.

In spite of the recent phenomenal rise in expenditures for publicly financed income maintenance programs, the United States is still far behind other industrialized countries in its commitment to income maintenance, especially with respect to social insurance. This relatively low commitment stems not only from the low level of expenditures for existing programs but also from lack of national health insurance, children's allowances, and maternity benefits and the near lack of temporary disability insurance (which exists only in five states and in Puerto Rico). Most Western countries provide all of these programs.

There is no accepted theory for explaining the growth of any particular income maintenance program. However, recent research findings are instructive. Henry Aaron, in his international study comparing expenditures for social security, found that per capita income and the duration of the social security program were statistically significant variables in explaining how much a nation spends for social security.[3] Harold Wilensky reports similar findings. Using path analysis, he found that "social security effort" (the percentage of the GNP that a nation devotes to social security) is a function of per capita income, the proportion of the aged in the population, and the duration of the social security program.[4]

When it comes to the question of this country's fiscal commitment to welfare programs, more than economic and demographic variables appear to be involved. In a study made for interstate comparison, this author found that states set a level of AFDC payments that was inversely related to the percentage of the nonwhite population and positively related to per capita income and tax effort. The percentage of the nonwhite population was the strongest predictor of the payment level, followed by per capita income and tax effort.[5]

However, societal commitment to income maintenance should not be assessed solely on the basis of how much the government spends for income maintenance programs. In some countries, Japan, for example, employers provide various benefits to supplement workers' incomes (housing allowances, dependents' allowances, transportation expenses, and food allowances), leaving the government relatively little to do about provisions for income maintenance. In some other countries, the intrafamilial and interrelative redistribution of income may facilitate income maintenance.[6]

In the course of its history, each country may have shifted the mix of provisions for income maintenance under different financing auspices. For example, during the preindustrial era in the United States, the family and the church were the primary providers of income support for those in need. As industrialization and urbanization advanced, state governments expanded their responsibilities for providing income support by enacting mothers' pensions and old-age pensions. After the Great Depression of the 1930s, the federal government began to assume primary financial responsibility for income maintenance. Since the 1950s, industry too has come to offer various types of income maintenance under the name of fringe benefits and employee assistance. In 1978, $166 billion was spent through private sources for social welfare purposes, compared with $27.8 billion in 1960 and $67.4 billion in 1970. [7] Private expenditures are especially high for health care.

Social welfare programs under private auspices have been positively affected by several developments during the last quarter-century. During World War II, wage stabilization policies of the federal government allowed the provision of fringe benefits as a substitute for increases in wages. High profits and legislation granting special tax treatment made it relatively easy for employers to finance pensions and other employee benefit plans. After the war, a court decision that required employers to bargain with unions on such pensions and benefit plans further encouraged the development of plans under collective bargaining. [8]

DESCRIPTIONS OF MAJOR INCOME MAINTENANCE PROGRAMS

See note 9 for a listing of publications consulted in writing this section.

Social Insurance

Old-Age, Survivors, and Disability Insurance (OASDI)

The current social security system originated in the Social Security Act of 1935. Old-age insurance was enacted in 1935, when the Social Security Act was originally passed; survivors insurance was enacted in 1939, and disability insurance in 1956. OASDI is federally financed by payroll taxes levied on both employers and employees and is administered by the Social Security Administration.

About 90 percent of the nation's labor force is now covered by OASDI. About 91 percent of the elderly in the nation are either receiving monthly cash benefits or will be eligible for benefits when they or their spouses retire; 95 percent of young children and their mothers can depend on monthly survivors insurance benefits if the head of the family dies; and about 80 percent of the people aged 21 to 64 are protected against a loss of income due to long-term disability. Currently, 36 million persons are receiving benefits from the OASDI program.[10]

How does a worker build credits for his work in covered employment? In general, before 1978, a wage earner acquired one quarter of coverage for each calendar quarter in which he was paid $50 or more in covered employment. A self-employed person acquired four quarters of coverage for each year in which net income from self-employment was $400 or more. Beginning in 1978, a worker acquires one quarter of coverage (up to a maximum of four) for each $250 of earnings paid in a year; the dollar measure is automatically increased each year to take account of increases in average wages ($260 in 1979, $290 in 1980, and $310 in 1981).

Generally, the worker is entitled to most types of benefits if he is "fully insured." The fully insured worker is one who has at least as many quarters of coverage (acquired at any time after 1936) as the number of years elapsing between ages 21 and 62 or the date of death or disability, whichever occurs first. For workers who became 21 years of age before 1951, one quarter of coverage is required for each year between 1950 and the year of attaining age 62, disability, or death. Therefore, as of 1981, 30 quarters of coverage are required to be fully insured so as to qualify for retirement or survivors benefits. However, a worker will eventually need 40 quarters of coverage to be fully insured.

To be eligible for disability benefits, the worker must not only be fully insured but must also meet the requirement of having been sufficiently attached to the labor force in the years just preceding the onset of disability. To meet the requirement regarding recent attachment, the worker must have at least 20 quarters of coverage out of the ten years before the onset of disability. More liberal requirements apply to workers who become disabled before age 31 and to those who are blind. Workers are defined as disabled if they are so incapacitated that they cannot earn a significant amount from work for at least 12 months. Disability is determined on the basis of the medical facts in the particular case and after evaluation of the individual's remaining capacity for work, considering age, education, and work experience. The applicant must present medical evidence establishing the existence, extent, and duration of the disability.

Benefits are also payable to certain categories of disabled widows and widowers who are between 50 and 59 years of age. The test of disability for these beneficiaries is much more strict than that applied to the disabled worker. That is, their disability is determined strictly on medical grounds. Disability is determined by state agencies—normally the state vocational rehabilitation agencies—under contract with the federal government.

Survivors benefits are paid to young widows and widowers with children if the worker was "currently insured," even though the worker may not have been fully insured. The status of currently insured was attained if the worker had acquired six quarters of coverage within the period of the past 13 calendar quarters ending with the quarter in which death occurred.

The level of social security benefits is related to the average indexed monthly earnings (AIME) of the worker. Two steps are involved in the calculation of benefits. First, the Social Security Administration calculates the worker's AIME. To obtain AIME, each year's taxable earnings are adjusted to account for the general rise in wages. Earnings are so adjusted until two years before the worker became 62 or died or became disabled before age 62. Later earnings (including those at age 62 or older) are used without adjustment. The Social Security Administration also calculates the computation period, which is equal to the number of years elapsed since 1951 (or age 21, whichever is later) through the year before the worker became 62 or died or became disabled (if disabled before age 62), minus five. The Social Security Administration then picks the highest earnings made during the number of years that will be used as the computation period. These earnings are then added and divided by the number of months in the computation period. The resulting figure is the worker's AIME. As implied above, five years of worker's low earnings are dropped when AIME is determined for the purposes of old-age insurance and survivors insurance. However, in the case of disability insurance, a lesser number of years is dropped in arriving at AIME for persons becoming disabled before age 47, depending upon the age at which the worker became disabled.

The second step is the calculation of the primary insurance amount (PIA), based on the worker's AIME. For workers who turn 62 in 1982 (or died or became disabled before age 62), the PIA is equal to 90 percent of the first $230 of AIME, plus 32 percent of the next $1,158 of AIME, plus 15 percent of AIME in excess of $1,388. The PIA is the basic benefit that will be paid to the worker when he retires or becomes disabled. When the worker retires before age 65, benefits are actuarially reduced. Thus, for example, when the worker retires at age 62, benefits are reduced by 20 percent. All other types of benefits are derived from the PIA. Each dependent of the retired or disabled worker is entitled to 50 percent of the PIA, subject to the provision of family maximum benefits. Aged widows and widowers are entitled to 100 percent of the PIA, subject to an actuarial reduction, if the benefit is claimed before age 65, depending on the age at which they claim benefits. Also, when the worker has claimed early-retirement benefits, the aged widow's and widower's benefit cannot be larger than the worker's retirement benefit, thus resulting in less than 100 percent of the PIA, although this cannot drop below $82\frac{1}{2}$ percent of the PIA. Young widows and widowers and their children are entitled to 75 percent of the PIA, subject to the provision of family maximum benefits. Family maximum benefits range from 1.5 to 1.88 times the PIA; that is, 1.5 times the PIA at the lowest level of earnings, moving up to 1.88 times the PIA as earnings increase to the upper-middle level, and tapering off to 1.75 times the PIA as earnings reach the maximum level.

The PIA is adjusted for rises in the cost of living from the year that the worker reaches age 62. Furthermore, under no circumstances may the PIA be less than $122—the so-called minimum PIA or minimum benefit; however, the 97th Congress repealed the minimum benefit for future retired workers. In addition, a special minimum PIA for workers with long histories of work at low wages is calculated by (1) multiplying $11.50 by the number of years of coverage in excess of ten (and up to 30) in which the worker's earnings were at least one quarter of the taxable maximum under social security and (2) adding cost-of-living increases effective after January 1979.

The retired worker who engages in gainful activities is subject to the earnings test (or the retirement test). The worker's dependents and survivors are also subject to the earnings test when they earn more than the amount stipulated under the law. The worker's earnings can result in reduction in benefits not only for himself but also for his dependents, depending on the extent of the worker's earnings. However, earnings by dependents or survivors subject only their own benefits to reduction. As of 1981, the beneficiary is permitted to earn $5,500 a year without having benefits reduced. (A lower amount— $4,080—applies to younger beneficiaries.) However, if earnings exceed $5,500, each additional earned dollar is subject to a 50 percent reduction in benefits. The earnings test was included in the law on the ground that benefits would be paid to a worker only when that worker had substantially retired and to dependents and survivors only when they did not have substantial earnings from work. However, retired workers 72 years of age and over receive full social security benefits, no matter how much they earn. (The age of 72 will be dropped to 70 effective January 1, 1983.)

Unemployment Insurance

Unemployment insurance programs are designed to provide income support for those who become unemployed involuntarily and who are able and willing to accept a suitable job. Unemployment insurance was enacted under the Social Security Act of 1935. However, Wisconsin had its own program as early as 1932. Many aspects of the Wisconsin program were adopted in unemployment insurance enacted under the Social Security Act of 1935.

Under the act, states and other jurisdictions were encouraged to develop unemployment insurance programs under a tax-offset scheme, which worked as follows. A uniform national payroll tax was imposed on industrial and commercial employers who employed at least eight workers for 20 weeks or more during a calendar year. Employers who paid a tax to a state with an approved unemployment insurance program could credit the state tax against the national tax up to 90 percent. This meant that the states without an unemployment insurance program would simply have lost national payroll taxes paid by employers in such states. Put another way, states with an unemployment insurance program could finance their unemployment insurance benefits with funds that might otherwise have gone to the federal treasury.

Unemployment insurance programs are under the jurisdiction of the Employment and Training Administration of the U.S. Department of Labor, which administers the programs through state employment security agencies. The federal government establishes minimum requirements for the states, and it finances state administrative costs of the program through grants-in-aid from the federal unemployment insurance trust fund.

Currently 97 percent of total employment is covered by the programs. Private employers come under the law if they have one or more individuals employed in each of 20 weeks during the current or the preceding year or if they paid wages of a certain minimum during any calendar quarter of the current or the preceding year. Certain types of agricultural workers, workers in domestic service in private homes, and self-employed workers are excluded from the programs. Generally, state and local governmental employees and employees of most nonprofit organizations are exempt from coverage. However, many states have extended coverage beyond the requirements under the law. For example, 42 jurisdictions cover state and local governmental employees. Hawaii and Puerto Rico have special coverage for agricultural workers excluded under the federal law. Hawaii, New York, and the District of Columbia cover domestic workers.

Eligibility requirements for unemployment insurance benefits differ widely among the states. In general, to be eligible for benefits, workers must have demonstrated their attachment to the labor force by a specified amount of recent work and/or earnings in covered employment. Furthermore, they must be ready, able, and willing to work and must be registered for work at a public employment office. Meeting all these requirements still will not ensure benefits to unemployed workers. They may be denied benefits if disqualified because of leaving the job voluntarily or being fired because of misconduct.

Benefits are paid weekly in cash. Benefit levels vary widely among the states. In general the formula is designed to provide a fraction of the usual weekly wage—normally about 50 percent—subject to a maximum. The majority of the programs use a formula that computes weekly benefits as a fraction of the wages in that quarter of the base period in which wages were highest, as it is assumed that such a quarter most closely reflects full-time work. A few states compute the amount of the weekly benefit as a percentage of annual wages; others base the weekly benefit directly on average weekly wages during a recent period.

All jurisdictions have a provision for minimum and maximum weekly benefits. Some states provide maximum weekly benefits that are fixed year after year, thus requiring a change in the law if maximum benefits are to be upgraded. Others provide flexible maximum weekly benefits, meaning the maximum is automatically established every year as a percentage—normally 50 percent—of the statewide average weekly wage. No state except Ohio adjusts its maximum according to changes in the consumer price index.

Because of the provision of maximum weekly benefits, not all unemployed workers receive 50 percent of lost wages in the form of benefits. For many workers who earn relatively high wages, unemployment insurance does not replace 50 percent of lost wages. Furthermore, because of eligibility requirements, disqualifications for benefits, and restrictions regarding maximum payments and the duration of benefit, unemployment insurance replaces only about 25 percent of aggregate wages lost because of unemployment.[11] Maximum duration of benefits varies between 26 and 36 weeks: Puerto Rico, however, limits benefits to a maximum of 20 weeks. In the past, during a period of high unemployment, an extended benefit period was often provided, allowing a claimant to draw benefits for 13 additional weeks. But currently these extended benefits do not exist. In 1979, about 7.5 million unemployed workers benefited from the unemployment insurance programs.[12]

Worker's Compensation

Worker's compensation programs are designed to provide cash benefits and medical care when workers are injured in connection with their job and to provide monetary payments to their survivors if they are killed on the job. Worker's compensation was the first social insurance program enacted in the United States. The federal government led the way with an act covering its civilian employees, passed in 1908 and reenacted in 1916. Similar laws were enacted by ten states in 1911; subsequently the rest of the states followed suit. Currently 54 different worker's compensation programs are in operation, with each of the 50 states and Puerto Rico having its own program. In addition, the federal government has three separate worker's compensation programs that cover not only federal governmental employees but also private employees in the District of Columbia and longshoremen and harbor workers throughout the country.

Before worker's compensation laws were passed, injured workers had to file a suit against their employer and prove that the injury was due to the employer's negligence in order to collect payments to recover from injury. The employer had the benefit of three types of common law defense. That is, the employer did not need to pay for the worker's injury if it could be proved that the injury occurred because of the normal risk of the work, that the negligence of a fellow worker was responsible, or that the injured worker was partly responsible through personal negligence. The enactment of worker's compensation laws changed the condition under which the injured worker is compensated. All programs are based on the principle of liability without fault, making it unnecessary to file a suit against the employer in order to receive compensation.

Over 80 percent of all workers are covered under worker's compensation programs. However, the coverage of workers varies among states. Workers in domestic service, agricultural employment, and casual labor are usually exempt. Many programs also exempt from coverage employees of nonprofit charitable or religious institutions. In some states only workers in hazardous occupations are covered.

There are various types of worker's compensation laws. Some state laws are compulsory for most of the private employment covered. Others are elective; that is, employers may accept or reject them. However, an employer who rejects the legislation loses the common law defenses against suits by employees. In some states, the laws are in part compulsory and in part elective.

To qualify for benefits an employee must have had an injury or have been killed while performing the duties on the job. However, the injuries must not have been caused by the employee's gross negligence, willful misconduct, or intoxication. The benefits provided include periodic cash payments and medical services to the worker during a period of disablement and death and funeral benefits to the worker's survivors. Lump-sum settlements are allowed under most laws. In many states, maintenance allowances and other services during rehabilitation are provided for injured workers; extra benefits are provided for minors injured while illegally employed.

The cash benefits for all types of disability—temporary total disability, permanent total disability, permanent partial disability—are usually calculated as a percentage of weekly earnings at the time of the accident. The percentage is from 60 to 67 percent, depending on the state. Survivors of workers killed in the course of employment are also paid benefits consisting of a percentage of lost wages. Some states differentiate the percentages according to the type of disability. For example, a few states lower the percentage when the status of the worker changes from temporary total disability to permanent total disability.

Permanent partial disability is compensated in one of the following two ways. When it involves a loss of part of the body—for instance, loss of a finger—the worker receives the same percentage of lost wages as in the case of temporary total disability, but is compensated for only a specified time according to a schedule stipulated in the law. When permanent partial disability involves less measurable loss of physical capability—such as injury to the head, back, or nervous system—the worker usually receives a smaller percentage of lost wages than in the case of permanent total disability, but is compensated for an indefinite time. In all cases, when the disabled worker becomes eligible for disability benefits under social security, the sum of the worker's compensation benefits and the social security benefits cannot exceed 80 percent of the worker's earnings before the injury occurred.

All laws stipulate maximum weekly benefits that the injured worker can receive. Thus some workers may not have their lost wages replaced at the statutory rate. Most laws limit the period during which benefits are paid. However, many states pay benefits as long as the disability lasts. A few states specify payment of benefits for the entire period of disability, but set maximum monetary limitations.

Veterans' Compensation Programs

The legislative objective of veterans' compensation programs is to compensate veterans or their families for disability or death incurred because of military service. The programs originated in 1917 and took the social insurance approach in providing service-connected disability and death benefits. Dependency and indemnity compensation were enacted in 1956. The programs are financed through open-ended federal appropriations providing for direct payments to beneficiaries. They are administered through regional offices of the Department of Veterans Benefits of the Veterans Administration.

To qualify for disability benefits a veteran must have contracted a disease, suffered an injury unrelated to misconduct, or aggravated an existing disease or injury in the line of active duty, and have been discharged with honor. Death compensations and dependency and indemnity compensation benefits are available to a widow, child, or dependent parents of a veteran whose death was due to service. There are no income tests for a disabled veteran, his wife, or children, but parents' income is considered in determining their dependency. Similarly, there is no income test for widows or children, but benefits to parents of a deceased veteran are income-tested (again to determine dependency).

Disability benefits payable in cash are determined by multiple factors, such as percentage of impairment, need for special care, certain anatomical losses or loss of the use of limbs or bodily function, marital status and sex of spouse, number of entitled children, and dependency of parents. Benefits are extended to wives, children, or dependent parents only if the veteran is entitled to compensation for a disability rated 50 percent or greater.

Under the death compensation and dependency and indemnity compensation programs, cash benefits are paid monthly. The amount of the benefits is calculated on the basis of the number of eligible children; the sex and health of the surviving spouse; the number, marital status, health, living arrangements, and income of dependent parents; and, under the dependency and indemnity compensation program, the pay grade of the deceased veteran. There are no work tests under these programs. Over 2.5 million individuals are benefiting from the veterans' compensation programs.[13]

Medicare

Medicare—Title XVIII of the Social Security Act—was enacted in 1965 to cover medical expenses for the aged. In 1972, coverage was extended to beneficiaries of disability insurance and to chronic renal disease patients. Medicare has two parts: hospital insurance (HI) and Supplemental Medical Insurance (SMI). HI is financed by payroll taxes levied on employers and employees and maintained in a federal trust fund. SMI is financed by a combination of beneficiary premiums and general federal revenues, all maintained in a federal trust fund. The programs are administered by the Health Care Finance Administration, which contracts with state health agencies for the certification of health care providers and with intermediaries such as Blue Cross and private insurance companies for the payment of claims.

To be eligible for HI, individuals must be (1) persons 65 years of age or over who are entitled to social security or railroad retirement benefits, or (2) disabled persons who have been eligible for social security or railroad retirement cash disability benefits for 24 or more consecutive months, or (3) chronic renal disease patients who have social security coverage.

To be eligible for SMI, individuals have to enroll in the program by paying monthly premiums. There are two types of enrollment periods. The first type begins at the third month preceding the month in which an individual attains age 65 and ends three months after the month of the 65th birthday—a total of seven months. The second type of enrollment period begins every year on January 1 and lasts through March 1. This is called the general enrollment period. Once the elderly drop out of SMI, they have only one chance to reenroll. Persons aged 65 and over who are not eligible for HI may voluntarily participate in the program by paying the full cost of coverage. However, enrollment in the SMI is required as a condition of buying into the HI program. State departments of human resources may enroll elderly individuals in SMI if these individuals are on SSI and/or Medicaid by paying monthly premiums on their behalf.

HI covers inpatient hospital care, which includes room and board in rooms containing two to four beds, nursing services (except for private duty nursing), drugs and biologicals, and all other services ordinarily furnished by a hospital to its inpatients. HI does not cover the services of physicians (including staff radiologists and anesthesiologists, pathologists, and psychiatrists) except for services provided by interns or residents under approved teaching programs. The program pays for all covered services for the first 60 days of hospitalization except for an initial deductible—a stated amount that the patient pays. The patient also has to pay a stated amount of coinsurance per day for the 61st through the 90th day of hospitalization, with the program paying the remainder. These payments for hospital care are provided for each benefit period. A benefit period begins when a person under Medicare first enters the hospital. When—after being out of a hospital or skilled nursing facility for 60 consecutive days—a person enters a hospital again, then a new benefit period starts.

The HI program provides skilled nursing facility benefits for up to 100 days per benefit period. Benefits are payable only when the stay in the nursing facility follows discharge from a hospital after a stay of three consecutive days or more. Full payment is made by HI for the first 20 days of skilled nursing care. For each of the remaining 80 days, the patient pays a stated amount of coinsurance. Furthermore, the HI program provides for all posthospital home health visits. The program pays the reasonable cost of home health visits.

The SMI program is designed to supplement the benefits under HI. SMI basically pays for physicians' services provided at home, hospital, or office. The program also pays for other services and supplies, such as drugs and biologicals that cannot be self-administered, if they are furnished as a part of the physician's professional service; diagnostic X-ray or laboratory tests, other diagnostic tests, materials, and technicians' services; surgical dressings, splints, casts, and other devices used for reduction of fractures and dislocations; the purchase or rental of durable medical equipment such as an oxygen tent, a hospital bed, or a wheelchair used in the patient's home (or in an institution that the patient uses as home); ambulance service when other means of transportation are not feasible; prosthetic devices (other than dental) that replace all or part of an internal organ; leg, arm, back, and neck braces; artificial legs, arms, and eyes, including replacements required because of changes in the patient's physical condition; and home health visits provided by a certified home health agency in accordance with a home health plan established by the patient's physician (no prior hospitalization being necessary in this case). Payment may be made for all home health visits in a calendar year without regard to similar services received under the HI program.

In each calendar year, the patient pays an initial deductible of a stated amount. After the deductible has been met the program pays for 80 percent of reasonable charges for goods and services allowed under the law, with the patient paying the remainder as coinsurance. Over 26 million persons were enrolled in HI and/or SMI in 1978, of whom 2.7 million were nonaged individuals. [14]

Welfare

Aid to Families with Dependent Children (AFDC)

AFDC was enacted as a part of the Social Security Act of 1935 to provide financial aid primarily to needy children of deceased or incapacitated parents. Before 1962 the program was known as Aid to Dependent Children (ADC). In that year it was named AFDC by Congress to reflect the changing nature of the program, which had covered needy parents of such children since 1950. In 1961 assistance was also extended, at state option, to needy children of unemployed parents (AFDC-UP). Since 1968 the state option has been limited to children deprived of care because of the father's unemployment. Currently 28 states participate in the AFDC-UP program. Since 1967 a Work Incentive program(WIN) has been in effect to require certain recipients to register for employment. In part, WIN aims to provide incentives to work.

The original objective of AFDC was to provide for needy children whose dependency was caused by a parent's incapacity, death, or continued absence from home. But over the years, the composition of the recipient groups has changed drastically. Now the majority of recipient families are those with a divorced, separated, or deserted parent. Some parents on AFDC have never been married. There are few families having a deceased or incapacitated parent, as income needs of such families are increasingly met by social security. Furthermore, the public has increasingly come to demand that AFDC mothers go out to work. These factors have led AFDC to become the most controversial welfare program, although it is not the largest of the welfare programs.

AFDC is financed and administered under federal-state partnership. The federal government finances 50 to 83 percent of the benefits paid to recipients (the rate depending on state per capita income) and additionally pays 50 percent of the administrative costs. State governments (in some cases local governments under state supervision) administer AFDC, but, to receive federal grants-in-aid for financing the program, states must comply with federal guidelines.

Under these guidelines developed by the federal government, the following requirements must be met:

- A person must be in need in order to receive assistance.
- The state must consider a person's available income and resources in determining eligibility and amount of assistance.
- The state must submit to the federal government a statewide plan for administering the program.
- The state must participate financially.
- The program must be statewide and administered by a single state agency.
- Opportunity must be provided for a fair hearing for any person whose application is denied or whose assistance is to be reduced or terminated.

In addition, states must not exclude individuals by establishing requirements of age and citizenship beyond those permitted by federal law. The U.S. Supreme Court has ruled that individuals cannot be disqualified for assistance simply because they fail to meet requirements for residence under state laws.

Beyond these broad guidelines, states have considerable leeway in setting up rules and regulations. Because there is no federal guideline in regard to the level of payments, assistance payments vary widely among states, with each state developing its own standards of need. Furthermore, payments in many states do not meet the standards so developed. In July 1978 less than half the states paid for 100 percent of the basic needs to families with no income. Among those that did not, Mississippi paid the lowest percentage of basic needs—32 percent.[15] Partly reflecting the variation in the level of payments, the average monthly payment per recipient varies considerably among states. As of October 1978, it ranged from $28.31 in Mississippi to $130.32 in Massachusetts and $135.44 in Alaska.[16]

In other areas also states have considerable latitude in deciding how the program will be organized and administered. For example, some states have a "suitable home" rule; that is, to be eligible for AFDC, a family must provide a home environment appropriate for raising children. Some states do not have such a rule. Furthermore, states differ regarding the time required, after a father deserts or becomes incapacitated, before his family can apply for AFDC. As another example, states differ regarding the maximum age at which children are no longer eligible for AFDC.[17]

An applicant must be proved needy through a means test in order to be eligible for AFDC. That is, the applicant must not have assets valued at more than a certain amount and must not have income more than a specified amount. Assistance payments are reduced $1 for each $1 of unearned income. Each $1 of earnings in excess of $30 a month reduces assistance payments by 67¢. Reasonable work expenses and expenditures for child care are subtracted from countable income. Before 1967, when the WIN program was put into effect, all income, whether unearned or earned, subjected AFDC payments to reduction at the rate of 100 percent. This meant that each earned dollar resulted in a $1 reduction in AFDC payments, making no difference in total family income. Thus additional work effort brought no additional income.

Except for children under 16 years of age or in school, the aged and the disabled, mothers with children under six years of age, and custodians for incapacitated persons, all AFDC recipients must register for the WIN program and may not refuse training or suitable employment. In states that provide assistance under AFDC-UP to needy families with unemployed fathers, the father must be registered with the state employment office. If a nonexempt person refuses to participate in the WIN program, that person—but not the rest of the family—becomes ineligible for AFDC. In states providing AFDC-UP, the father's refusal to accept employment offered by the state employment office makes the whole family ineligible for assistance. As of June 1980, 11 million persons benefited from the AFDC program, 69 percent of whom were children.[18]

Supplemental Security Income (SSI)

Enacted through the 1972 amendments to the Social Security Act, SSI is a federal income assistance program for the poor who are aged, blind, or disabled. This program became effective in January 1974, superseding the previous state public assistance programs for these three categories. The program, which federalized financial and administrative responsibilities, provided the first nationwide guaranteed income for these poor. States are responsible for financing supplementary benefits so that conversion will not decrease the level of benefits for those transferred from former state public assistance programs. However, a state is not required to finance state supplements beyond the "hold-harmless" level—that is, the level of that state's share of assistance expenditures in calendar year 1972. Nevertheless, many states do provide optional supplements beyond what is required under the law. States can arrange (through the Social Security Administration) for the federal government to administer both the federal payments and state supplementary payments, or state governments can administer both components, or the federal government and state governments can each administer their respective SSI component.

SSI requires tests of both assets and income. To be eligible for assistance, an individual must not have assets that exceed $1,500 in value; a couple must not have assets that exceed $2,250. Not all resources are counted in determining the cash value of assets. Major exclusions are a home and adjacent land and outbuildings, household goods and personal effects of reasonable value, property necessary for self-support, an automobile, life insurance with a face value up to $1,500, and, for the blind and disabled, resources necessary to achieve an approved self-support plan. Income cannot exceed stipulated amounts.

Eligibility requirements for the blind and the disabled under SSI are similar to those under disability insurance of social security, except that SSI involves tests of income and assets as well. Individuals must be diagnosed as blind or disabled to the extent that they have not been able to earn a significant amount from work for at least 12 months. Blind children and disabled children are covered under SSI, although they were excluded from former state public assistance programs of Aid to the Blind (AB) and Aid to the Totally and Permanently Disabled (APTD). For child recipients, prognosis of employability is not as important as for adult recipients.

Relatives bear no responsibility for SSI recipients. However, when an SSI recipient lives in the household of another, the SSI payments are automatically reduced by one third. It is presumed that the other person or persons in the household can assist the recipient to the extent of one third of SSI. It is also presumed that the income and resources of the parents with whom a blind or disabled child recipient lives are available to the recipient. Such income and resources are therefore included when calculating benefits.

Basic federal assistance payments vary according to the type of living arrangements. Recipients living independently get the full amount of assistance payments; recipients living in the household of another, two thirds of the full amount; those residing in nursing homes, $25 a month. A married couple receives one and one-half times as much as a single person. A person essential for maintaining the welfare of the recipient gets half of the federal basic payment of the single recipient. Increases in benefits are commensurate with the rise in the cost of living.

A work incentive is incorporated in the benefit formula. When the recipient earns from work, payments are reduced by $1 for each $2 of earned income over $195 per quarter (or over $255 if there is no unearned income). Unearned income over $60 per quarter—from rent, dividends, interest, and other private or public transfer payments—reduces SSI by its full amount.

Many states provide optional supplementary payments beyond what is required by the law. When states choose to administer such optional supplements, they may provide them under specific state laws. Thus, at least for paying optional supplementary amounts, some states place a lien on property, although this is not permitted for the federal SSI payments or for mandatory state supplements. Some states require that a wider range of relatives be financially responsible for aiding those receiving state optional supplements than is implied under the federal law. Because of state supplements, the level of payments varies among states, although not as widely as for AFDC. The average monthly payment per SSI recipient in October 1980 ranged from $116.35 in South Dakota to $255.60 in California. [19]

The number of the disabled on SSI has been increasing significantly over the years. This contrasts with the stable numbers of the blind and the aged on SSI. As a matter of fact, the number of the disabled is close to being the majority of all SSI recipients. All told, as of October 1980, over 4.2 million persons received benefits from the SSI program. [20]

General Assistance

General assistance is a generic term for a wide variety of income maintenance programs financed and administered solely by state and/or local governments. It is known by various names across the country, including general assistance, general relief, emergency relief, and home relief. Programs of this kind have a history that dates back to early statehood when states provided for paupers and indigents. Before the federal government became involved in various types of income maintenance programs, general assistance programs were the major means through which poor people were supported.

General assistance is designed to assist families who do not qualify for help under the federally aided assistance programs or, in a few states, families who are not receiving from federally aided programs enough assistance to meet their needs. This type of assistance often is the only resource for many temporarily or permanently unemployable persons and for persons out of work who either have exhausted or cannot qualify for unemployment insurance benefits or who receive inadequate benefits under that program. However, about a third of the states do not pay general assistance to families with an employable person in the household, except for carefully defined emergency situations.

The basic condition for eligibility is need, but definitions of eligibility vary widely among and within states. Other factors determining eligibility usually relate to employability, residence, assets, eligibility for federal income support programs, and the presence of relatives who are legally required to provide support. As of June 1980, 929,000 persons were assisted by the program. [21]

Under general assistance, the type and level of payments are generally more restricted than under any other type of assistance program. The most common forms of assistance are cash or vendor payments for such items as food, rent, utilities, and medical service. Many states assist families only during periods of emergency. Others limit the maximum time that an eligible person can receive assistance. In many states, there is a maximum payment, and recipients cannot receive more regardless of whether or not needs exceed this maximum. As of June 1980, the average monthly payment per recipient was $126.58, with Mississippi paying the lowest amount ($13.64) and Hawaii the highest ($167.75).[22]

Veterans' Pensions

The veterans' pension program, enacted in 1933, is designed to assist wartime veterans whose income and resources are insufficient and who have disabilities that are not service-connected but are permanent and total. The program is income-tested as compared with veterans' service-connected compensation programs, which take the form of social insurance. In 1960, changes were made so that benefits were to be reduced by less than 100 percent of earnings (the rate of reduction previously had been 100 percent) and to take into account the number of dependents when determining benefits. The program is administered through regional offices of the Department of Veterans' Benefits of the Veterans Administration. It is financed solely by the federal government.

To be eligible for pensions, recipients must have served 90 days or more in active wartime duty or, if less than 90 days, must have been released because of a service-related disability. In addition, they must be permanently and totally disabled or over 65. The level of assistance payments is determined by current income and the number of dependents. For each $1 of countable income, benefits are reduced between 36 and 96 percent. The exact rate at which benefits are reduced varies with the number of dependents and the amount of income received. There are no work requirements. Over 2.2 million individuals are benefiting from the program.[23]

Medicaid

Medicaid—Title XIX of the Social Security Act—was enacted to enable each state, at its option, to provide medical assistance to needy families with dependent children and to needy individuals who are aged, blind, or permanently and totally disabled; also, to provide rehabilitation and other needed services to help such families and individuals attain or retain capability for independence and self-care. Medicaid was enacted in 1965 along with Medicare, the former being a welfare program, the latter a social insurance program. Before the enactment of Medicaid, the federal government, under the 1950 amendments to the Social Security Act, participated in financing direct vendor payments for medical care for recipients of public assistance. In 1960 the federal government expanded its participation in financing direct vendor payments for the medically indigent. Medicaid was an attempt to consolidate and expand grants-in-aid to the states for their medical assistance to these groups of recipients and the medically indigent. At present all states except Arizona provide Medicaid. The federal share of the payments to providers of medical care ranges from 50 to 83 percent, depending on state per capita income. The program is administered by state and local governments, but the federal government pays more than half of the administrative costs.

Basically, three types of families are eligible for Medicaid: those who receive either AFDC or SSI; those who come under the "categorically needy" group, meaning individuals and families who would have been eligible for money payments except for an eligibility condition or requirement that is prohibited under Title XIX; and those who do not receive such aid but whose income is below 133 percent of state AFDC payment levels when their medical expenses are subtracted from their income.[24] Medicaid recipients in this third category are called the "medically indigent." At present only 25 states and the District of Columbia provide for the medically indigent. Other requirements for eligibility are more liberal than those under the former state medical assistance programs. Under Medicaid a state cannot impose a citizenship requirement that excludes any citizen of the United States, cannot place a lien on the recipient's property in order to recover the costs of medical assistance after the recipient's death, and cannot require that any relative be financially responsible for the Medicaid recipient except the recipient's spouse or the parent of a recipient 21 years old or less.

Medicaid provides two types of medical care services: required services and optional services. Required services include provision of inpatient hospital services (except in institutions for treatment of tuberculosis or mental diseases); outpatient hospital services; other laboratory and X-ray services; skilled nursing home services for persons aged 21 or over and home health care services to persons entitled to skilled nursing home services; physician's services; early screening, diagnostic, and treatment services for children under age 21, as provided by the regulations set forth by the secretary of the Department of Health and Human Services; and transportation to obtain medical care services.

Optional services include provision of prescribed drugs, dental services, eyeglasses, physical therapy, prosthetic devices, private duty nursing, nursing home services for persons under 21 years of age, care for persons aged 65 and over in institutions for the treatment of tuberculosis or mental illness, family planning services, and clinical services other than outpatient hospital services. Optional services also include care of individuals in intermediate care facilities.

Under the law, limited cost sharing is permitted for outpatient services, but few states impose it. For almost all AFDC and SSI recipients, covered medical services are provided free of charge. States pay medical expenses for the medically indigent only when recipient families "spend down" their income for medical care until their income reaches 133 percent of the state AFDC payment level. Currently more than 25 million persons benefit from the Medicaid program.[25]

Food Stamps

The food stamp program as we know it today was first enacted in 1964.[26] However, the practice of providing food stamps goes back to 1939, when Rochester, New York, provided them.[27] The program is administered by the Food and Nutrition Service of the U.S. Department of Agriculture through state and local welfare offices. The federal government pays over 50 percent of all administrative costs and the entire cost of benefits.

Income-testing and asset-testing are required, as well as work requirements for some recipients. There are no other requirements for eligibility. Thus the food stamp program is the only noncategorical welfare program in the United States. It is a sort of negative income tax program, offering recipients food stamps rather than cash.

Until 1979, recipients had to purchase food stamps. The bonus value—that is, the difference between the food stamp allotments and the purchase requirements—was the net benefit to the recipient family. This provision created difficulty for poor families, as many of them could not come up with cash to pay for the stamps. Because of this the law was changed to simply provide food stamps of the bonus (or net) value. The benefit levels are uniform across the country, except in Hawaii and Alaska, where higher benefits are provided.

Income level and family size are taken into account when calculating food stamp benefits. Payroll taxes, expenses for child care, medical expenses, and a portion of any excessive costs for shelter are deducted in calculating countable income. Public assistance payments are included as income. When a family's income increases, food stamp benefits are reduced by 30¢ for each additional dollar of net income.

There is a work requirement for able-bodied recipients who are 18 to 64 years of age; they must register at the local employment office and accept any bona fide offer of suitable employment. Children, students, mothers of children under six years of age, and those already working at least 30 hours a week are exempt from this requirement of work registration. If any member of the family refuses to accept a job, the entire household becomes ineligible for food stamps. In 1977, 24.7 million individuals received food stamps.[28]

Housing Assistance

Several forms of housing assistance exist for low-income families. The most widely used form is provided through rental subsidies under Section 8 of the Housing and Community Development Act of 1974, which was enacted as an amendment to the Housing Act of 1937. This was intended eventually to replace the more traditional forms of housing subsidy. The program is funded through annual appropriations to the Department of Housing and Urban Development (HUD), which enters into annual contribution contracts with local housing authorities. In turn, the local housing authorities may enter into subsidy contracts with owners of rental housing, on behalf of low-income families.

To be eligible for assistance under Section 8, a family must have a total family income that is below 80 percent of the area median income (at the time of application). Income is defined comprehensively, although some exclusions are allowed, and it is estimated on a prospective annual basis. There is no assets test, but income is imputed, at a rate of 10 percent per year, on assets in excess of $5,000. There is no work test or job search requirement.

Benefits are in kind, but are not as restrictive as for traditional public housing. The certified family pays an income-conditioned rent to the owner of an eligible rental unit, and the local housing authority makes up the difference between the income-conditioned rent and the market rent (which cannot exceed 110 percent of the area "fair market rent" established by HUD). The family contribution to rent is 15 or 25 percent of family income. A large family with very low income or a family with exceptionally high medical expenses pays 15 percent of countable income; all other families pay 25 percent of countable income, but no less than 15 percent of gross annual income. The benefit to the family, then, is the amount that the local housing authority pays to the landlord, that is, the difference between 15 or 25 percent of family income and the market rent. Thus, when family income increases, the amount of assistance decreases at the rate of 15 or 25 percent of the increase, depending on the family's contribution rate.

In addition to the program under Section 8, there are other types of housing assistance for low-income families. Under Section 235 of the Housing Act, for example, low-income families are helped to own a home; under Section 202, low-cost housing is provided for the elderly; and under Section 236, low-interest loans are made to builders of rental and cooperative housing for persons with low and moderate income. Many other programs also assist suppliers of housing for low-income families.

CHARACTERISTICS OF INCOME
MAINTENANCE PROGRAMS

It is difficult to generalize about the characteristics of the more than
40 different income maintenance programs. However, it is possible
to distinguish in broad terms between welfare programs and social
insurance programs, as well as between social insurance programs
and private insurance programs.

Distinguishing Between Welfare and
Social Insurance Programs

The most important difference between welfare programs and
social insurance programs is that the former invariably involve a test
of income or a test of assets or both, while the latter do not. [29] Welfare payments are provided on the basis of current financial need,
but social insurance benefits are calculated on the basis of past earnings and employment records. Associated with this difference is the
fact that welfare payments have generally been based on individual
need, and social insurance benefits have been based on presumptive
need. Individual need refers to the financial support a particular family needs, giving due consideration to the cost of its food, clothing,
and shelter. Presumptive need refers to a presumed amount of need,
given certain characteristics of a group of beneficiaries. Thus, under
a social insurance program, benefits are the same for individuals
within a group of beneficiaries who have similar earnings and employment records and the same family composition.

In recent years, however, welfare payment levels have been
established more and more on the basis of presumptive need. SSI is
a good example. Under SSI, the basic levels of federal assistance
payments were developed by taking into account the national average
cost of food, clothing, and shelter for families of various sizes under
various living arrangements such as independent domicile or congre-
gate care.

Another distinguishing mark between welfare and social insurance is the concept of entitlement to benefits. An individual's contributions to a social insurance program entitle that person to specified
benefits upon meeting the requirements for eligibility. This concept
does not apply to a welfare program. Although the Social Security Act
of 1935 adopted the concept of the right to assistance from public
assistance programs, the concept has not been implemented. If it
were to be implemented, all states would be required to assist all
eligible needy families. But such is not the case.

Last, welfare programs tend to be more concerned with work

incentives for recipients than social insurance programs are. Thus many welfare programs not only incorporate work incentives in the payment formulas but also specify work requirements. Welfare's pre-occupation with work incentives seems to stem from the public's belief that the recipient is getting "something for nothing," the public's wish to influence recipients' behavior, and the public's fear that more people may cross the line and become welfare recipients.

Distinguishing Between Social Insurance and Private Insurance

Social insurance is similar to private insurance in various respects. Both try to pool risks; both explicitly state all conditions related to coverage, benefits, and financing; both calculate benefits impartially according to a set formula; and both specify the rates of contributions (or premiums). At the same time, social insurance differs from private insurance in important ways. First, private insurance is based strictly on the principle of individual equity, whereas social insurance implements the principle of social adequacy as well. Individual equity is generally understood to mean that the contributor receives benefits directly related to the contributions made. Social adequacy is generally understood to mean that benefits are calculated so as to provide the insured with an acceptable standard of living. Second, participation in compulsory under social insurance and voluntary under private insurance. Third, social insurance creates a statutory relationship between two parties, whereas private insurance creates a contractual relationship. The statutory provision can be changed by the legislature but the contractual provision cannot. Fourth, private insurance must be fully funded so as to protect the right of the insured, but social insurance does not need to be fully funded because its financial soundness depends on the government's taxing power and because it is compulsory and statutory.[30]

NOTES

1. Alma W. McMillan and Ann Kallman Bixby, "Social Welfare Expenditures, Fiscal Year 1978," Social Security Bulletin 43 (May 1980): 8.

2. Ibid.

3. Henry Aaron, "Social Security: International Comparisons," in Studies in the Economics of Income Maintenance, ed. Otto Eckstein (Washington, D.C.: Brookings Institution, 1967), pp. 13-48.

4. Harold L. Wilensky, The Welfare State and Equality: Struc-

tural and Ideological Roots of Public Expenditures (Berkeley: University of California Press, 1975).

5. Martha N. Ozawa, "An Exploration into States' Commitment to AFDC," Journal of Social Service Research 1 (Spring 1978): 245-59.

6. For detailed discussion on income redistribution as social process, see Robert J. Lampman, "Transfer and Redistribution as Social Process," in Social Security in International Perspective, ed. Shirley Jenkins (New York: Columbia University Press, 1969), pp. 30-54.

7. McMillan and Bixby, op. cit., p. 17; and Alfred W. Klodrubetz, "Two Decades of Employee-Benefit Plans, 1950-70: A Review," Social Security Bulletin 35 (April 1972): 10-22.

8. U.S. Department of Health, Education, and Welfare, Social Security Administration, Social Security Programs in the United States: 1973 (Washington, D.C.: U.S. Government Printing Office, 1973), p. 17.

9. U.S. Department of Health, Education, and Welfare, Social Security Administration, Social Security Programs in the United States: 1973; U.S. Congress, Subcommittee on Fiscal Policy of the Joint Economic Committee, 92nd Congr., 2d Sess., Handbook of Public Income Transfer Programs, Studies in Public Welfare, Paper no. 2 (Washington, D.C.: U.S. Government Printing Office, 1972); and Martha N. Ozawa, "Income Maintenance Programs," in Handbook of the Social Services, ed. Neil Gilbert and Harry Specht (Englewood Cliffs, N.J.: Prentice-Hall, 1981).

10. U.S. Department of Health and Human Services, Social Security Administration, Office of Research and Statistics, Monthly Benefit Statistics, no. 10 (Washington, D.C.: Social Security Administration, November 6, 1981).

11. Robert J. Lampman, "Employment Versus Income Maintenance," in Jobs for Americans, ed. Eli Ginzberg (Englewood Cliffs, N.J.: Prentice-Hall, 1976), pp. 165-66.

12. Social Security Bulletin 43 (May 1980): 65.

13. U.S. Congress, Subcommittee on Fiscal Policy of the Joint Economic Committee, Handbook of Public Income Transfer Programs, pp. 83, 87.

14. U.S. Department of Health, Education, and Welfare, Social Security Administration, Social Security Bulletin: Annual Statistical Supplement, 1977-1979 (Washington, D.C.: Social Security Administration, 1980), p. 202.

15. U.S. Department of Health, Education, and Welfare, Social Security Administration, AFDC Standards for Basic Needs, July 1978 (Washington, D.C.: Social Security Administration, March 1979), p. 14.

16. Social Security Bulletin 43 (May 1980): 61.

17. U.S. Department of Health, Education, and Welfare, Social and Rehabilitation Service, Assistance Payments Administration, Characteristics of State Plans for Aid to Families with Dependent Children, 1974 ed. (Washington, D.C.: U.S. Government Printing Office, 1974).

18. Social Security Bulletin 44 (February 1981): 55.

19. Ibid., p. 48.

20. Ibid., p. 47.

21. Ibid., p. 59.

22. Ibid.

23. U.S. Congress, Subcommittee on Fiscal Policy of the Joint Economic Committee, Handbook of Public Income Transfer Programs, pp. 156, 163.

24. Categorical assistance programs generally refer to income-tested cash assistance programs provided for certain categories of poor. Currently, SSI and AFDC represent categorical assistance programs.

25. U.S. Department of Health, Education, and Welfare, Office of the Assistant Secretary for Planning and Evaluation, "General Approaches to Welfare Reform," Discussion Paper, February 12, 1977.

26. For an excellent review of the development of the food stamp program, see Maurice MacDonald, "Food Stamps: An Analytical History," Social Service Review 51 (December 1977): 642-58.

27. Irwin Garfinkel and Felicity Skidmore, "Income Support Policy: Where We've Come From and Where We Should Be Going," Discussion Paper no. 490-78 (Madison: Institute for Research on Poverty, University of Wisconsin, April 1978).

28. U.S. Department of Health, Education, and Welfare, "General Approaches to Welfare Reform," op. cit.

29. For detailed discussion, see Eveline M. Burns, The American Social Security System (New York: Houghton Mifflin, 1949), pp. 28-39.

30. Robert J. Myers, Social Insurance and Allied Government Programs (Homewood, Ill.: Irwin, 1965), pp. 6, 9-10.

3

MEASUREMENTS OF
POVERTY AND INEQUALITY

Since Michael Harrington wrote his famous book The Other America, poverty has been rediscovered in the United States.[1] President Lyndon B. Johnson declared war on poverty and set forth social policy to eradicate poverty from our then increasingly affluent society. Numerous antipoverty programs, including the major income maintenance programs reviewed in Chapter 2, have since been initiated or expanded; and public expenditures for such programs have increased greatly.

If the main purpose of domestic policies under the Johnson administration was to eradicate poverty, it is important to understand the definitions of poverty before evaluating antipoverty effects of specific programs. How were poverty thresholds drawn up by the government? In drawing up thresholds, which concept of income was used? Was it gross money income or net disposable income? Was it annual income or income received over a longer period of time? What was the unit of analysis: family or household income? Did the government calculate the percentage of families who were poor or the percentage of persons living in a poor family? What are the implications of using one definition instead of another?

There is still another problem in defining poverty. What was the policy goal of eradicating poverty? Did it aim to eradicate absolute poverty and thus ensure that all the nation's families would have a basket of goods and services of a definite size? Or did it aim to decrease relative poverty?

Once poverty is considered as a relative concept, the question of inequality is bound to be raised. Even after the war on poverty is won, can income stay as unequal as it is now? Can society be content with such a state of being? If not, what price must be paid to lessen inequality, and under what circumstances can it be lessened?

43

DEVELOPMENT OF POVERTY THRESHOLDS

The poverty thresholds as we know them today were developed in 1964 by Mollie Orshansky of the Social Security Administration (SSA) and became the official SSA poverty thresholds. Since 1969, the official poverty thresholds have been used by the Bureau of the Census to estimate the percentage of the population who are poor. The idea of poverty-line income is not new, however. Charles Booth, a pioneering student of poverty in England, developed eight income classes and de-fined families to be poor if they fell into one of the bottom four. The poverty thresholds were set at 21 shillings per week for a small family and 25 shillings for a large family.[2] With thresholds so defined, Booth found that 32 percent of the London population were living in poverty in 1891. B. Seebohm Rowntree's study in York, eight years after the Booth study, further refined the concept of poverty thresholds. He established two types of poverty: "primary poverty" and "secondary poverty." A family was living in primary poverty if it had an income below the minimum subsistence level described in Rowntree's family living budgets. A family was living in secondary poverty if it had an income higher than the subsistence level but was existing under the same miserable economic conditions as a result of the mismanage-ment of income. Based on these criteria, Rowntree found 28 percent of the York population living in primary poverty and an additional 10 percent in secondary poverty.[3] In the United States in 1904, Robert Hunter defined poverty-line income to be $460 a year for a family of ordinary size who lived in the northern industrial states. He found that 20 percent of the population living in New York, Massachusetts, Connecticut, Indiana, and Michigan were poor.[4]

Oscar Ornati traced budgets based on living standards that vari-ous social service agencies defined over the period 1905-60. He traced three different levels of family budgets: "minimum subsistence," "minimum adequacy," and "minimum comfort." He found that all three levels moved upward in real terms as time went on.[5] In his analysis, the minimum subsistence level applied to a "charity" class. Social service agencies had selected the charity class as their target for the provision of assistance. These agencies used the minimum subsistence level of income to establish eligibility for income support and other related social services.

Lee Rainwater surveyed public opinion polls for the period 1946-69 and found a similar upward trend in the public's perception of poverty-line income. He surveyed the findings from 18 public opinion polls taken during this period, which asked: "What is the smallest amount of money a family of 4 needs (weekly) to get along in this com-munity?" He found that the public's perception of poverty-line income increased from $80.30 a week in 1946 to $119.72 in 1969, in constant dollars.[6]

The federal government's first pronouncement of poverty thresholds was made in 1964, when the Council of Economic Advisors defined an unrelated individual as poor who had an income below $1,500 and a family as poor who had an income below $3,000. Based on such definitions, the council found that 8.8 million families (or 19 percent) and 4.9 million unrelated individuals (or 44 percent) were living in poverty in 1963.[7] The poverty thresholds developed by Mollie Orshansky were a refinement of the concept first operationalized by the Council of Economic Advisors.

Orshansky developed the poverty thresholds in a three-step process.[8] First she obtained weekly food budgets for individuals grouped by age and sex, based on an "economy food plan" developed by the Department of Agriculture. The economy plan was intended for temporary or emergency use when family funds were low. Thus it assumed that all meals would be prepared at home from foods purchased at retail. Furthermore, to have a viable economy plan and to ensure an acceptable level of nutrition within the budget constraints, the homemaker had to be able to manage money sensibly. As a matter of fact, the food budget in the economy plan was only about 75 to 80 percent as much as the basic "low-cost" plan that the Department of Agriculture had also developed. This low-cost plan, adapted to patterns of food consumption by families in the lowest third of the income range, had been used by state welfare departments as a basis for food allotments to needy families. Therefore the food budget Orshansky used in developing the poverty thresholds is modest indeed.

The second step was to calculate food budgets for various types of families, differentiated by the age and sex of the head of the household and by family size. The third step was to calculate the weighted average poverty thresholds for various types of families by estimating the percentage of income spent for food. Orshansky assumed that the poor generally spend a larger percentage than do the nonpoor. The Bureau of Labor Statistics reported that in 1961 urban families spent between 22 and 28 percent of their income for food, with large families generally spending a higher proportion than small families.[9] Thus Orshansky believed that the idea that the poor would spend a third of their total income for food was a reasonable one. She therefore multiplied the annual food budget by three to obtain the poverty threshold.

Poverty thresholds were further differentiated to apply to nonfarm and farm families. Orshansky assumed that farm families could benefit from homegrown foods and from the real property on which they live. Thus she developed a separate set of thresholds for farm families, using 85 percent of the poverty thresholds applicable to nonfarm families. The poverty thresholds have been updated to account for changes in the consumer price index and also have been extended backward to 1959.

TABLE 3.1

Weighted Average Thresholds at the Poverty Level in 1978,
by Size of Family and Sex of Head, by Farm-Nonfarm Residence
(in dollars)

Size of Family Unit	Total	Nonfarm			Total	Farm	
		Total	Male Head*	Female Head*		Male Head*	Female Head*
1 person (unrelated individual)	3,302	3,311	3,460	3,196	2,795	2,898	2,690
14 to 64 years	3,386	3,392	3,516	3,253	2,913	2,987	2,764
65 years and over	3,116	3,127	3,159	3,118	2,661	2,685	2,650
2 persons	4,225	4,249	4,258	4,206	3,578	3,582	3,497
Head 14 to 64 years	4,363	4,383	4,407	4,286	3,731	3,737	3,614
Head 65 years and over	3,917	3,944	3,948	3,923	3,352	3,354	3,313
3 persons	5,178	5,201	5,231	5,065	4,413	4,430	4,216
4 persons	6,628	6,662	6,665	6,632	5,681	5,683	5,622
5 persons	7,833	7,880	7,888	7,806	6,714	6,714	6,700
6 persons	8,825	8,891	8,895	8,852	7,541	7,543	7,462
7 persons or more	10,926	11,002	11,038	10,765	9,373	9,386	8,813

*For one person (that is, unrelated individual), sex of the individual.

Source: U.S. Bureau of the Census, Current Population Reports, Series P-60, no. 124, Characteristics of the Population Below the Poverty Level, 1978 (Washington, D.C.: U.S. Government Printing Office, 1980), Table A-3, p. 208.

Based on the poverty thresholds developed according to the fore-going three-step process, Orshansky arrived at an annual poverty-line income in 1963 for families of varying composition—for example, $3,130 for a nonfarm family of four, headed by a nonaged person, and $1,540 for a nonfarm, nonaged individual. She applied the poverty threshold to estimate the proportion of families and individuals who were poor. She found that 15 percent of families and 44 percent of unrelated individuals were living in poverty. These findings were re-markably similar to those of the Council of Economic Advisors. How-ever, when the incidence of poverty was investigated for specific groups of families, rates of the incidence of poverty differed greatly from those found by the council. For example, a higher percentage of large families fell below the poverty level under the council's defini-tion of poverty than under Orshansky's definition. This difference stemmed from the fact that Orshansky's thresholds were more sensi-tive to family size than the thresholds developed by the council.

Table 3.1 shows poverty thresholds for 1978 for various types of families, and Table 3.2 shows the number of persons and the per-centage of the population below the poverty level for selected years. Both tables were developed from data provided by the Current Popu-lation Survey (CPS), which is conducted annually by the Bureau of the Census. The CPS uses gross annual money income of families and unrelated individuals to identify those who are poor and then counts the number of persons living in such families or as unrelated individ-uals. Table 3.2 shows that the number of poor persons declined both in absolute terms and as a percentage of the population until the early 1970s. Since then, the number and the percentage have been relatively stable.

Few governmental indexes have been used so widely for various political and academic purposes as the SSA poverty thresholds devel-oped by Orshansky: They have facilitated the establishment of grant-in-aid formulas for various federal welfare and manpower programs, and they have enabled academic and governmental researchers to measure the effectiveness of various antipoverty programs. However, a great deal of controversy surrounds the SSA poverty thresholds and the way that the federal government has used them to estimate the incidence of poverty.

Substandard Level of Poverty Thresholds

A widespread criticism points to the extremely low level of the economy plan food budget used in developing the SSA poverty thresh-olds. The budget allowed for no meals purchased outside the home. If a husband bought a lunch at the work place or a child spent money

TABLE 3.2

Persons Below the Poverty Level, by Family Status: Selected Years

Year	All Persons (in millions)	Percent Below Poverty Level		
		All Persons	Persons in Families	Unrelated Individuals
1960	39.8	22.2	20.7	45.2
1965	33.1	19.0	17.4	42.7
1970	25.4	12.6	10.9	32.9
1975	25.8	12.3	10.9	25.1
1978	24.4	11.4	10.0	22.1

Source: U.S. Bureau of the Census, Current Population Reports, Series P-60, no. 124, Characteristics of the Population Below the Poverty Level, 1978 (Washington, D.C.: U.S. Government Printing Office, 1980), Table 1, p. 16.

for a school lunch, these expenses had to be deducted from the already low budget. It may be unreasonable to impose, as a permanent concept of income, an income based on an economy food plan intended for temporary use. Also, it may be unreasonable to expect homemakers of low-income families to have the knowledge and the management skills required to provide an acceptable level of nutrition on so meager a budget.

Inaccurate Method of Calculating the Incidence
of Poverty

Ever since the SSA poverty thresholds were developed, the CPS reports regarding the incidence of poverty have been based on these thresholds. However, in estimating the incidence of poverty, CPS has used—as did Orshansky in 1964—gross annual money income received by a family or by an unrelated individual before taxes. Gross annual money income means the total income that a family (or an unrelated individual) receives in the form of money during the course of one year from all sources, including governmental transfer programs. The use of such a measure of income tends to overstate the true incidence of poverty in some ways and to understate it in others. Furthermore, it may not be possible to estimate precisely the true incidence of poverty on the basis of gross annual money income.

Why is this the case? The reason is that gross annual money income does not precisely measure economic well-being. To measure economic well-being based on the principle of horizontal equity—that is, similar treatment of families with the same economic well-being—one needs to make various adjustments to gross annual money income received by a family or an unrelated individual.

First, there are certain costs involved in obtaining income, for instance, taxes, child care costs, and commuting costs. When these items are not considered and gross annual money income is not adjusted accordingly, the incidence of poverty tends to be understated. Furthermore, failure to consider them may put many families into a wrong income class. Take the following example: Family A receives income from rent, interest, and dividends. Family B earns the same amount of income from work. Family B has to pay social security taxes, child care costs if it has small children to care for, and transportation costs. Family A does not pay all these costs. Both families may or may not pay income taxes, depending on the level of income. Thus the level of net money income, which is a more sensible concept of economic well-being, is quite different for the two types of families, although they receive the same amount of gross annual money income.

Second, gross annual money income does not include other, nonmonetary income. Many governmental programs provide assistance to low-income families, not in cash but, for example, in food stamps, public housing, medical care, or day care. Some individuals may receive free housing as a fringe benefit at the work place or from relatives and friends. Failure to include these types of income would overstate the true incidence of poverty. Also, money income figures cannot differentiate between the economic well-being of the home owner and the renter. The home owner "receives" imputed rent through ownership of the house. In contrast, the renter has to pay for a rented apartment or a house from money income on hand. Therefore, given the same level of money income and the same monthly payments for housing, the home owner is better off than the renter.

Third, annual gross money income reported by CPS does not correct for the underreporting of income by the respondent. It is estimated that the aggregate amount of underreporting is as much as 10 to 12 percent. Some types of income are underreported more than others. Wages and salaries are underreported by 12 percent, public assistance by 25 percent, social security benefits by 10 percent, unemployment insurance benefits and government pensions by 40 percent, and dividends and interest by as much as 45 percent.[10] Underreporting of income inevitably results in overstatement of the incidence of poverty.

Fourth, the annual gross money income published in the Current Population Survey applies to families and unrelated individuals. But many persons live with others who are not related to them by blood. Those who live with other individuals benefit from the collective use of a house and the economy of scale involved in paying for food and other living necessities. Thus failure to use the household as a unit of analysis of income would overstate the incidence of poverty.

Fifth, the use of gross annual money income is deficient in differentiating the poor from the nonpoor in the long run. For a promising young person attending school, inadequate income for a few years does not mean being poor years hence. If income is averaged over a number of years, that person may well belong in the nonpoor category. On the other hand, a low-income level may be repeated year after year in the case of a large family headed by an uneducated person. In short, the annual income concept cannot account for life-cycle fluctuations that affect the level of income over time. Thus annual income, as used by Orshansky and the CPS, cannot measure a family's true economic status over the family's entire life span; nor can it measure the percentage of the population whose lifetime average income falls below the poverty level.

To compound the problem involved in measuring income to calculate the percentage of the population who are poor, the SSA poverty thresholds are based on a static notion of poverty. That is, the poverty thresholds have not been upgraded commensurate with the rise in standards of living but only with the rise in the consumer price index. As a result, the poverty thresholds tend to lag behind average family income over time. To be more specific, during the period 1960-75, the median family income increased by 34 percent in real terms, but the purchasing power of poverty-line income was constant. As a result, the poverty threshold for a family of four expressed as a percentage of the median family income decreased from 53 percent in 1960 to 40 percent in 1975.[11]

It is ironic that before the government's official poverty thresholds were announced, the definition of poverty had been made in an ad hoc manner, as the study by Ornati showed, but the level of poverty-line income nonetheless had increased over time, reflecting the rise in standards of living and the public's perception of what constitutes a subsistence level of living. But since the federal government's pronouncement of the official definition of poverty in the early 1960s, the level of poverty-line income has been frozen in real terms and has not been allowed to move upward commensurate with the rise in standards of living. The federal government's adoption of the static concept of poverty thresholds has profound implications in evaluating and interpreting the effects of income maintenance programs and other related antipoverty programs.

Research Efforts to Make Adjustments
to Gross Annual Money Income

Many research projects have focused on the foregoing problems. The intent of such projects has been to make proper adjustments to gross annual money income and to obtain a more accurate estimate of the incidence of poverty.

The Congressional Budget Office investigated the incidence of poverty and used income figures much closer to the net disposable income of individuals and families.[12] The study adjusted the CPS figures of gross annual money income in several ways. It included income received in the form of in-kind benefits (food stamps, child nutrition, housing assistance, Medicare and Medicaid), corrected income figures to account for underreporting of certain types of income, and deducted taxes paid by families and individuals. In adding in-kind income transfers to income figures, the study used the average benefits received by participants of a particular program, not the actual benefits of each recipient. Individuals were treated as a one-person family. The findings from the study are startling. When all the adjustments were made, the incidence of poverty among all families in 1976 went down from 13.5 to 8.3 percent. Let us elaborate this finding in more detail.

When in-kind income transfers were added to gross annual money income, the incidence of poverty among all families went down from 13.5 to 8.1 percent. When taxes—mainly payroll taxes, as low-income families pay little income tax—were reduced from income figures (which already included in-kind income transfers), the incidence of poverty increased from 8.1 to 8.3 percent. One can say from this finding that the addition of in-kind income transfers does make a considerable difference in the incidence of poverty, but that the deduction of taxes from income does not. Such a tendency is especially pronounced in the case of the elderly. The inclusion of in-kind income transfers decreased the incidence of poverty among the elderly from 16.7 to 6.1 percent. The deduction of taxes from income did not increase their incidence of poverty at all; it stayed at 6.1 percent.

Some might object to the inclusion of benefits from Medicare and Medicaid as part of in-kind income. Mollie Orshansky, for example, objects to this inclusion because it tends to pull artificially out of poverty the sickness-prone segments of the population, who benefit greatly from Medicare and Medicaid.[13] Certainly, there is an awkward relationship between the level of illness and the level of income. The sicker certain groups of individuals are, the richer they are. This may be especially true in the case of the elderly, as they tend to become ill more often and stay ill longer than the nonaged. On the other hand, it should be remembered that the study by the

Congressional Budget Office used the average benefits, not individual benefits, of Medicare and Medicaid and included the market value of such benefits in income of the elderly. Such average benefits can be, in a way, considered as a value of insurance premiums that people normally pay from their own income. At any rate, the case of the elderly warrants closer scrutiny.

| | Incidence of Poverty Among Families by Age of Head, 1976 (in percentage) | |
	65 and Over	Under 65
When gross money income alone is considered	16.7	12.7
When in-kind income transfers other than Medicare and Medicaid are added	14.1	10.6
When Medicare and Medicaid are added as well	6.1	8.6
When taxes are deducted	6.1	8.9

It is clear that the inclusion of Medicare and Medicaid benefits as part of income makes a dramatic difference in the incidence of poverty among families headed by the elderly. When in-kind income transfers other than Medicare and Medicaid were taken into account, the incidence of poverty among the elderly was 14.1 percent. However, when Medicare and Medicaid were also included as part of in-kind income, it dropped to 6.1 percent—a 57 percent drop in the rate of poverty. Is it reasonable to include these benefits as part of income? This is hard to answer. The elderly would have to pay for medical care if it were not for Medicare and Medicaid. But because they do not pay directly from their own pockets for a sizable part of medical bills under Medicare, and none at all under Medicaid, their use of medical care services may be greater than if they were not under these programs. If this is true, adding the value of these benefits as part of income would artificially inflate income among the elderly. The result would be an understatement of the incidence of poverty among the elderly.

Morton Paglin made a study similar to that of the Congressional Budget Office. His study attempted to examine the incidence of poverty by adjusting gross annual money income to correct for the underreporting of income, for taxes paid, and for the market values of in-kind income transfers received (food stamps, housing assistance, medical care, other food and nutrition benefits, and maternal and child health care). And it did more. The study used the households as the unit for analyzing income instead of the family and the unrelated individual, which the Congressional Budget Office used. The study then counted the persons living in a poor household or as unrelated individuals to calculate the incidence of poverty. After the adjustments were made, Paglin found that only 3.6 percent of all persons in the United States were living in poverty in 1975.[14] Although there are some methodological problems in Paglin's study, it seems clear that in-kind benefits substantially lower the incidence of poverty.[15]

These studies by the Congressional Budget Office and by Paglin still do not deal with the problem of the CPS income figures, which are annual in concept. Because annual income tends to fluctuate, the incidence of poverty based on annual income figures tends to be biased upward. A study by Richard Coe dealt with this, in addition to some other problems studied by the Congressional Budget Office and by Paglin.

Coe developed average annual income figures for families during the five-year period 1967-71.[16] The income level for each year was adjusted for the cost of earning the income (federal individual income taxes) and income received in kind (imputed rent to home owners, rent value of free housing, amount saved on food at work or school, and the net value of food stamps). When annual income figures for 1971 were used, Coe found that, after these adjustments were made, the incidence of poverty among families was 5.9 percent. However, he found that 41.3 percent of those poor in 1971 were not poor when the five-year annual average income was used. On the other hand, 29.9 percent of those poor when the five-year average annual income was used were not poor in 1971. Taking the forces from the two directions into account, the incidence of poverty based on the five-year average was 4.9 percent; that is, it was one percentage point lower than the incidence of poverty based on the one-year figures. Coe's findings indicate that the poor one year are not necessarily poor other years. They also indicate that the reverse is true, but to a lesser extent: Some may have been poor in other years who were not poor in the one year when the rate of poverty was calculated.

The probability of being poor during the entire five-year period differs according to the demographic backgrounds of families. For example, 10.1 percent of poor black families stayed poor for the entire five years, compared with only 1.3 percent of white families. One out of every six poor families headed by a person with a fifth-grade education or less stayed poor for the entire five-year period, compared with only 0.9 percent of families headed by a person with a 12th-grade education. Only six-tenths of 1 percent of poor families headed by a person who was not disabled stayed poor for the entire five-year period, but 10.1 percent of poor families headed by a person who was disabled all along stayed poor for the entire period.[17] In the final analysis, the most statistically important predictor of how many years a family would stay poor during the five-year period was education, followed by race, and then disability status of the head of the family.

The study by Coe sheds some light on what might happen to the incidence of poverty when income figures are obtained by averaging income over a longer period than one year. It shows that a smaller percentage of families would be poor if the five-year average annual income was used than if annual income was used. However great caution should be taken in interpreting such a finding. There is a built-in bias in a study such as Coe's. It should be remembered that the poverty thresholds are based on a static concept, and that income levels tend to move upward in real terms as years go by. Therefore, as long as American families benefit from economic growth, and thus from rising standards of living, one would expect a smaller percentage of families to fall below the poverty line. A similar result would be expected when the average annual income during a five-year period is used. That is, the average annual income tends to be higher than the annual income in the first year of the period because of the rise in living standard; therefore, the incidence of poverty based on the five-year average annual income would tend to be lower than the incidence based on the annual income in the first year of that five-year period.

The study by Coe, however, compared the incidence of poverty based on the five-year average annual income with that based on 1971—the last year of the period—and still found the incidence for the five-year period lower than for the one year. Thus one would expect that the difference would be even more pronounced if the incidence of poverty based on the five-year average annual income was compared with the incidence based on the income in the first year, 1967. The point that needs to be made is that, whichever way the comparison is made, a built-in bias exists as long as a static concept of poverty thresholds is used. To neutralize such a bias when investigating changes in the incidence of poverty over time, a dynamic concept of poverty thresholds needs to be developed.

Researchers at the Institute for Research on Poverty at the University of Wisconsin have made some efforts to neutralize such a built-in bias. Robert Plotnick and Felicity Skidmore, for example, developed a relative measure of poverty thresholds by keeping constant over time the ratio of poverty thresholds to the median family income.[18] They found that in 1965 the poverty-line income for a family of four was 44 percent of the median income for families of the same size. They developed poverty thresholds that stayed at 44 percent of the median family income. Using this relative measure of poverty thresholds, Sheldon Danziger and Robert Plotnick calculated the incidence of poverty for different years.[19] The findings are startling. When this relative measure of poverty thresholds was used, the incidence of poverty decreased infinitesimally during the period 1956-78. In 1965, 15.6 percent of all persons in the United States were poor; 15.5 percent were poor in 1978. But when the absolute (or static) poverty thresholds were used, the incidence of poverty decreased from 15.6 to 11.4 percent during the same period. It should be noted that in making these calculations, Danziger and Plotnick used annual gross money income figures before taxes.

What are the implications of using the concept of relative poverty instead of the concept of absolute poverty? A study by Sidney Zimbalist sheds light on this. His study compares the British and the American poverty thresholds and investigates the effects of the use of these poverty-line concepts. The British poverty thresholds are based on a dynamic concept; the American, on a static.[20] That is, the British poverty thresholds have been upgraded every year to account for the rise in general standards of living. But the American poverty thresholds have been upgraded just to account for the rise in the consumer price index. Because of this difference, it appears that the United States has been conquering poverty much more quickly than Britain. But this is an illusion, because basically absolute poverty in the United States is being compared with relative poverty in Britain. Because the United States has adopted a static notion of poverty thresholds, one would naturally expect that a smaller and smaller percentage of the population would fall below these thresholds as long as general standards of living increase over time. But in Britain, which adopted a dynamic notion of poverty thresholds, one would expect that a relatively stable percentage of the population would fall below the poverty thresholds.

On top of all these adjustments to gross annual money income made by researchers, some economists believe that current economic well-being should also reflect the annuity value of the net worth of the wealth a family holds. A study by Burton Weisbrod and W. Lee Hansen indicates that if families had drawn annuity income in 1962 from all the wealth they held, the average family income would have been about 9 percent higher. If such a measure of income were used to calculate the percentage of the population who are poor in the United States, the incidence of poverty would be lower than otherwise.[21]

Marilyn Moon expanded the Weisbrod-Hansen study. In studying the income levels of the elderly in 1966, she included in income not only the value of net worth held by the elderly but also intrafamily transfers. She further adjusted earnings by the elderly, so that earnings made during the years of labor force participation could be spread over the entire lifetime of the elderly. Based on such a broad measure of income—or "economic welfare" as Moon calls it—she found that the mean income of the elderly was one and a half times larger than the mean gross annual income, and the proportion of aged families with less than $2,000 was only 14 percent compared with 40 percent when the annual money income measure was used.

A broad income measure such as the one used by Moon transforms gross annual money income into something quite different conceptually. Whereas gross annual money income measures the level of flows of money income during the course of one year, the broad income measure used by Moon captures the level of total "consumption possibilities" that are available steadily during the lifetime of a person living in a household. Such a broad measure indeed can capture the level of economic well-being more precisely than gross annual money income figures normally used by government agencies to measure the economic well-being of individuals and families.[22]

The foregoing discussion indicates that controversy and complexity abound both with regard to the poverty thresholds themselves and also with regard to how the incidence of poverty is calculated. The question of how many people are poor in the United States can be answered in countless ways. The answer depends on whether one uses a static concept of poverty thresholds or a dynamic one, and how one defines income. Is it annual income or the average annual income over a number of years? Is it gross money income or net disposable income, which includes in-kind income transfers? Is it income before or after taxes are paid? Finally, the incidence of poverty differs according to the unit of analysis of income and living arrangements—family, household, or individual.

POVERTY AND INEQUALITY

Are the poor in the United States becoming better off? In relation to what? Do we have fewer poor people now than in years before? These questions are often asked but seldom answered precisely. A part of the confusion, as alluded to earlier, is that one can calculate the percentage of the population who are poor by various types of measurements. Confusion also stems from the varying interests and attitudes of the investigators who are measuring the economic well-being of the poor. Some believe that poor people are adequately dealt with if they are ensured certain minimum living standards. Others feel that the poor are not becoming better off unless their share of personal income in the nation increases over time.

For the moment, let us focus on the notion of minimum living standards. If this means that the poor should be guaranteed a basket of food, clothes, and shelter, we certainly have fewer poor people now, in both absolute and proportionate terms, than we used to in the early 1960s. But if the size of the basket of food, clothes, and shelter is to become larger—as it has for nonpoor families—what then? The review of research findings showed earlier that, when the size of the basket is to increase in size (or in quality) commensurate with the increase in living standards enjoyed by nonpoor families, then we have the same proportion of the population who are poor as we used to in the 1960s. Because the population has increased since then, we have a larger number of poor people than we had in the early 1960s. This implies that the economic well-being of the poor in relation to the nonpoor has not improved but has stayed the same over the years.

Are poor people increasing their share of personal income in the nation? When this question is raised, one needs to look into the pattern of distribution of income in the United States. The pattern in Table 3.3 appears to indicate that there has been no measurable change in distribution. The lowest fifth of the families has been receiving just about the same proportion of gross annual money income for more than three decades. In contrast, however, the lowest fifth of unrelated individuals has been receiving a slightly increasing proportion of gross annual money income during the period. It should be remembered that this table is based on the Current Population Survey, and income figures are therefore not adjusted for the underreporting of certain types of income. Also, because the income figures used to develop Table 3.3 are based on gross annual money income, the data in the table have the limitations discussed earlier in relation to Table 3.2.

Has the distribution of income become less unequal over the years? An understanding of the Lorenz curve and the resulting Gini coefficient should be helpful in answering this question. In Figure 3.1, cumulative percentages of families are shown on the horizontal axis and cumulative percentages of income on the vertical axis. The diagonal line indicates perfectly equal distribution of income, because it shows 10 percent of the families receiving 10 percent of the income, 20 percent of the families receiving 20 percent of the income, and so on. If we calculate the cumulative percentages of income going to each progressing cumulative quintile of families and plot them, we can draw a curve similar to that shown as L in Figure 3.1. This curve is called the Lorenz curve. Only in a perfectly egalitarian society is the Lorenz curve identical to the diagonal line. Otherwise, the Lorenz curve is always drawn below the diagonal line. The Gini coefficient is the ratio of the area between the diagonal line and the Lorenz curve to the total area below the diagonal line. Thus the greater the Gini coefficient, the greater the inequality of income.

Gini coefficients are presented in the last column of Table 3.3. The Gini coefficients in various years for families are generally lower than those for unrelated individuals. This shows that the distribution of income among families is less unequal than among unrelated individuals. The trend in Gini coefficients over the years indicates that the distribution of income has changed very little among families since

TABLE 3.3

Distribution of Money Income: Mean Income and Share of Aggregate Income Received by Each Fifth and Top 5 Percent of Families and Unrelated Individuals: Selected Years, 1950–78

| Year and Group | Mean Income Before Tax (current dollars) | Percentage Distribution of Aggregate Income | | | | | | | Gini Coefficient |
		Lowest Fifth	Second Fifth	Middle Fifth	Fourth Fifth	Highest Fifth	Top 5 Percent	
Families								
1950	3,815	4.5	12.0	17.4	23.4	42.7	17.3	0.379
1955	4,962	4.8	12.3	17.8	23.7	41.3	16.4	0.363
1960	6,227	4.8	12.2	17.8	24.0	41.3	15.9	0.364
1965	7,704	5.2	12.2	17.8	23.9	40.9	15.5	0.356
1970	11,106	5.4	12.2	17.6	23.8	40.9	15.6	0.354
1975	15,546	5.4	11.8	17.6	24.1	41.1	15.5	0.358
1978	20,091	5.2	11.6	17.5	24.1	41.5	15.6	0.364
Unrelated Individuals								
1950	1,585	2.3	7.1	13.8	26.5	50.3	19.3	0.492
1955	2,009	2.5	7.2	13.3	24.7	52.4	22.5	0.506
1960	2,501	1.7	7.3	13.7	26.0	51.4	20.2	0.506
1965	3,175	2.9	7.6	13.6	25.0	50.9	20.0	0.486
1970	4,560	3.3	7.9	13.8	24.4	50.7	20.8	0.478
1975	6,623	4.0	9.0	14.7	24.3	47.9	18.7	0.442
1978	8,919	4.1	9.0	14.9	23.9	48.2	19.5	0.443

Source: U.S. Bureau of the Census, Current Population Reports, Series P-60, no. 123, Money Income of Families and Persons in the United States, 1978 (Washington, D.C.: U.S. Government Printing Office, 1980), Table 13, pp. 63–65.

FIGURE 3.1

The Lorenz Curve

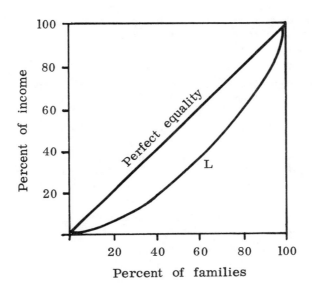

1950, but it has become slightly less unequal among unrelated individuals. However these data still do not indicate whether or not the distribution of income among all families and unrelated individuals put together has become less unequal.

Are the rich getting richer and the poor getting poorer? Or is the trend in the opposite direction? Past trends in the distribution of income indicate that inequality measurably declined between the Great Depression of the 1930s and World War II.[23] Since World War II, however, the distribution of income has been relatively stable with slight upward and downward shifts in inequality in more recent years. A study by Danziger and Plotnick indicates that between 1965 and 1974 the Gini coefficient of gross annual money income received by families and unrelated individuals increased 4 percent from 0.399 to 0.4077, thus showing a slight increase in inequality among all families and unrelated individuals.[24]

It is important to note that a part of the change in inequality in income is due to a shift in demographic composition. During the period 1965-74, the number of families headed by a young or an elderly person or a prime-age female increased greatly. Also the number of unrelated individuals who lived alone also increased. This resulted in a larger proportion of low-income families and individuals. Thus one would expect that part of the increase in the Gini coefficient is due to a demographic shift. Danziger and Plotnick attribute about half of the increase in the Gini coefficient to such a demographic change. The other half reflects the net deterioration in income inequality.

Whereas Danziger and Plotnick report the slightly deteriorating situation of distribution of income during the period 1965-74, a study by G. William Hoagland shows the opposite trend for the period 1976-80. He reports that the Gini coefficient of gross annual money income received by families and individuals declined by 6 percent.[25]

Would the level of the Gini coefficient, and therefore the level of income inequality, be different if transfer payments did not exist? The answer is yes. The study by Danziger and Plotnick indicates that the Gini coefficient for 1974 would have been greater by 16.9 percent if it had not been for cash transfer payments. This difference is especially marked for the elderly segment of the population. If it had not been for cash transfer payments, the Gini coefficient for the aged female individuals would have been greater by 105 percent. In the case of aged male individuals it would have been greater by 71 percent. These figures show that provision of cash transfer payments is greatly mitigating income inequality, which otherwise would have been much worse than it appears to be.

What happens to the degree of income inequality when in-kind transfer payments—such as food stamps, housing assistance, and medical care—are included in income? When these types of income are added to gross money income, the degree of inequality further decreases. The study by Hoagland, which considers all public in-kind transfers plus the burden of federal income and payroll taxes, reports a 4 percent reduction in the Gini coefficient in 1980 as a result of the inclusion of such in-kind transfers and the exclusion of taxes.

Aside from researchers' interest in investigating how the inclusion of public in-kind transfers in income affects the pattern of distribution of income, there is a question as to whether it is appropriate to include these transfers in order to study income inequality. It seems quite appropriate to investigate the percentage of the population who fall below a certain threshold when, depending on the purpose of the study, public in-kind transfers are included or not included. But it is quite another thing to study the degree of inequality by including in income public in-kind transfers that are targeted mostly to low-income families. If one is to study the shape of income distribution and not the percentage of the population who fall below a certain poverty threshold, one needs to include both public and private in-kind transfers. (Fringe benefits for health insurance are a good example of private in-kind transfers. Private in-kind transfers tend to be targeted to middle- and upper-income families.) This is the case because the study of income inequality deals with the relative share of income by all income classes. Therefore the measures of income for studying income inequality must be uniform across all income classes. Thus it is not appropriate to obtain the Gini coefficient based on income figures that include public in-kind transfers alone. A study such as Hoagland's should have included all in-kind transfers, from both public and private sources, in order to obtain a more realistic estimate of income inequality.

A study by Timothy Smeeding deals with in-kind transfers from both public and private sources. He found that in 1972 public in-kind transfers indeed increased the share of income by the lowest quintile of families to a significant degree. But such an improvement in their share of income was offset by the distribution of fringe benefits provided by employers, which tend to favor middle- and upper-class families. Thus in-kind transfers from both public and private sources resulted in only a slight improvement in the share of income by the lowest quintile. The net effect of in-kind transfers from both sources was only a 6 percent increase in the share of income by the lowest quintile. He further reports that the improvement in the share of net income by the lowest quintile since 1962 is attributable in part to the increase in in-kind public transfers received by families in this quintile.[26]

What about the level of the Gini coefficient itself? Are we supposed to despair that the Gini coefficient of income received by families is too high in the United States? Normally economists measure the degree of inequality as a distance between perfectly equal distribution of income and actual distribution of income. Here they assume that for a society to be perfectly egalitarian, all families—whether headed by a young person, a middle-aged person, or an elderly person—are to have absolutely the same level of income. On the basis of this assumption, they measure the distance between this ideal condition and the actual distribution of income. Gini coefficients measure such a phenomenon.

In recent years, however, Morton Paglin has stirred up a controversy by presenting a totally new way of constructing the notion of perfectly equal distribution of income.[27] He argues that it is absurd to state that in order to be perfectly equal in economic well-being, all families of all types of demographic backgrounds must have equal income. The level of income need is different, depending on stages of the life cycle. Young families without children may need less than families with growing children, and families headed by the elderly may need even less. Thus he argues that equality should be measured among families headed by persons who fall in a given age cohort. To Paglin, a perfectly egalitarian society is one in which all families with heads in a particular age group have equal income. Families across age groups may have different levels of income but, to Paglin, this does not constitute income inequality. The measurement of income inequality is the degree to which family income deviates from the average income of families within a particular age cohort. In short, Paglin attempts to deduct from the Gini coefficient that part attributable to income inequality because of difference in the age of the head of the family. He developed a new concept of the Gini coefficient based on this interpretation of income inequality and called it the Paglin-Gini coefficient.

Another way to explain the Paglin-Gini coefficient is to use the analogy of analysis of variance. Instead of using the total variance, which is analogous to the Gini coefficient, Paglin proposes to deal with only the within-group variance in income inequality, deducting the between-group variance from the total. The within-group variance is analogous to the Paglin-Gini coefficient; the between-group variance is analogous to income inequality between cohorts.

Using this new framework and the procedure that grew out of it for measuring inequality in income, Paglin calculated Paglin-Gini coefficients of income received by families for the years 1947 through 1972. His calculations show that Paglin-Gini coefficients steadily declined during that period, due primarily to a great increase in income inequality between age cohorts. Put another way, according to Paglin's analysis, if one disregards that part of inequality attributable to the growing number of families headed by young adults and elderly individuals, the distribution of income among families has been becoming less unequal over the years.

Paglin's new framework of inequality also opens up a new way to measure the relative share of income received by the lowest fifth of families. Traditionally, one would say that the lowest fifth received in 1970 only 27 percent of the share that would have been due them if income had been distributed equally (5.4 percent, as seen in Table 3.3, divided by 20 percent). But, according to Paglin's framework, in 1970 the bottom fifth of families received 42 percent of their equal share, as their equal share should have been 12.9 percent instead of 20 percent (42 percent equals 5.4 percent divided by 12.9 percent).

The concept of the Paglin-Gini coefficient invited severe criticism from other economists. For example, Sheldon Danziger, Robert Haveman, and Eugene Smolensky argue—on the basis of a study by Bhattacharya and Mahalanobis—that the Paglin-Gini coefficient does not nearly measure income inequality among families within cohorts, as Paglin seems to claim it does. Rather, the Paglin-Gini coefficient fluctuates over time, depending on the distribution of families by cohorts and the mean income of each cohort as well.[28] The ambiguity involved in the Paglin-Gini coefficient as a measure of income inequality may raise the question as to whether this coefficient is any more useful than the normal Gini coefficient, which also has a built-in ambiguity similar to that in the Paglin-Gini coefficient.

Besides the technical aspects of the Paglin-Gini coefficient, there are policy implications of its use. These are discussed by Danziger, Haveman, and Smolensky. If for the moment we adopt the Paglin-Gini coefficient as a measurement of inequality, we assume that the perfectly egalitarian society is one in which all families within a specific age group have equal income. However, many of the income transfers in the United States, for example, social security, go from the nonaged to the aged segment of society. When income transfers are between cohorts and not between families within the same cohort, the Paglin-Gini coefficient does not decrease much. On the other hand, perfect equality, as conceived by Paglin, would be attained if income was completely equalized within cohorts, even though there might be wide variation in income levels between cohorts.

Is this the type of equality that policymakers envision when they attempt to redistribute income from one segment of society to another? Probably not. Rather, policymakers attempt to transfer income from the rich to the poor segment of society. Even in age-specific programs such as social security, the implicit goal is to equalize distribution of income in society as a whole. In social security, the aged are primary recipients and the nonaged are distributors of funds precisely because the aged are presumed to be poor in relation to the typical standards of living perceived by society. If this is true, the normal Gini coefficient still has a useful role to play, because it measures overall inequality in income, not just inequality within cohorts.

What does all this discussion about inequality indicate? As in the case of the poverty thresholds and the resulting percentage of the population who are poor, the explanation of Gini coefficients and Paglin-Gini coefficients shows the complexity involved in measuring the degree of inequality in distribution of income. But at least a few thoughts emerge from the foregoing discussion. First, to understand whether the rich are getting richer and the poor poorer, or vice versa, one needs to make sure that researchers are using an income concept applied uniformly to all income classes. Second, the inclusion of cash transfer payments in income tends to lower the level of income inequality. The question of whether the inclusion of in-kind transfers in income would further decrease income inequality is hard to answer at this point, because researchers are finding it difficult to include all in-kind transfers from both public and private sources. Failure to do so tends to understate income inequality because private in-kind transfers such as employer-provided health insurance, which are generally excluded from data analysis, tend to favor middle- and upper-income families.

Another thought that emerges from the foregoing discussion is

that one needs to first understand the shifting composition of households, families, and unrelated individuals and see whether such a
shift is contributing to changes in the pattern of distribution of income.
After the effect of demographic shift is accounted for, the net change
in income inequality can be measured.

If a large part of the increasing inequality in income from 1965
through 1974 is due to a demographic shift, as shown by Danziger and
Plotnick, should society worry about such a phenomenon? Take, for
example, the growing number of elderly persons who establish their
own households rather than live with their adult children or other
relatives. The increasing number of households headed by the aged
is contributing to a greater degree of inequality in income. As Alice
Pivlin stated, the aged now have the luxury of living apart from relatives thanks to social security benefits and other transfer payments,
but at the same time they are taking a greater chance of being poor
than they otherwise would. [29]

Here the question seems to boil down to whether the elderly in
fact choose to live apart from their children or other relatives, or
whether they are forced to do so. If the elderly voluntarily choose to
live independently, they are making a calculated trade-off of social
amenity versus income deficiency. Through such a trade-off, they are
maximizing their total well-being. If this hypothesis is correct, it
does not seem to be the government's business to intervene.

Suppose, however, that elderly persons are forced to live on
their own against their wishes. What then? They may be forced to
live apart from relatives because they do not have the financial resources to move to the town where their relatives live, because they
do not have any relatives to live with, because the relatives would find
living with them inconvenient, or for some other reason. If this is the
case, social intervention may be called for. If they can be helped to
live with others—and if that is their wish—they may greatly increase
their well-being, as a result of both the economy of scale and the
social interaction that a larger household may bring about.

At any rate, little is known about the interaction between economic variables and sociological and psychological variables in regard
to living arrangements among American families. Certainly greater
research effort in such areas would enable the policymaker to understand better the dynamic relationship between the degree of income
inequality and living arrangements among American families.

BEYOND THE NUMBERS

Since the declaration of the war on poverty by President Johnson, the
public has accepted the eradication of absolute poverty as a desirable

goal of social policy. This has brought about an enormous number of antipoverty programs and, in addition, has created public recognition that all publicly financed social welfare programs must pay attention to what they do for the poor.

In contrast to the wide acceptance of the eradication of absolute poverty as a goal, the question of lessening income inequality has not been openly discussed nor has it been uniformly accepted as a desirable goal of social policy. Opinions are divided on this issue.

Some economists worry that equalizing distribution of income prevents the rich from saving, which is necessary for economic growth. Classical economists worry that equalizing distribution of income disturbs the natural order of distributing factor income to workers according to marginal productivity. When such a disturbance occurs, not only are industrial resources maldistributed but also workers are demoralized, with the consequence of slower economic growth and bitterness among the working population.

Some may even oppose lessening income inequality from sociological and psychological viewpoints. A sociological theory states that for a complex society like the United States to function effectively, it inevitably needs social stratification to make sure that each diverse function is carried out and each task is fulfilled. Moreover, according to a psychological theory, an egalitarian spirit provoked by a public announcement on lessening income inequality may be bad for the mental health of the citizenry. Exaggerated expectations about life opportunities may drive many young persons to strive to become something they cannot, for example, to become the president of the United States. Because so few eventually get to occupy such highly prestigious positions, all others are doomed to failure. But such failures are in fact caused by false expectations. Many people can be prevented from becoming failures if society does not inject in the minds of the young unlimited expectations from life processes.[30]

In contrast to this pessimistic view regarding the question of whether income inequality should be lessened, some argue that equalizing income is not only a just goal of society but also an effective tool for achieving social, and in the long run, economic progress. For example, R. H. Tawney argues that society suffers from extreme inequality caused in part by such unfair social institutions as inheritance of wealth, tax treatment of certain types of incomes, racial discrimination, and monopoly generated by guilds (or unions) and professions. Here Tawney is arguing that, under the circumstances created largely by these institutions, individuals are not allowed to extract the income justly due them in return for their contribution to an industrial society. Instead there seem to be many artificial barriers that obstruct the natural distribution of income based on individual productivity so loudly defended by classical economists. At any rate, extreme inequality in income, according to Tawney, is detrimental to developing human capital effectively and nurturing the maximum number of sophisticated minds necessary to maintain democracy in a basically capitalistic society.[31]

Faced with general ambivalence about the issue of lessening inequality in income, public policy in the United States seems to have taken an obscure road toward helping the poor. The approach has been to redistribute income to the poor to help them meet basic needs but at the same time to avoid changing the fundamental shape of distribution of income. How can society help the needy through governmental transfers without making the rest of the society worse off? Economists call such a criterion Pareto optimality. How has the government approached the problem?

During the 1960s and through the early 1970s, policymakers in Washington launched an enormous number of antipoverty programs, believing that healthy economic growth would create an atmosphere of "superabundance." In times of superabundance, with the economic pie becoming larger and larger, nobody feels hurt even if the government increases transfer payments for the poor because everybody else is becoming better off than before. It should be noted also that the government has never tried to fulfill unmet wants among the poor. It simply intended to meet unmet needs. And these needs were translated into the poverty thresholds. But both the poor and the rich have a sense of want. The level of want is always higher than the level of need. Specific needs can be met by providing certain items essential for faily living. But a sense of want never seems satisfied because it constantly moves upward as soon as basic needs are met and because it is felt in relation to the economic well-being of others.

If the government tried to satisfy wants perceived by the poor, it probably would have to move toward reshaping distribution of income. But if the government simply deals with unmet needs, it does not have to be much concerned with such reshaping. Moreover, needs as translated into poverty thresholds in the United States are static in concept. Put another way, government has been dealing with absolute, not relative, poverty.[32]

In a perpetually growing economy, the absolute level of need would eventually be met for a greater number of poor families, making governmental intervention increasingly unnecessary. However, ironically, in a growing economy, the perception of what constitutes basic needs eventually changes, as shown by Rainwater's study.[33] Thus the government cannot deal with a static notion of need indefinitely. The levels of both need and want tend to move upward in a society that is becoming more affluent with time.

In the final analysis, what is the relationship between income inequality and governmental intervention in eradicating poverty? In

Chapter 2, we observed that the government has been spending increasingly large sums of money to help the poor escape poverty, but that the shape of distribution of income has been relatively stable over the years (see Table 3.3). Also, we saw from the study by Danziger and Plotnick that in the absence of income transfers, inequality in income would have been even greater. Finally, we saw in Smeeding's study that in-kind transfers from both public and private sources tended to increase slightly the share of income by the lowest quintile. All this means that increasing governmental expenditures in antipoverty efforts have been just enough to keep the status quo in terms of income inequality and to reduce slightly income inequality if in-kind transfers—both public and private—are included. Thus the poor in America are just about as poor in relation to others are they used to be years ago.

The real war on poverty in modern society should not be a war to eliminate absolute poverty but rather a war to mitigate the extreme relative poverty and inequality perceived by those in the bottom layers of society. The Council of Economic Advisors implicitly acknowledged this fact in 1964, when it said, "By standards of contemporary American society most of the population of the world is poor; and most Americans were poor a century ago. But for our society today a consensus on an approximate standard can be found."[34] Martin Rein succinctly points out how combating relative poverty and inequality is the real challenge of modern society:

> Poverty cannot be understood by isolating the poor and
> treating them as a special group. Society is seen as a
> series of stratified income layers and poverty is con-
> cerned with how the bottom layers fare relative to the
> rest of society. Hence, the concept of poverty must be
> seen in the context of society as a whole. The study of
> the poor then depends on an understanding of the level
> of living of the rich, since it is these conditions relative
> to each other that are critical to the conception of inequal-
> ity. To understand the poor we must study the affluent.[35]

In a stagnant economy, the redistribution of income to combat relative poverty would make nonbeneficiaries of such redistribution worse off both absolutely and relatively. Even in a growing economy, the redistribution of income to reshape distribution of income would make nonbeneficiaries worse off in relation to what they would have been if the redistribution policies had not been in effect. Such policies could take many forms. Income could be taken away from some and directly redistributed to others. To redistribute opportunities for developing human capital, taxes could be levied on some for training others. Through legislation—for example, affirmative action programs—

opportunities for certain groups of individuals to obtain better jobs or to be promoted to higher-ranking positions may be enhanced.[36] Combating inequality in these ways shakes up relative positions between economic classes. Certainly a war to lessen inequality would involve much more painful social processes than would a war to combat absolute poverty.

Finally, the social policy goal of equalizing income distribution may raise the issue of the trade-off between economic efficiency and equality.[37] Equalization of income through public income transfers—if pursued too vigorously—may stifle work efforts among the population, which in turn may impede the growth of new capital and hence the growth in economy. On the other hand, economic growth cannot be attained if society is plagued with a high level of social disintegration.[38] A high level of crime and delinquency is one manifestation of social disorganization. Some degree of equalization of income distribution is necessary to mitigate social disintegration. The challenge facing the policymaker is to find the delicate balance between economic efficiency and equality. These policy objectives must go hand in hand because it is impossible to achieve one without attending to the other.

NOTES

1. Michael Harrington, The Other America: Poverty in the United States (New York: Macmillan, 1962).

2. Charles Booth, Life and Labour of the People of London (London: Williams and Norgate, 1891).

3. B. Seebohm Rowntree, Poverty: A Study of Town Life (London: Macmillan, 1903).

4. Robert Hunter, Poverty (New York: Macmillan, 1909).

5. Oscar Ornati, Poverty Amid Affluence (New York: Twentieth Century Fund, 1966).

6. Lee Rainwater, "Poverty, Living Standards, and Family Well-Being," in The Family, Poverty, and Welfare Programs: Household Patterns and Government Policies, Welfare Paper no. 12 (Part II), 93rd Congr., 1st Sess., Subcommittee on Fiscal Policy of the Joint Economic Committee (Washington, D.C.: U.S. Government Printing Office, 1973), pp. 231-33.

7. The Economic Report of the President, 1964 (Washington, D.C.: U.S. Government Printing Office, 1964).

8. Mollie Orshansky, "Counting the Poor: Another Look at the Poverty Profile," Social Security Bulletin 28 (January 1965): 3-29.

9. U.S. Department of Commerce, Bureau of Labor Statistics, Consumer Expenditures and Income, Supplement 3, Part A, to BLS Report no. 237-38 (Washington, D.C.: U.S. Government Printing Office, 1964).

10. Morton Paglin, Poverty and Transfers In-Kind (Stanford, Calif.: Stanford University, Hoover Institution Press, 1980), p. 23; and U.S. Congress, Congressional Budget Office, Poverty Status of Families Under Alternative Definitions of Income (Washington, D.C.: U.S. Government Printing Office, 1977), p. 6.

11. U.S. Department of Health, Education, and Welfare, Social Security Administration, Social Security Bulletin: Annual Statistical Supplement, 1976 (Washington, D.C.: Social Security Administration, 1976), p. 50; and U.S. Bureau of the Census, Statistical Abstract of the United States, 1976 (Washington, D.C.: U.S. Government Printing Office, 1976), p. 404.

12. U.S. Congress, Congressional Budget Office, op. cit.

13. Mollie Orshansky et al., "Measuring Poverty: A Debate," Public Welfare 36 (Spring 1978): 46–55.

14. Paglin, op. cit.

15. For methodological problems involving Paglin's study, see Timothy M. Smeeding, "The Anti-Poverty Effect of In-Kind Transfers: A 'Good Idea' Gone Too Far?" (Provo: Department of Economics, University of Utah, June 1981).

16. Richard D. Coe, "Sensitivity of the Incidence of Poverty to Different Measures of Income: School-Aged Children and Families," in Five Thousand American Families: Patterns of Economic Progress vol. IV, ed. Greg J. Duncan and James N. Morgan (Ann Arbor: Institute of Social Research, University of Michigan, 1976), pp. 357–409.

17. In calculating the probability of staying in poverty for the five-year period, Coe subtracted from income the net value of food stamps and social security taxes.

18. Robert D. Plotnick and Felicity Skidmore, Progress Against Poverty: A Review of the 1964–1974 Decade (New York: Academic Press, 1975), p. 43.

19. Sheldon Danziger and Robert D. Plotnick, Has the War on Poverty Been Won? (in press).

20. Sidney E. Zimbalist, "Recent British and American Poverty Trends: Conceptual and Policy Contrasts," Social Service Review 51 (September 1977): 419–33.

21. Burton A. Weisbrod and W. Lee Hansen, "An Income—Net Worth Approach to Measuring Economic Welfare," in Improving Measures of Economic Well-Being, ed. Marilyn Moon and Eugene Smolensky (New York: Academic Press, 1977).

22. Marilyn Moon, The Measurement of Economic Welfare: Its Application to the Aged Poor (New York: Academic Press, 1977).

23. Lester Thurow, "Toward a Definition of Economic Justice," Public Interest 31 (Spring 1973): 56–80.

24. Sheldon Danziger and Robert Plotnick, "Demographic Change, Government Transfers, and Income Distribution," Monthly Labor Review 100 (April 1977): 7–11.

25. G. William Hoagland, "The Effectiveness of Current Transfer Programs in Reducing Poverty," paper presented at Middlebury College Conference on Economic Issues, Middlebury, Vt., April 19, 1980.

26. Timothy Smeeding, "On the Distribution of Net Income: Comment," Southern Economic Journal 45 (January 1979): 932-44; see also Timothy Smeeding, "The Antipoverty Effectiveness of In-Kind Transfers," Journal of Human Resources 12 (Dummer 1977): 360-78.

27. Morton Paglin, "The Measurement and Trend of Inequality: A Basic Revision," American Economic Review 65 (September 1975): 598-609.

28. Sheldon Danziger, Robert Haveman, and Eugene Smolensky, "The Measurement and Trend of Inequality: Comment," American Economic Review 67 (June 1977): 505-12.

29. Alice M. Pivlin, "Income Distribution—Can Economists Help?" American Economic Review 65 (May 1976): 1-15.

30. For detailed discussion on the subject, see Robert J. Lampman, Ends and Means of Reducing Income Poverty (Chicago: Markham, 1971), pp. 16-42.

31. R. H. Tawney, Equality (London: Allen & Unwin, 1964), p. 33, 138-40.

32. For detailed discussion, see Thurow, op. cit.

33. Rainwater, op. cit.

34. The Economic Report of the President, 1964, op. cit.

35. Martin Rein, "Problem in the Definition of Measurement of Poverty," in The Concept of Poverty, ed. Peter Townsend (London: Heineman Educational Books, 1970), p. 71.

36. Lester C. Thurow, "The Political Economy of Income Redistribution Policies," Annals of the American Academy of Political and Social Science 409 (September 1973): 146-55.

37. Arthur M. Okun, Equality and Efficiency: The Big Tradeoff (Washington, D.C.: Brookings Institution, 1975).

38. Kenneth E. Boulding, "The Boundaries of Social Policy," Social Work 21 (January 1967): 3-11.

4

DISTRIBUTIVE IMPACT OF INCOME MAINTENANCE PROGRAMS

FRAMEWORK FOR STUDYING DISTRIBUTIVE IMPACT

As stated earlier, income maintenance programs in the United States take two distinctly different approaches to redistributing income: social insurance and welfare. The principles involved in these two approaches differ fundamentally. In general, social insurance attempts to stratify benefits according to the previous levels of earnings. Thus the higher the previous earnings, the higher the benefits. In contrast, the levels of benefits that welfare programs provide are related inversely to the family's available income. Thus, under welfare, the lower the current income, the higher the benefits. Philosophically speaking, social insurance attempts to reward beneficiaries on the basis of their work records. Welfare, in contrast, selects the financially less capable and supplements the financial resources available to them. This difference between social insurance and welfare in the basis for providing income is one source of the tension in the current system of income maintenance. Many policy issues and problems stem, in part, from this difference.

Another way to distinguish between the patterns of redistribution of income through social insurance and welfare is that under social insurance vertical income redistribution from the rich to the poor is attempted only implicitly and inefficiently, whereas under welfare it is attempted explicitly and efficiently. Old-age insurance under social security, for example, redistributes income from the young to the old, and in effect money is redistributed to a certain degree from the economically better-off to the economically worse-off. Also, under unemployment insurance, income is redistributed from the securely employed to the less securely employed, accomplishing some degree of vertical redistribution of income. Welfare programs, in contrast, explicitly redistribute income vertically—from the rich to the poor—through income-testing. Recipients must prove they are needy by meeting a program's requirements of eligibility. The level of payments is determined by the standards of need and the resources available to a recipient family.

Another difference between the distributive patterns of social insurance and welfare is that family size, and therefore family need, is more explicitly recognized under welfare than under social insurance. Social insurance benefits are conceptually tied to previous earnings and represent a stated proportion of what the worker earned. If a social insurance program provided the same benefits for each additional dependent as for the first one, total family benefits for workers with large families would surpass previous earnings. To prevent this, social security, for example, has a rule for maximum family benefits. Beneficiary families cannot receive more than this maximum, regardless of the number of dependents. Unemployment insurance does not provide for dependents in the majority of states. Welfare programs, on the contrary, explicitly incorporate family size into their benefit formulas. The level of assistance payments is always higher for a large family than for a small family, other things being equal.

Because welfare programs are income-tested and redistribute income vertically, they are often called "target-efficient" programs. These characterizations indicate that income-tested programs redistribute a larger proportion of the total benefits to low-income beneficiaries than do less target-efficient programs. Thus it is considered that given a fixed program budget, welfare programs are more efficient in helping the poor than are social insurance programs.

However, the question of how much low-income families benefit in terms of dollar amounts cannot be answered by the criterion of target efficiency alone. To answer this question, one needs to know the total outlay of a program as well. It is conceivable that a program that seems to be less target-efficient may redistribute a larger amount of income to low-income families, if the program involves a large total outlay. Conversely, it is conceivable that a program that seems to be target-efficient may redistribute a relatively small amount of income to low-income families if the program involves only a small total outlay. Only when the level of total outlay is the same can one say with certainty that a target-efficient program helps low-income families more than does a less target-efficient program.

All income maintenance programs—whether social insurance or welfare—transfer income from one segment of society to another, with the government acting as a transfer agent. This being so, transfer payments as such do not contribute to the gross national product. Only when families who are beneficiaries of income maintenance programs spend the distributed income, thus generating economic activities, do they contribute to the GNP.

The spending of transfer payments by beneficiary families implies that money changes hand. Once out of the hands of the beneficiary family, the original income may pass through the hands of different owners several times a year. Economists call such a phenomenon the "multiplier effect." The interesting question, then, is: Where does the money go once beneficiary families spend their transfer payments? Is it not probable that it goes right back to taxpayers, many of whom are suppliers of goods and services bought by beneficiary families?

One needs to keep in mind some caveats in studying the redistributive impacts of income maintenance programs. The data presented in Tables 4.4 and 4.5 show what Sheldon Danziger et al. call the "measured" redistributive effects of income maintenance programs. Measured redistributive effects are obtained by simply comparing the distributions of income before and after income transfers are provided. Thus the concept of measured redistributive impacts assumes that people do not change their work behavior and/or living arrangements in response to income transfers. In reality, however, people do respond to the government provision of income transfers. For example, if the government stopped providing income transfers, current recipients might increase their work effort. Others might keep a high level of work effort because they know there would be no governmental income support to fall back on. Or others—like elderly persons and single-parent families—might choose to live with others to increase their standards of living. On the other hand, some taxpayers might work less if they did not need to pay for such programs, because in that case they could stay even in disposable income by working less. When all these dynamic effects of income maintenance programs are further taken into account, the "true" redistributive impacts of income maintenance programs may be quite different from the "measured" redistributive impacts. As Danziger et al. speculate, the magnitude of true redistributive impacts of income maintenance programs is probably less than that of measured redistributive impacts.[1]

With these aspects involved in income redistribution through social insurance and welfare, and keeping these caveats in mind, we shall review distributive impacts of income maintenance programs. Tables 4.2, 4.3, 4.4, and 4.5 have been developed on the basis of data published by the Congressional Budget Office. As mentioned earlier, the Congressional Budget Office adjusted the CPS income figures to account for the underreporting of income. Individuals living alone are considered as one-person families. In these tables, income maintenance programs are categorized into four groups: social insurance, cash assistance, in-kind transfers other than Medicare and Medicaid, and Medicare and Medicaid. Table 4.1 shows the programs

TABLE 4.1

Summary of Transfer Income by Source, 1976

	Benefits in Fiscal Year 1976 (millions of dollars)
Social Insurance	
Social security and railroad retirement	73,665
Government pensions	22,720
Unemployment insurance	18,524
Worker's compensation	3,791
Veterans' compensation	5,259
Cash Assistance	
Veterans' pensions	2,687
Supplemental Security Income	6,029
Aid to Families with Dependent Children	9,257
In-kind transfers other than Medicare and Medicaid	
Food stamps	5,304
Child nutrition	2,026
Housing assistance	2,265
In-kind transfers: Medicare and Medicaid	
Medicare	16,947
Medicaid	14,900

Source: U.S. Congress, Congressional Budget Office, Poverty Status of Families Under Alternative Definitions of Income (Washington, D.C.: U.S. Government Printing Office, 1977), Table A-2, p. 22.

included in each category and the expenditures for benefits in each program. All programs categorized as cash assistance are income-tested and therefore welfare programs. So are all programs under "in-kind transfers other than Medicare and Medicaid." Medicare is a social insurance program that takes the form of in-kind provision. Medicaid is a welfare program and provides in-kind assistance.

ASPECTS OF DISTRIBUTIVE IMPACT

Target Efficiency

Table 4.2 shows the percentage of benefits going to each quintile of families. Families are ranked by their income before receiving any transfer income and before paying any tax. Broadly speaking, welfare programs are more target-efficient than social insurance programs. This generalization is made by comparing the distributive pattern of social insurance benefits with those of cash assistance and in-kind transfers other than Medicare and Medicaid. A larger proportion of benefits under cash assistance or in-kind transfers goes to the lowest 20 percent of families than under social insurance. Together, Medicare and Medicaid seem just as target-efficient as other in-kind transfers, although Medicare is a social insurance program and thus does not involve income-testing.

The degree of target efficiency differs among various social insurance programs. For example, social security is much more target-efficient than other social insurance programs. A study by Robert Plotnick and Felicity Skidmore shows that in 1972, 53 percent of social security benefits went to pretransfer poor families, compared with 38 percent of benefits under government pensions, 21 percent under unemployment insurance, and 33 percent under worker's compensation.[2]

Why this difference? One might speculate as follows: As regards unemployment insurance, poor people tend to be more unemployment-prone than the nonpoor. But they are also more likely to be out of the labor force. If they ever get employed, they may not stay in a job long enough to establish employment records that make them eligible for benefits. Even if they do, they may quit the job for personal reasons, or they may be fired for misconduct. Furthermore, for those who do qualify for benefits, previous earnings are likely to have been meager and thus bring only meager benefits. Indeed a study by this author and one by Martin Feldstein indicate that unemployment insurance is not particularly pro-poor.[3] This program seems basically for lower-middle-income and middle-income families who have heads with relatively stable attachment to the labor force. Of course the program does not do much for upper-income families because they seldom encounter unemployment.

Similar speculations may apply to worker's compensation. That is, the poor, if they are employed, tend to be in more hazardous jobs than the nonpoor. However, the poor are less likely to be in covered employment than are the nonpoor. Furthermore, their low earnings entitle them only to low benefits.

That government pension programs are less target-efficient than social security can be explained by the fact that the benefit formulas

TABLE 4.2

Distribution of Income Transfer Benefits to Families Classified
by Pretax/Pretransfer Income Quintiles: Fiscal Year 1976*

Quintile[†]	Social Insurance	Cash Assistance	In-Kind Transfer Other than Medicare and Medicaid	Medicare and Medicaid
Low 20%	31.9	61.5	47.6	55.0
Second 20%	28.4	20.5	31.2	24.8
Third 20%	16.2	9.2	12.2	9.7
Fourth 20%	12.0	5.0	5.5	5.7
High 20%	11.5	3.8	3.5	4.7
Total[‡]	100.0%	100.0%	100.0%	100.0%
Total dollars (in billions)	$124.0	$18.0	$9.6	$31.8

*Social insurance includes social security and railroad retire-
ment, government pensions, unemployment insurance, worker's compensation, and veterans' compensation. Cash assistance includes
veterans' pensions, Supplemental Security Income, and Aid to Families with Dependent Children. In-kind transfers other than Medicare
and Medicaid include food stamps, child nutrition, and housing
assistance.

[†]The upper limits of each quintile are as follows: low 20%
($1,812), second 20% ($7,871), third 20% ($13,994), and fourth 20%
($21,682).

[‡]Components may not add to totals because of rounding.

Source: U.S. Congress, Congressional Budget Office, Poverty
Status of Families Under Alternative Definitions of Income (Washington, D.C.: U.S. Government Printing Office, 1977), Table 2, p. 4.

under government pension programs tend to be slanted less in favor
of low-income families than the formulas under social security. Government pension programs are based more strongly on the principle
of individual equity (or the insurance principle) than social security,
which is based as well on the principle of social adequacy (or the
welfare objective). Furthermore, the poor are less likely to be in
government jobs than in other types of jobs. The poor can benefit
from social security if they have any type of job; but they do not bene-

fit from government pension programs unless they have worked for the government.

In general, then, social security is less restrictive in its eligibility for benefits, and its benefit formulas are slanted more in favor of low-income families than are the formulas for other social insurance programs.

Because welfare programs are income-tested, one can expect a larger proportion of program benefits to go to low-income families. Plotnick and Skidmore show, for example, that in 1972 pretransfer poor received 87 percent of public assistance payments, 70 percent of food stamps, 74 percent of public housing, and 75 percent of Medicaid.[4] These proportions are generally higher than the proportions of benefits received by the poor from social insurance programs.

Although income-tested programs generally are more target-efficient than social insurance programs, there is some variation in target efficiency between income-tested programs. Such variation has to do with two factors. First, the benefit formula in one type of welfare program has been developed so as to target benefits more efficiently to low-income families than the formula in another type. For example, public assistance programs (AFDC and SSI) target benefits more efficiently to low-income families than does the food stamp program or Medicaid. Public assistance programs, especially AFDC, succeed in achieving a high level of target efficiency by withdrawing benefits at a faster rate as the income of recipient families rises than occurs in the case of other welfare programs.

Another factor involved in target efficiency is the rate of participation in welfare programs among low-income families. Studies show that the rate of participation by such families in the food stamp program is only 42 percent,[5] compared with 50 percent for SSI[6] and 78 percent for AFDC.[7] When low-income families do not participate, whatever the reason, benefits will not be targeted to them regardless of how well designed the welfare program may be for helping the poor.

Distributive Impact in Dollar Terms

Target efficiency alone, however, cannot tell the whole story about how important an income maintenance program is with respect to distributing income in actual dollar terms to low-income families. The real impact of an income maintenance program can be measured only when both the target efficiency and the total outlay are known. That is, the amount of benefits going to an income class is a product of the total outlay and the proportion of that outlay accruing to that income class.

By inspecting the level of aggregate income that each quintile of

TABLE 4.3

Income from Various Sources: Aggregate Income for Families Classified by
Pretax/Pretransfer Income Quintiles: Fiscal Year 1976
(amounts in billions of dollars)

Source of Income	Low 20%		Second 20%		Third 20%		Fourth 20%		Fifth 20%		All Families	
	Amount	Percent	Amount	Percent	Amount	Percent	Amount	Percent	Amount	Percent	Amount	Percent
Income before transfers	3.3	4.3	76.3	60.5	173.7	87.0	276.2	93.9	534.0	97.0	1,063.5	85.3
Social insurance	39.5	53.0	35.2	27.9	20.0	10.1	14.8	5.0	14.3	2.6	123.9	9.9
Cash assistance	11.1	14.6	3.7	2.9	1.6	.8	.9	.3	.7	.1	18.0	1.4
In-kind transfers other than Medicare and Medicaid	4.5	5.9	3.0	2.4	1.2	.6	.5	.1	.3	.0	9.6	.8
Medicare and Medicaid	17.5	23.0	7.9	6.3	3.1	1.6	1.8	.6	1.5	.3	31.8	2.6
Total*	75.9	100.0	126.1	100.0	199.7	100.0	294.2	100.0	550.8	100.0	1,246.8	100.0

*Components may not add to totals because of rounding.

Source: Derived from U.S. Congress, Congressional Budget Office, Poverty Status of Families Under Alternative
Definitions of Income (Washington, D.C.: U.S. Government Printing Office, 1977), Table A-4, p. 25.

families received in 1976 from various sources, one can clearly discern the impact of each sector of income maintenance (see Table 4.3). Focusing on the lowest 20 percent of families, the largest amount of aggregate income (39.5 billion, or 52 percent) came from social insurance programs. The impact of social insurance programs on the level of income received by the lowest quintile of families is clearly greater than the impact of cash assistance programs, or for that matter, the impact of all income-tested programs put together. This occurs despite the relatively low target efficiency involved in social insurance programs compared with that of welfare, or income-tested, programs. The greater impact of social insurance programs is a result of their relatively larger outlay, especially for social security programs.

Comparing sources and amounts of income received by families in different quintiles tells a startling story about the economic conditions of American families. Families in the lowest quintile depend heavily on government transfer payments for their living. Although there may be some question about the appropriateness of including Medicare and Medicaid benefits as part of income, the pattern is clear. Low-income families receive an overwhelming proportion of income from income maintenance programs, not from work or other private sources. As one goes up the quintiles, families rely increasingly on income from private sources—whether earned (such as wages and salaries) or unearned (such as rent, interest, and dividends).

Another observation from Table 4.3 is that the total aggregate income of the lowest 20 percent of families is small—$75.9 billion—compared with the total received by families in higher quintiles. It is only 60 percent of the total aggregate income received by families in the second quintile and only 14 percent of the total aggregate income received by the top 20 percent of families. Great disparity in aggregate income exists even after the transfer of the enormous amounts devoted to income maintenance programs, most of which redistributes income heavily to the lowest 20 percent of families. Another way to describe the situation is to say that family income before transfer payments is distributed even more unequally than after these payments. This observation confirms the findings from the study on inequality of income by Danziger and Plotnick cited in Chapter 3.[8]

Antipoverty Effects

How effective is each sector of the income maintenance programs in bringing families out of poverty? The question of whether a family is brought out of poverty by receiving benefits from an income maintenance program depends both on the amount of benefits and on the

TABLE 4.4

Percentage of Pretransfer Poor Families Taken Out of Absolute Poverty by Government Transfers, by Demographic Groups and by Regions: Fiscal Year 1976

	Pretransfer Poor Families Taken Out of Poverty by Social Insurance	Pretransfer Poor Families Taken Out of Poverty by Cash Assistance	Pretransfer Poor Families Taken Out of Poverty by In-Kind Transfers Other than Medicare and Medicaid	Pretransfer Poor Families Taken Out of Poverty by Medicare and Medicaid	Pretransfer Poor Families Taken Out of Poverty by All Transfers
All Families	41.9	8.1	8.1	11.8	69.9
Age					
Under 65	23.7	8.2	11.2	10.6	53.7
65 and over	64.1	8.0	4.3	13.4	89.8
Race					
White	46.3	7.5	11.3	6.4	71.5
Nonwhite	23.3	10.7	14.2	15.4	63.6
Region					
South	36.7	5.5	7.9	11.3	61.4
West	40.3	13.1	7.0	9.0	69.4
Northeast	47.1	9.4	9.4	12.9	78.8
North Central	46.6	6.9	8.0	14.0	75.5

Source: Derived from U.S. Congress, Congressional Budget Office, Poverty Status of Families Under Alternative Definitions of Income (Washington, D.C.: U.S. Government Printing Office, 1977), Tables 3, 5, 6, and 7, pp. 8, 11, 12, 13.

family's pretransfer income. That is, given a certain amount of benefits, the probability is higher for the family to be brought out of poverty when it has a relatively high pretransfer income than when it has
low pretransfer income. Put another way, benefits from a program
can fill the poverty gap (the difference between poverty-line income
and the income available before transfer payments) with relative ease
if that gap is small. When interpreting the data in Tables 4.4 and 4.5,
these underlying forces should be recognized.

Another thing that is important to keep in mind when interpreting
these data is the order in which benefits from different income maintenance programs are added to income. In Table 4.4 benefits from
social insurance programs are added first to pretransfer income of
families. Then benefits from cash assistance programs are added,
followed by benefits from in-kind transfers other than Medicare and
Medicaid, and last, benefits from Medicare and Medicaid. The Congressional Budget Office, which constructed the original table from
which Table 4.4 is derived, added benefits in the order shown in
Table 4.4 for the logical reason that benefits from income-tested programs are designed to supplement those from social insurance.

The order of adding benefits is also important for measuring
validly the antipoverty effectiveness of income maintenance programs.
Thus first-added social insurance benefits must be relatively large in
amount to help a family pull out of poverty, because the poverty gap
is greatest at this stage of computation. In contrast, the antipoverty
effect of last-added Medicare and Medicaid benefits comes out stronger
than if these benefits were added at an earlier stage of computation,
as some families, although not all, receive benefits (already added to
pretransfer income) from other income maintenance programs.

Closely related to the two factors involved in distributive impact
of income maintenance programs (the level of pretransfer income and
the order in which benefits from different income maintenance programs are added to income) is this fact: Families who benefit solely
from social insurance programs tend to have relatively higher pretransfer income than families who benefit solely from welfare programs.
Thus, at least for beneficiaries receiving only social insurance benefits, social insurance programs are called upon to fill a relatively
small poverty gap, making it relatively easy to pull such families out
of poverty. In contrast, income-tested programs are called upon to do
a more difficult job in bringing out of poverty families who benefit
solely from welfare, because these families tend to have a low pretransfer income to start with. In general, when measuring the distributive impact of the various sectors of income maintenance programs,
the order of adding benefits to income does not matter for families
who benefit from only one sector of the income maintenance programs.
This, too, should be kept in mind in inspecting Tables 4.4 and 4.5.

TABLE 4.5

Incidence of Poverty Before and After Transfers, by Demographic
Groups and by Regions: Fiscal Year 1976
(in percentage and numbers in thousands)

	Poor Families Before Transfers		Poor Families After Transfers Excluding Medicare and Medicaid	Poor Families After Transfers Including Medicare and Medicaid
	Number	Percent		
All Families	21,436	27.0	11.3	8.1
Age				
Under 65	11,789	18.6	10.6	8.6
65 and over	9,647	59.9	14.1	6.1
Race				
White	17,330	24.7	9.8	7.1
Nonwhite	4,106	43.8	22.7	15.9
Region				
South	7,873	30.8	15.4	11.9
West	3,918	26.2	10.2	8.6
Northeast	4,754	26.4	9.0	5.6
North Central	4,881	23.3	9.0	5.7

Source: U.S. Congress, Congressional Budget Office, Poverty
Status of Families Under Alternative Definitions of Income (Washington, D.C.: U.S. Government Printing Office, 1977), Tables 3, 5, 6,
7, pp. 8, 11, 12, 13.

Table 4.4 shows the percentage of pretransfer poor taken out of
poverty, in a sequential order, by each sector of the income transfers.
Table 4.5 shows the incidence of poverty at three stages: before transfers, after all transfers except Medicare and Medicaid, and after all
transfers including Medicare and Medicaid.

In 1976, there would have been 21 million families (or 27 percent
of all families) who were poor, if it had not been for income maintenance programs (see Table 4.5). Table 4.4 shows that social insurance
programs helped 41.9 percent of pretransfer poor families pull out of
poverty. After social insurance programs did their work in preventing
poverty, cash assistance programs (AFDC, SSI, and veterans' pen-

sions) pulled an additional 8.1 percent of pretransfer poor families
out of poverty. In-kind benefits other than Medicare and Medicaid
pulled another 8.1 percent of pretransfer poor families out of poverty.
After all this, benefits from Medicare and Medicaid helped an additional 11.8 percent of pretransfer poor families pull out of poverty.
When benefits from all income maintenance programs were distributed,
69.9 percent of the original pretransfer poor were no longer poor.
Thus the incidence of poverty went down to 8.1 percent from 27 percent (see Table 4.5), thanks to these income maintenance programs.

Because some may question the appropriateness of considering
Medicare and Medicaid benefits as part of income, let us disregard
the antipoverty effectiveness of these programs for the moment. Even
when these programs are not included, 58.1 percent of the original
pretransfer poor were no longer poor after they had received the benefits for which they were eligible from all income maintenance programs except Medicare and Medicaid.

Of all the various income maintenance programs, clearly social
insurance programs offer by far the most effective weapon for attack-
ing poverty. Compared with the powerful antipoverty effect of social
insurance programs, the effect of welfare programs is relatively
weak in helping poor families pull out of poverty. Cash assistance
and in-kind welfare programs put together helped only an additional
16.2 percent of pretransfer poor families become nonpoor.

The powerful antipoverty effect of social insurance programs
stems in part from their huge outlay. Table 4.2 shows that nearly
four and one-half times as much public money was expended for social
insurance programs as for cash assistance and in-kind welfare programs put together (excluding Medicare and Medicaid). Also, as
already indicated, beneficiaries of social insurance programs may
have had a relatively small poverty gap to fill before they received
social insurance benefits; therefore these benefits alone could pull
many of them out of poverty without additional help from welfare programs. This speculation is plausible because, to be eligible for
social insurance benefits, the beneficiary must have had relatively
strong attachment to the labor force. In other words, among the pretransfer poor, families who are beneficiaries of social insurance are
relatively well-off poor to start with.

Age

Many income maintenance programs are age-biased owing to
legislative intent or sometimes to socioeconomic conditions that certain age groups are placed under. Bias related to age is clearly dis-
cerned in the third row of Table 4.4. Thanks to social security, which
constitutes a large part of the social insurance sector, many families
headed by elderly persons are prevented from becoming poor. As

many as 64.1 percent of otherwise poor elderly families became non-poor after social insurance benefits were distributed. After that, an additional 8 percent were pulled out of poverty by cash assistance payments, followed by 4.3 percent by other in-kind transfer payments and 13.4 percent by benefits from Medicare and Medicaid. All told, 89.9 percent of the original pretransfer poor elderly families were no longer poor thanks to benefits from all income maintenance programs. Thus the incidence of poverty among the elderly went down to 6.1 percent from 59.9 percent (see Table 4.5). When Medicare and Medicaid were excluded, their poverty incidence went down to 14.1 percent.

A different picture emerges for families headed by persons under 65. All social insurance put together helped only 23.7 percent of the pretransfer poor families headed by persons under 65 pull out of poverty. Because the antipoverty effect of social insurance programs is relatively weak for these families, income-tested programs tend to play a larger part in preventing poverty for them—but not very much larger. For example, 11.2 percent of pretransfer poor families headed by nonaged persons, compared with 4.3 percent headed by the elderly, were made nonpoor by in-kind transfer payments. But the percentage of the pretransfer poor families pulled out of poverty by benefits from Medicare and Medicaid was greater if they were headed by elderly persons (13.4 percent) than if they were headed by nonaged persons (10.6 percent). All told, 53.7 percent of the pretransfer poor families headed by nonaged persons became nonpoor thanks to benefits from all income maintenance programs. Their incidence of poverty after receipt of benefits was 8.6 percent compared with 18.6 percent before receiving such benefits (see Table 4.5).

Indeed, these data indicate that the American system of income maintenance has been developed as though it were designed to help the aged. If it were not for income maintenance programs, the majority of families headed by elderly persons (59.9 percent) would have been poor, compared with only 18.6 percent headed by the nonaged. After benefits from all programs were added to income, the incidence of poverty of the aged was actually lower (6.1 percent) than that for the nonaged (8.6 percent). Thus the incidence of posttransfer poverty for the aged and for the nonaged converged to a great extent. Although the appropriateness of including benefits from Medicare and Medicaid in income may be questioned, it is still reasonable to reiterate that the American system of income maintenance is doing an effective job in preventing the elderly from becoming poor.

One can speculate about the sources of the differential impacts of social insurance benefits on the aged and nonaged pretransfer poor as follows. First, a large proportion of the outlay for social insurance programs is for social security, which is designed basically to help the elderly. Second, it may be that the aged pretransfer poor became so because they withdrew from the labor force; however, their previous attachment to the labor force made them eligible for social insurance benefits—mainly social security benefits. In contrast, it may be that the nonaged pretransfer poor became so because they had little or no previous attachment to the labor force, thus making them unable to benefit adequately from social insurance programs. Third, the social insurance programs that are likely to benefit the nonaged pretransfer poor are for short-term contingencies: notably unemployment insurance and worker's compensation. Fourth, as mentioned earlier, the benefit formula of social security, from which the aged benefit heavily, is slanted more in favor of low-wage beneficiaries than the formulas of other types of social insurance programs, which are basically designed for the nonaged. Last, the benefit formula under social security more adequately meets the needs posed by family size for the elderly than the benefit formulas under other social insurance programs do for the nonaged.

Race

As expected, social insurance programs prevented white families from becoming poor more than nonwhite families. As many as 46.3 percent of pretransfer white poor families compared with 23.3 percent of their nonwhite counterparts were brought out of poverty by social insurance benefits. After the effects of these benefits were felt, income-tested programs proved themselves relatively less effective in helping white families pull out of poverty. An additional 7.5 percent of pretransfer white families were brought out of poverty by cash assistance programs, 11.3 percent by in-kind transfer programs other than Medicare and Medicaid, and 6.4 percent by Medicare and Medicaid. In all, 71.5 percent of the original pretransfer white poor families were brought out of poverty when benefits from all income maintenance programs were counted.

Because social insurance programs did less in preventing poverty among nonwhite families than among white families, income-tested programs had a greater part to play in filling the poverty gap for nonwhite families. This seems clear from the relatively large percentage of pretransfer nonwhite poor families that were brought out of poverty by cash assistance programs and in-kind transfer programs. Medicare and Medicaid also played a larger part in preventing poverty among nonwhite families than among white families. All told, 63.6 percent of the original pretransfer nonwhite poor families were brought out of poverty when benefits from all income maintenance programs were counted.

As alluded to earlier, the sources of the differential impacts of social insurance programs are multiple. First, nonwhite families' pretransfer income is lower; thus their poverty gap is greater than that for white families. The size of the poverty gap depends on pretransfer income and family size. On both counts nonwhite families are more disadvantaged. Second, because social insurance benefits are based on previous earnings, benefit levels are expected to be lower for nonwhite families than for white families. Furthermore, the probability for nonwhite poor families to receive social insurance benefits is lower than for white poor families, given the same risks they encountered. However, it is important to remember that, even for nonwhite families, social insurance programs still are a powerful means of preventing poverty.

That income-tested programs are more effective in preventing poverty among nonwhite families than among white families may be explained as follows: First, because social insurance programs help relatively less to prevent poverty for nonwhite families, these families are forced to resort more heavily than white families to income-tested programs for obtaining their income. Put another way, income-tested programs in general play a larger part in preventing poverty for nonwhite families than for white families. Second, it may be that a larger proportion of nonwhite families participate in these programs than do white families. There is evidence to indicate this. For example, the rate of participation in AFDC is greater among nonwhite families than among white families.[9] Similar findings were made in regard to the food stamp program and SSI.[10]

Underlying the differential impacts of social insurance and welfare programs on whites and nonwhites, in part, is different compositions of white and nonwhite populations. For one thing, the rate of female head is much higher among nonwhite than among white families. Because female heads cannot participate in the labor force as frequently as male heads of families, and because they cannot earn as much as male counterparts if they do participate, they tend to benefit less from social insurance programs. As a result, female-headed families are forced to resort to welfare more frequently and depend on it more heavily than male-headed families.

Another important demographic factor is that there are proportionately fewer nonwhite persons among the aged population than all nonwhite persons among the total population. Likewise, nonwhites are underrepresented among beneficiaries of old-age and survivors insurance under social security, in relation to all nonwhites in the total population. Because of such differences in demographic compositions, the nonwhite poor families draw a relatively smaller proportion of their transfer income from social security than do white poor families: Social security is a significant part of social insurance. As a result, welfare programs are forced to play a larger role in meeting income needs of nonwhite families.[11]

What about the antipoverty effects of the system of income maintenance programs as a whole? As Table 4.5 shows, in the absence of
income maintenance programs, 24.7 percent of white families would
have been poor, compared with 43.8 percent of nonwhite families.
The system as a whole decreased the number of white poor families
by 71.5 percent, compared with 63.6 percent of nonwhite poor families.
After benefits from all income maintenance programs were counted,
only 7.1 percent of white families were left in poverty, compared
with 15.9 percent of nonwhite families.

What these data indicate is rather startling. Nonwhite families
had a higher incidence of poverty before benefits from any of the programs were distributed. When all programs were put to work in helping
them pull out of poverty, a smaller proportion of the relatively large
pool of nonwhite poor families was helped to escape poverty. Thus, in
the end, the incidence of poverty of nonwhite families in relation to
that of white families (expressed as the ratio of the incidence of poverty of nonwhite families to the incidence of poverty of white families)
further deteriorated after all these income maintenance programs did
their work in helping them not to be poor. Another way to describe
the distributive impact here is to say that, after the government did
all it could to prevent poverty, nonwhite poor families came to constitute an even larger proportion of poor families; in short, nonwhite
poor families became further poorer compared with white poor families.

Region

Antipoverty effects of income maintenance programs in different
regions can best be illustrated by comparing the effects in the South
with those in other regions. Because social insurance benefits are
tied to previous earnings and because wage levels in the South lag behind those in other regions, it is not surprising to find that social
insurance programs cannot do as much to prevent poverty in the South
as in other regions. Only 36.7 percent of pretransfer poor families in
the South were pulled out of poverty by social insurance benefits, compared with at least 40 percent in other regions. Another factor in the
inability of social insurance to help poor families in the South pull out
of poverty is their lower levels of pretransfer income—thus a greater
poverty gap to fill—than in other regions. Income-tested programs are
supposed to pick up where social insurance programs leave off. Therefore, one would expect that the antipoverty effects of income-tested
programs would be greater in the South than in other regions. However,
one does not observe this phenomenon working for the South. Income-
tested programs pulled out of poverty a relatively small additional
percentage of pretransfer poor families. For example, cash assistance programs pulled out of poverty only an additional 5.5 percent—
a much smaller percentage than in most other regions. In-kind transfer

programs and Medicare and Medicaid did better in preventing poverty in regions other than the South, except for the West. These effects were contrary to what was expected. What could be the reason?

There are two plausible explanations. First, most income-tested programs still follow state standards for benefits. (The food stamp program, which has uniform benefit standards nationally, is an exception.) Because the southern states provide lower benefits in income-tested programs than the states in other regions, it is hard to bring poor families out of poverty with such relatively low benefits. Second, income available to poor families in the South before the distribution of benefits from income-tested programs tends to be small compared with that in other regions. However, if a much larger proportion of poor families in the South participated in income-tested programs than did poor families in other regions, this would influence the distributive effect in the opposite direction. There is evidence to indicate that this may be beginning to occur. A study shows that eligible families in the South participate in SSI at a higher rate than in other regions. [12] Therefore, in time the trend of the distributive effect in the South may change.

What are the overall effects of all income maintenance programs combined? As expected, the South, of all regions, succeeded least in preventing poverty even with the help of all income maintenance programs. When benefits from all programs were distributed, only 61.4 percent of pretransfer poor families in the South were brought out of poverty, compared with 69.4 percent in the West, 78.8 percent in the Northeast, and 75.5 percent in the North Central.

All this paints a gloomy picture for the South. Before transfers, the South had the highest incidence of poverty—30.8 percent. But all programs combined brought a relatively small percentage of that relatively large body of pretransfer poor out of poverty. In the end, the incidence of poverty after transfers was 11.9 percent—much higher than in other regions. Like the situation of nonwhite families, the incidence of poverty for families in the South deteriorated further in comparison with other regions after all these benefits were distributed. Put another way, poor families in the South came to constitute an even larger proportion of poor families in the nation after the government did all it could to combat poverty.

After all this has been said, however, one needs to recognize that, in studying differential antipoverty effects of income maintenance programs on different regions, the nationally uniform measurement of poverty thresholds was used with no consideration of the difference in cost of living. One needs to be aware of a relatively low level of cost of living in the South. For one thing, the cost of living is somewhat lower there because of climate. Heating costs are less; lightweight clothing costs a bit less; in agricultural areas, which are considerable, homegrown foods are available for a longer period of the year. There are probably other differences too. Thus a family may be able to obtain basic essentials for less money.

Feedback Effects

Does income distributed to the poor stay in low-income segments of society? Put another way, who benefits from recipients spending transfer payments? Findings from a study by Fredrick Golladay and Robert Haveman on the stimulation analysis of a hypothetical negative income tax (NIT) program are instructive. [13] They indicate that the South received a disproportionately large share of NIT payments. However, money so distributed went right back to more productive regions, especially to the North Central and Northeast. At the same time, in the more productive regions, relatively more high-skill, high-wage jobs were created than low-skill, low-wage jobs as a result of the feedback effects of NIT payments. Why did this happen? The secondary distribution of NIT payments to richer regions took place because recipients bought goods and services that tended to be produced not by those like themselves—the poor—but by highly educated and highly skilled workers in regions of high productivity. This kind of feedback effect of an income maintenance program is bound to occur in a highly industrialized society. One can conclude that an income maintenance program for the poor, such as NIT, has a long-range distributive impact that is not favorable to low-income regions of the country as the initial impact suggests.

It is reasonable to expect that the feedback effects of the income maintenance programs under consideration are similar to those indicated in the study by Golladay and Haveman. Such effects are expected in most income-tested programs, which are geared to low-income families. However, the feedback effects of social insurance programs are not so clear. For one thing, benefits from social insurance programs may be more evenly distributed across states than benefits from income-tested programs. For another, many beneficiaries of social security—which constitutes a large piece of the social insurance pie—may not live where they used to work but may live in places favorable for retirement with a warm climate and so on.

There are degrees of the feedback effects of income maintenance programs within states in addition to such effects across states. Thus if one talks about the feedback effects of income maintenance programs within a particular state, it still holds that money spent by beneficiaries of any income maintenance program—whether social insurance or welfare—feeds back to producers of goods and services in that state. These providers are at the same time taxpayers who support income maintenance programs. They also tend to be better off economically than beneficiaries of income maintenance programs.

IMPLICATIONS

What do the data so far presented tell us? They indicate that absolute poverty has diminished greatly in the United States thanks to public income transfers. Social insurance programs are contributing more toward this end than income-tested programs. However, the anti-poverty effectiveness of social insurance programs is felt unevenly by different demographic groups. These program benefits, a large proportion of which are distributed to the elderly through social security, are primarily helping the aged escape poverty. Similarly, because benefits from social insurance are related to previous earnings, and because white families are likely to have higher previous earnings than nonwhite families, social insurance programs tend to be more effective in helping white families escape poverty than nonwhite families. For the same reason, more families in the industrial North escape poverty through social insurance benefits than do families in the South.

Benefits from income-tested programs are supposed to supplement inadequate benefits from social insurance programs. But this does not always occur. Supplementation seems to be working for nonwhite poor families, but it does not seem to work for the poor in the South or for poor families headed by nonaged persons. Furthermore, income distributed to poor regions through income-tested programs tends to come right back to rich regions.

So where do we go from here? Can we at least eliminate absolute poverty? How much would it cost to do it? As of 1976, the poverty gap, after the government did all that it did to distribute income to the poor, stood at $11.8 billion (in 1978 dollars). The comparable figure for 1965 was $16.9 billion (in 1978 dollars).[14] The $4.1 billion reduction in the poverty gap was achieved after an enormous increase in overall expenditures for income maintenance programs. We cannot say therefore that, with another $11.8 billion in public expenditures, poverty could be wiped out altogether. It takes a lot more money than the amount of the poverty gap to fill it. The goal seems so close but in fact is so hard to reach.

One very serious reason is that, when the benefits transferred through income maintenance programs are not counted in, the poverty gap has been widening over the years. It stood at $64 billion in 1976, compared with $45.8 billion in 1965 (both in 1978 dollars).[15] What this means is that, without considering public income transfers, the difference between what the public thinks the poor at least ought to have and the aggregate income that the poor themselves obtained in the private sector has been growing. Thus over the years the government has been called upon to fill an ever-increasing—bottomless?—poverty gap. This helps explain why, after all that increase in public expenditures for income maintenance, there is still a gap of $11.8 billion to fill in order to eliminate absolute poverty. This is also a reason why it will probably mean spending many times the amount of this poverty gap to fill it. It is difficult to parcel out the causes of the growing poverty gap before transfers. Part of the answer may be found in the diminishing opportunities for the poor to obtain income through work in the private sector. Another part may be found in the growing public expenditures of the income maintenance programs themselves. That is, the private sector may be adjusting to an increasing governmental intervention in providing income. The interacting forces coming from these directions are so dynamic and complex that it is hard to pin down the causes of the growing poverty gap before transfers.

Second, social insurance programs, and social security in particular, have proved to be effective in redistributing income to the poor; however, it would be extremely expensive for them to do an additional job of eliminating poverty if this was attempted by the traditional means of across-the-board increases in benefits. As mentioned earlier, social insurance programs are not specifically targeted to the poor; benefits go also to the nonpoor. And benefits to nonpoor families tend to be higher than those to poor families. Thus when the government resorts to across-the-board increases in social insurance benefits in order to help poor families, the result is that nonpoor families are helped more. For example, based on the data in Table 4.3, if the total expenditures of $123.9 billion for social insurance benefits were increased by 10 percent, or $12.4 billion, the lowest 20 percent of families would receive an additional $3.9 billion. This would represent an increase of only 5.1 percent in the aggregate income of this quintile—hardly a worthwhile venture.

The large outlay involved in social insurance programs, and social security in particular—which as noted earlier gave these programs strength in distributing large sums of money to low-income families—becomes a disadvantage when one attempts to mobilize further social insurance programs to help the poor. Only when the benefit formulas of social insurance programs are changed can a sizable redistribution of income be achieved through social insurance without incurring disproportionate additional expenditures. To bring this about, one needs to develop a new structure of benefits in social insurance. Can social insurance benefits be targeted more effectively to low-income families without making social insurance programs into another type of welfare? This is a difficult and challenging question to answer and will be touched on in later chapters.

Even income-tested programs designed to target their benefits to the poor should not do this so efficiently that they undermine the work incentive of recipients. For example, filling the poverty gap of $11.8 billion with additional public expenditure of $11.8 billion would require a 100 percent withdrawal rate in benefits. In this case, target efficiency would be perfect—100 percent—but the work incentive would diminish to zero. Thus it always takes more dollars to fill a given poverty gap, even through an income-tested program.

Third, it is difficult to fill the poverty gap because, as discussed earlier, many individuals may change their work behavior and/or living arrangements in response to income transfers. If the government expands income maintenance programs in an attempt to fill the poverty gap, some individuals may reduce work effort. Others may change their living arrangements and decide to live independently because they can afford to do so as a result of expanded income transfers. But, by their so doing, the number of low-income families may further increase. Thus the government's attempt to fill the poverty gap may further expand the gap, which in turn may require further governmental intervention to fill it.

In broad perspective, income-tested programs, although designed to supplement inadequate wages and inadequate benefits from social insurance programs, cannot in fact do so without creating some ideological and economic constraints in a work-oriented capitalist society. For example, if benefits from cash assistance programs or from in-kind transfer programs so completely supplement inadequate income from work or from social insurance programs that they radically change the pattern of income distribution existing before such income transfers, then they provoke discontent among those who do not participate in these programs. Such discontent has both political and economic connotations.

Politically, a capitalist society needs to disseminate a clear and consistent signal that work brings more reward than nonwork. Unlike socialism, capitalism is predicated on the value of free enterprise and depends on people's voluntary economic behavior. Yet paradoxically, a nation developed on the basis of voluntary work cannot afford to have people opt for nonwork. That is why the free enterprise economic system needs to be organized to reward work more than nonwork. When the economic system fails to do this, political coercion will be introduced to make certain groups of people work against their will. At that time society ceases to be one of free enterprise.

Economically, income-tested programs cannot radically distort the structure of incentives to work without eroding economic efficiency in deployment of the labor force. Transfer income from income-tested programs to supplement the factor income from work distorts the price level at which persons are willing to sell their labor. The result is that workers withdraw from the labor force unless the employer is willing to pay more than the market value of their labor, thus inviting inefficiency in the labor supply function. Even those who are not affected by income transfers and who consistently stay in the labor force will see that providing transfer income to nonworkers diminishes the net difference between the value attached to workers and the value attached to those who do not work. Thus income-tested programs cannot go so far that they undo completely the pattern of distribution of income created by the way wages and salaries are distributed and by the way benefits from work-related social insurance programs are distributed. In short, there is a limit to how much income-tested programs can do to eliminate absolute poverty, let alone relative poverty, without creating political discontent and economic inefficiency.

It may be reasonable to argue that the income maintenance system, as it exists today, is doing all it can to minimize absolute poverty. Another attempt merely to expand the present system proportionately may bring only a diminishing return in abolishing poverty. The goal of abolishing poverty seems impossible to achieve if pursued in a manner of business as usual. To achieve the goal, one needs to look at the distribution of income before benefits from income maintenance programs are distributed and attempt to reshape it. This means, for example, that work opportunities need to be increased for the poor so that their income from work would increase. One also needs to look into the benefit structures of social insurance programs and attempt to reform them, without making these programs into another type of welfare or without inviting undue disincentives for work among social insurance beneficiaries.

Another approach for further minimizing poverty in the United States is to establish a new program that does not involve the conflict created by disincentives for work; that is, a program that does not influence the work behavior of the population one way or another. Such a program may be costly. However, if the objectives of providing an adequate income to the poor and preserving work incentives can be simultaneously achieved, then a relatively large outlay may be tolerated for a program.

NOTES

1. Sheldon Danziger, Robert Haveman, and Robert Plotnick, "How Income Transfer Programs Affect Work, Savings, and the Income Distribution: A Critical Review," Journal of Economic Literature 19 (September 1981): 975-1028.

2. Robert D. Plotnick and Felicity Skidmore, Progress Against Poverty: A Review of the 1964-1974 Decade (New York: Academic Press, 1975), Table 3.4, pp. 56-57.

3. Martha N. Ozawa, "Social Insurance and Redistribution," in Jubilee for Our Times: A Practical Program for Income Equality, ed. Alvin L. Shorr (New York: Columbia University Press, 1977), pp. 123-77; and Martin S. Feldstein, "Unemployment Insurance: Time for Reform," Harvard Business Review 53 (March-April 1975): 51-61.

4. Plotnick and Skidmore, op. cit., Table 3.4, pp. 56-57.

5. Maurice MacDonald, Food Stamps and Income Maintenance (New York: Academic Press, 1977), Table 6.1, pp. 94-95.

6. U.S. Department of Health, Education, and Welfare, Social Security Administration, "Supplemental Security Income: The Aged Eligible," Social Security Bulletin 36 (July 1973): 31-35; and Jennifer N. Warlick, "The Relationship of the Supplemental Security Income Program and Living Arrangements of the Low-Income Elderly," paper presented at the National Conference on Social Welfare, Philadelphia, May 15, 1979.

7. Barbara Boland, "Participation in the Aid to Families with Dependent Children Program (AFDC)," Urban Institute Working Paper 971-02 (Washington, D.C.: Urban Institute, 1973).

8. Sheldon Danziger and Robert Plotnick, "Demographic Change, Government Transfers, and Income Distribution," Monthly Labor Review 100 (April 1977): 7-11.

9. Boland, op. cit.

10. Richard D. Coe, "Participation in the Food Stamp Program Among the Poverty Population," in Five Thousand American Families, Patterns of Economic Progress, vol. VII, ed. Greg J. Duncan and James N. Morgan (Ann Arbor: Institute of Social Research, University of Michigan, 1977), pp. 249-71; Martha N. Ozawa, "Who Seeks SSI? An Empirical Study of the Determinants of Seeking SSI Payments Among the Low-Income Elderly." Final Report to the Administration on Aging. St. Louis, Washington University, 1981. Mimeographed.

11. In 1978, 10.5 percent of all white families were female-headed, but 36 percent of all nonwhite families were female-headed. In the same year, 11.6 percent of the total population were nonwhite, but only 8.3 percent of the aged population were nonwhite. Also, in 1977, 8.3 percent of OASI beneficiaries aged 62 and over were nonwhite. See U.S. Bureau of the Census, Current Population Reports, Series P-60, no. 124, Characteristics of the Population Below the Poverty Level: 1978 (Washington, D.C.: U.S. Government Printing Office, 1980), Tables 8 and 19, pp. 38, 83; and U.S. Department of Health and Human Services, Social Security Administration, Social Security

Bulletin: Annual Statistical Supplement, 1977-1979 (Washington, D.C.:
Social Security Administration, 1980), Tables 65, pp. 117-28.

12. Warlick, op. cit.

13. Fredrick Golladay and Robert Haveman, "Regional and Distributional Effects of a Negative Income Tax," American Economic Review 66 (September 1976): 629-41.

14. Sheldon Danziger and Robert D. Plotnick, Has the War on Poverty Been Won? Chap. 4 (in press).

15. Ibid.

5

POLICY ISSUES IN
WELFARE REFORM

President Richard M. Nixon and President Jimmy Carter both attempted
to reform welfare—and failed. The situations involving the welfare mess
have since been deteriorating. Is there any way out? The present chapter discusses how the welfare mess was created and illustrates the
basic problems involved. It reviews and discusses the attempts at welfare reform by Nixon and Carter in order that we may better understand the complexity of welfare reform. We may also be able to learn
the limitations inherent in welfare programs, both proposed and in
operation, for helping the poor improve their economic condition.

DEVELOPMENT OF THE WELFARE MESS

When Lyndon B. Johnson took over the presidency, he gave this nation
a vision of a "Great Society." The elimination of poverty was an important ingredient of that vision. Thus his declaration of war on poverty
was quickly translated into the enactment of the Economic Opportunity
Act (EOA), which he signed into law on August 20, 1964. However,
the excitement surrounding EOA notwithstanding, the approach it took
in helping the poor was basically conservative. The approach was
changing the poor instead of enriching them through direct income redistribution; adapting the poor to the economic system rather than
changing the system; and above all, instilling in the minds of the poor
new attitudes and stronger motivation to work and encouraging a lifestyle more compatible with the mainstream of society.[1] In short, the
programs under EOA adopted the strategy of service orientation, which
was reflected in the Job Corps, the Neighborhood Youth Corps, Head
Start, and Upward Bound—all administered by the Office of Economic
Opportunity (OEO).

Another approach that EOA took was to make the then existing social services more responsive to the needs of the poor. Community action programs that developed across the nation confronted local and state agencies so as to make them serve the poor better than they had before. Legal aid services for the poor, also developed under EOA, were to supplement the community action programs and accelerate the movement toward making local and state agencies more responsive to the needs of the poor.

In spite of the tremendous publicity that EOA commanded during the Johnson administration, the scope of the programs directly related to the act was relatively small. In 1965, when such programs were just beginning to be put into effect, the expenditures for them were $359 million, or 0.5 percent of total social welfare expenditures. Seven years later, when OEO programs were well in operation, the expenditures for these programs were only $3.3 billion, or 3 percent of total social welfare expenditures.[2] As soon as Nixon entered the White House, the mission of OEO, as well as the programs administered by the office, was quickly undermined. Many controversial programs were terminated, and some popular programs—such as Head Start—were transferred to other federal agencies.

The legacy of Johnson in his quest for helping the poor pull out of poverty did not end with the downhill of OEO programs, however. The effects of the Equal Opportunity Act spilled beyond the programs directly related to the act. One important effect was to raise a basic question for all federal agencies administering all sorts of programs: What does it do for the poor? Perhaps no other president ever raised this question in evaluating federal programs. Before, only the question of efficiency was asked. In this case governmental programs were to be evaluated on the basis of how much they contributed to the stability and growth of the economy. The question of "What does it do for the poor?" uses equity instead of efficiency as a focal point of national policy[3] and focuses on the redistributive impact of federal programs on the poor.

With the enactment of EOA, the momentum seemed to set in motion the expansion of the extant welfare programs and the institution of new ones, all responding to the question, "What does it do for the poor?" As a result, public expenditures for social welfare programs targeted to the poor increased rapidly during the decade 1965-74. Per capita expenditures in constant dollars for income-tested programs increased by 217 percent, in contrast to a 122 percent increase in per capita expenditures for social insurance programs during the same period. Expressed as a percentage of the gross national product, public expenditures for income-tested social welfare programs constituted only 1 percent in 1965, but in 1974 they were 2.3 percent of GNP.[4] This indicates that public expenditures for these programs were expanding more than twice as fast as the economy as a whole.

The expansion of income-tested programs (welfare) occurred on many fronts, of which inauguration of new programs was one. Medicaid was enacted in 1965 to provide free medical care to recipients of categorical public assistance programs—then Aid to Families with Dependent Children (AFDC), Old-Age Assistance (OAA), Aid to the Permanently and Totally Disabled (APTD), and Aid to the Blind (AB)—and to the medically indigent whose income decreased below a stated amount as a result of meeting medical bills. The food stamp program was enacted in 1964 and was amended later to nationalize eligibility requirements and benefits. By 1974 the program came to cover every part of the nation. In essence, it became a nationwide negative income tax program under the guise of food stamps. In 1972 yet another important cash assistance program was enacted and put into effect in 1974. It was Supplementary Security Income, which consolidated the former state categorical public assistance programs of OAA, AB, and APTD. SSI became the first national guaranteed income program for the poor who are aged, blind, or disabled.

On a second front, existing programs were liberalized. AFDC, for example, expanded enormously during the decade following the enactment of EOA. In 1965, $1.6 billion was spent for this program, but in 1975 expenditures were $9.2 billion. The number of recipients increased to 11.2 million in 1975 from 3.2 million in 1965.[5] This rapid expansion took place paradoxically in a steadily growing economy.

There were multiple forces at work to expand the scope of the AFDC program: some structural, some not. In 1967, the AFDC benefit formula was changed to allow a disregard of work expenses and the first $30 of earnings in calculating AFDC payments. AFDC payments were then reduced by two thirds of the net earnings. Before that, a $1 increase in earnings resulted in a $1 decrease in cash payments, giving AFDC recipients no incentive to work. Under the revised benefit formula, after AFDC recipients kept the first $30 in earnings and an extra amount to meet work expenses, they would be able to keep 33¢ out of every $1 earned. Thus the change in the benefit formula created a structural change in the program, resulting not only in an improvement in the work incentive but also an increase in program expenditures.

The expansion of AFDC also stemmed from several court rulings that resulted in liberalizing eligibility requirements. Through the case of Shapiro vs. Thompson, the U.S. Supreme Court in 1969 eliminated the residency requirement. It struck down in 1968 the man-in-the-home rule through the King vs. Smith case. Furthermore, it overturned the rule that assistance may be discontinued prior to a fair hearing and ruled instead that public assistance should be continued until an evidentiary hearing was held. Two cases, Wheeler vs. Montgomery (1969) and Goldberg vs. Kelly (1970), were involved in the decision. All

these decisions helped break down barriers and enabled the poor to
take better advantage of AFDC.

The movement involving the National Welfare Rights Organizations that sprang up across the nation accelerated the expansion of
AFDC also. The organizations helped the poor—especially black poor
families—to change their attitudes about receiving AFDC. They succeeded, to a great extent, in enabling blacks to feel that they had a
right to AFDC payments if they were needy. The transformation of
AFDC payments from doles to benefits by right helped dilute the sense
of stigma that had been traditionally attached to the program.

The shift in the demographic characteristics of American families also contributed to the expansion of AFDC. In 1965 only 9 percent
of white families were female-headed; in 1975, the proportion increased
to 10.5 percent. In absolute terms, the number of female-headed white
families increased from 3.8 million to 5.2 million, or a 37 percent
increase. The change was even more pronounced among black families.
The number of black female-headed families increased from 1.1 million in 1965 to 2.4 million in 1975, more than doubling in numbers.
Thus as many as 32 percent of all black families were female-headed
in 1975, compared with only 23 percent in 1965.[6] These female-headed
families are generally immune to economic growth. Even if female
heads are in the labor force, the probability that they will be poor is
higher than for the general population.

Since the 1967 amendments to the Social Security Act separated
cash payments from the provision of social services, a variety of
social services have been developed, and traditional ones have been
expanded. This, too, contributed toward increasing public expenditures
for welfare programs for the poor. Not only casework-type counseling
services but also services of a more tangible type came to be provided,
including, for example, meals on wheels for the elderly, home-chore
services for the disabled, day care for children, employment-related
medical services and education and training programs for adults, and
a lot more. Furthermore, the eligible pools of recipients of services
was enlarged to include not only those on categorical cash assistance
programs but also those who were not on such programs and whose
income sometimes exceeded the median income in the community.[7]

Thus when Nixon entered the White House in 1969, the nation
was in the midst of an expansion spree for all types of welfare programs. He was concerned about the alarming rate at which these
programs expanded. But just as important, it seems, he was concerned about the chaotic structure of the whole system of welfare.
The system was full of inadequacies and inequities. First, the levels
of payments for most welfare programs varied widely across states,
and in low-paying states they were far below the poverty line. For
example, when Nixon took office, the average monthly payment per

recipient under AFDC was only $11.95 in Mississippi but was $70 in Massachusetts.[8] Second, working families with two parents at home were excluded from most welfare programs even though they might have been just as needy as single-parent families. Third, there was an unequal distribution of the number of programs from which families benefited. Some families were benefiting from AFDC, food stamps, public housing assistance, Medicaid, and perhaps more. But other needy families benefited from none of these programs. All this amounted to horizontal inequity, as families with the same level of financial need were treated differently.

Above all, Nixon seemed to be concerned about a disincentive effect created by a particular welfare program or several programs in combination. As a matter of fact, concern about the question of the work incentive was prevalent among policymakers in Washington before he took office. Thus OEO, during the Johnson administration, funded the New Jersey Income Maintenance Experiment to test whether working poor families would reduce their work effort if they were provided a guaranteed income by the government. The experiment began in 1968 and lasted three years. Researchers involved in the project reported that, while the wives in the experimental group worked significantly less than the wives in the control group, the work effort of husbands in the experimental group did not significantly differ from that of their counterparts in the control group. Specifically, the wives in the experimental group worked 23 percent fewer hours and earned 20 percent less than their counterparts in the experimental group. But the husbands in the experimental group actually earned 3.5 percent more, although they worked 2 percent fewer hours than their counterparts in the control group.[9] These rather benign findings notwithstanding, the Nixon administration seemed to make a serious issue of the work incentive.

PRESIDENT NIXON'S PROPOSAL ON THE
FAMILY ASSISTANCE PLAN

On August 8, 1969, President Nixon proposed the Family Assistance Plan (FAP) to provide a nationally financed and administered cash assistance program to all families with children whose income fell below stated amounts.[10] The plan was the first attempt by the federal government to provide income support to working families with children with two parents at home.

FAP as proposed in H.R. 16311 of the 91st Congress provided an income guarantee of $500 per year for each of the first two family members, plus $300 per year for each additional member. Thus, in the absence of other income a family of four was to receive $1,600 a year. When the family earnings exceeded $720, the cash payment would decrease by 50¢ for each $1 earned. (However each $1 of unearned income—such as rent, interest, dividends, social security benefits—would result in a $1 reduction in FAP benefits for each $1 of such unearned income.) Thus FAP benefits would be reduced to zero when the family earnings reached $3,920.

Concerned about the issue of the work incentive, FAP included the requirement that unemployed recipients must accept suitable work or training. If this was refused, the fourth person's allowance ($300) would be deducted from the grant. Researchers involved in the New Jersey Income Maintenance Experiment reported that male heads of families did not reduce their work effort as a result of income transfers. Nevertheless, Nixon's proposed plan included the work requirement to ensure passage of the bill through the House Committee on Ways and Means chaired by Wilbur Mills (D.-Ark.), who had been known to be concerned about the work incentive.

The underlying objectives of FAP were multiple, all attempting to address the prevailing criticisms in regard to welfare. FAP was proposed on the principles that (1) poverty among all poor families with children should be alleviated; (2) FAP should improve the situation in regard to disincentives involved in AFDC and other income-tested programs; (3) FAP should not encourage family breakups but rather encourage family stability; (4) FAP should treat all poor families with children equally, regardless of residence or source of income; and (5) FAP should be administered in such a way as to promote the dignity and self-reliance of its recipients. [11]

The reaction of the general public at first appeared positive when FAP was announced. Indeed, the reform proposal seemed to arouse the enthusiasm of practically everyone. Each one saw what he wanted to see: State governors saw a possible fiscal windfall in the plan; conservatives liked the work requirement for the able-bodied; liberals welcomed an introduction of a national floor of income; egalitarian academics believed that the inclusion of the working poor in the plan would eliminate discrimination against them and would diminish the incentive for poor families to break up in order to become eligible for public assistance; conservatives and liberals alike believed that the economic incentive (as opposed to the provision of social services) would be the key to getting recipients off welfare and halting the increase in welfare expenditures.

Congressional debate and public hearings on FAP eventually created more complex problems than the bill could ever hope to solve. Even the initial supporters of the plan began to find fallacies where none seemed to have existed before. In the area of benefits, the dilemma involved in the provision of a uniform basic guarantee and an economic incentive at the same time—regardless of the employability of the family head and subject only to family size—was soon exposed. With a given amount of fiscal resources, the provision of a greater degree of work incentive would inevitably result in a smaller basic guarantee. The working poor would escape the impact, but it would operate with cruel effect on those who could not work. Again, with a given amount of fiscal resources, the provision of an adequate basic guarantee would have to be matched by a weaker incentive measure. In this case, one of the basic goals of FAP—the preservation of the work incentive—would be defeated.

The northern states, which already provided more liberal public assistance than the national minimum proposed under FAP, recognized that the federal assumption of fiscal responsibility for such a minimum would greatly help the states in the South, but not the states in the North. Welfare mothers in the North, organized under the leadership of George Wiley of the National Welfare Rights Organization, saw no additional increment to what they were already receiving; worse yet, they were afraid that they might benefit less from FAP than from AFDC.

Perhaps FAP met the most critical opposition from Senator John J. Williams (Delaware), who had been determined to kill the bill. He exposed in a Senate Finance Committee hearing the problem of the work disincentive caused by the receipt of multiple welfare benefits. Using the situation in Chicago as an example, Williams asserted that a family of four receiving an FAP payment, the state supplement to the FAP payment, food stamps, Medicaid (average vendor payment per family), and public housing assistance would receive $5,541 in total benefits in 1970. When the family earned $720, the FAP payment would not be reduced but the bonus value of food stamps would be reduced by $96. Furthermore, the family would have to pay $37 in social security taxes. As a result, the total net income would be $6,128. In essence, earning $720 would bring a $587 net increment to family income. When the family earned $5,560, the family would lose all transfer payments (the FAP payment, the state supplement, food stamps, and Medicaid) except public housing assistance. As a result, the total net income would go down to $6,109, or a $19 deduction. A typical notch problem was exposed here. (A notch problem refers to a situation when extra work effort results in a decrease in the net family income.) By earning more, the family lost income. The notch problem in this case was created for two reasons: Other income-tested programs as well as FAP withdrew benefits simultaneously as the family earned more, resulting in a cumulative implicit tax rate of more than 100 percent on its earnings; and the family was dropped completely from Medicaid when it became ineligible for FAP. The exchange of arguments between Senator Williams and Robert Patricelli, deputy assistant secretary of HEW (now HHS), was perhaps the most dramatic scene encountered by FAP. It went as follows:

> Williams: If they increase their earnings from $720 to $5,560 under this bill, they have a spendable income of $6,109, or $19 less than they would have if they sit in a rocking chair earning only $720. Is that not correct?
> Patricelli: That is correct, Senator. They would have less if they earned $5,560 than if they earned $720, provided they get public housing, medical payments, and so forth. [In Chicago, he said, only 18 percent of AFDC families lived in public housing.]
> Williams: They are penalized $19 because they go out and earn $5,560?
> Patricelli: That is correct. [12]

On November 20, 1970, the Senate Finance Committee killed the 1970 FAP bill by a 10-6 vote.

Come the 92nd Congress, the Nixon administration launched another attempt at welfare reform. The revised scheme was introduced as H.R. 1 of the 92nd Congress. The revised plan cashed out the value of the food stamp bonus and included it in cash payments. Thus the bill provided $2,400 (instead of $1,600) for a family of four. It provided for a benefit cut of 66.7¢ for each $1 earned in excess of $720 a year. The break-even point—at which benefits became zero—was set at $4,140.*

At a glance, the implicit tax rate on earnings of 67 percent appears greater than the 50 percent rate provided in FAP (H.R. 16311). But the actual impact on recipients would have been quite similar. Because the original FAP was to operate side by side with the food stamp program, which had its own implicit tax rate of 30 percent, recipients benefiting from both programs would have given up 65¢ worth of combined benefits as they earned each extra $1. Under H.R. 1, which incorporated the food stamp bonus value in cash payments, benefits were to be withdrawn by 67¢ as earnings increased by $1. Therefore, the impact of the benefit-loss rates under both plans would be quite similar even though the nominal rates were different.

---

*H.R. 1's break-even point should have been $4,320 ($720 plus 1.5 times $2,400) but to save money the Ways and Means Committee decided to disallow payments smaller than $10 monthly. At the expense of poor families, this reduced the cutoff point by $180 a year ($45 a quarter).

The difference between FAP and H.R. 1 was more pronounced in the treatment of different categories of recipient families. Whereas FAP treated equally all families with children, H.R. 1 singled out families with fully employed fathers and offered them a program called Opportunities for Families, under which they would receive wage supplements. If no jobs were found for them and they had no other income, these families were to receive the full basic guarantee—$2,400 for a family of four. When they earned income, their benefits were to be cut by a percentage of earnings, except for the first $720, which would be disregarded. Nonemployable families—those headed by an incapacitated father or by a mother with a child below the age of three—would be treated in the same way as the original FAP would have treated them. That is, they would receive the basic guarantee, and only when they worked would their payments be reduced by a portion of their earnings in excess of $720.

H.R. 1 also provided separate income support (Title III) for the elderly, blind, and disabled. The program provided $130 a month per individual and $195 a month per couple. H.R. 1 passed the House of Representatives without difficulty but met formidable opposition in the Senate.

Senator Russell Long of Louisiana, chairman of the Senate Finance Committee, had long opposed the idea of a negative income tax—a scheme embraced by FAP. He succeeded in having the Senate Finance Committee reject H.R. 1 in favor of his own "workfare" plan. The plan was to withdraw federal welfare aid from mothers whose youngest child is six years or older and instead guarantee them a job at $1.20 an hour. It also provided wage supplements for those who take low-paying private jobs. For low-paid family heads at private jobs covered by social security, the plan was to pay a tax credit of 10 percent up to earnings of $4,000.

In the meantime Senator Ribicoff (Connecticut), who always represented the liberal wing of the Senate, introduced an amendment to H.R. 1. His bill proposed a basic benefit of $3,000 for a family of four—$600 above H.R. 1—and a gradual increase in benefits each year so that the level would reach the poverty threshold by 1976. The bill proposed that benefits would be reduced by 60¢ for each $1 of earnings beyond $720, as compared with 67¢ under H.R. 1. Thus the break-even point under the Ribicoff bill would be $5,720, considerably higher than $4,140 under H.R. 1. The bill covered single persons and childless couples as potential beneficiaries as well and exempted mothers with preschool children from work requirements.

The Senate Finance Committee thus had to entertain three different versions of welfare reform, representing a wide range of the political spectrum. Unlike the earlier time when the introduction of FAP was embraced by many groups of supporters, this time each party involved in the debate insisted on its own viewpoint and concern and saw the ideas advocated by others as unacceptable.

Nixon refused to make any compromise on H.R. 1. In spite of the president's stance, the Senate Finance Committee reported out its own version of H.R. 1, which included Long's welfare plan for families and the federal income guarantee for the aged, the blind, and the disabled. The Senate later rejected Ribicoff's amendment. Senate-House conferees subsequently deleted the program involving families with children (FAP). Finally, on October 17, 1972, the House and the Senate passed H.R. 1, deleting FAP but including Supplemental Security Income. Thus out of the prolonged national debate on welfare reform, which originally focused on families with children, a national guaranteed income for the aged, the blind, and the disabled—SSI— emerged with little controversy and not much debate.

In seeking to understand why Nixon's attempt at welfare reform went the way it did, one cannot help but appreciate the political realities and the complexity involved in welfare reform. As the public debate on welfare reform continued and the presidential election approached, Nixon seemed to sense which side the electorate was on. The electorate was not ready for a for a sweeping welfare reform. He chose to trade off welfare reform in exchange for improved reelection prospects. Ironically, Senator George McGovern (Democrat, South Dakota), who tried to champion the cause of the poor by offering "$1,000 for everyone," in effect bailed Nixon out of the controversy on welfare reform.

A more critical problem was the set of conflicting goals that FAP embodied: an attempt to provide adequate assistance, a work incentive provision, equal treatment of working and nonworking poor families, fiscal relief to the states, and reduced welfare costs for the federal government in the long run. The goals, however worthy, proved almost paradoxical in their relationship to one another. They could not be reconciled.

PRESIDENT CARTER'S ATTEMPT TO REFORM WELFARE

Upon taking office, President Jimmy Carter, too, established welfare reform as a major national policy goal.[13] On August 6, 1977, he announced a major proposal for welfare reform—the "Program for Better Jobs and Income." The main purpose of this proposal was to streamline the welfare system by consolidating the three major existing welfare programs: AFDC, SSI, and food stamps. Although some features were new, many derived from earlier attempts to reform welfare, especially Nixon's FAP. The major features of Carter's plan were as follows: This plan, for the first time in the American welfare history, provided for all low-income individuals and families with no exclusion. Combining welfare reform in regard to cash assistance payments with the creation of jobs and integrating an earnings supplement with cash assistance payments were also important new features of the proposal. Consolidating three major existing programs constituted a bold move.

Carter's plan had two parts: income provision and work requirements.

Income Provision

To provide income support, Carter proposed a dual system that was further supplemented by earned income tax credits (or earnings supplement). The first part of the dual system—called the income support program—was targeted to the nonworking poor, namely, the aged, the blind, the disabled, and single-parent families with children 6 and under. Single-parent families with children age 7 to 13 would also come under this program when a job and day care were not available. The program would provide basic income support of $4,200 per year for a family of four. Income support payments would decline by 50¢ as earnings increased by $1. The break-even point, therefore, would be $8,400. The basic income support for the aged, blind, or disabled individuals would be $2,500 a year. The level of support for a couple falling in any of these three categories would be $3,750 a year.

The second part of the dual system was a work-benefit program for the working poor. Single individuals, childless couples, intact families with children, and single-parent families with children age 14 and over came under this category. Single-parent families with children age 7 to 13 would be covered under this program when a job and day care were available.

For these groups, the Carter plan provided work benefits of $2,300 per year for a family of four until its earnings reached $3,800. Thereafter, work benefits were to be reduced by 50¢ for each $1 of earnings. Thus the break-even point would be $8,400. For example, a family of four earning $5,000 a year would receive work benefits of $1,700 per year, resulting in a total annual family income of $6,700. Single-parent families would be able to deduct 20 percent of earned income up to $150 per month to pay for child-care expenses necessary for the parent to go to work.

On top of the dual system, the Carter plan provided "earned income tax credits": 10 percent of earnings up to $4,000 and 5 percent of earnings between $4,000 and $9,080, at which point the credits would start declining at the rate of 10 percent of each extra $1 earned and reach zero when family earnings reached $15,620. Earned income credits were provided only to those who were employed in private or nonsubsidized public jobs.

A four-member family earning less than $8,400 a year would receive both work benefits and an earned income tax credit. When the family earned more than $8,400, it would receive only the earned income tax credit. Beyond the $9,080 level, the family would start paying income taxes, yet it would continue to claim earned income tax credits until its earned income reached $15,620, when tax credit no longer applied.

Work Requirements

Like Nixon, Carter was concerned about the issue of the work incentive. His emphasis on work was shown in two ways: through the work incentive built into benefit formulas and the specific work requirements imposed on the employable. The Carter plan required unemployed single persons, childless couples, single parents with children age 14 and over, and heads of intact families to sign up for job training, counseling, and placement services. Single parents with children age 7 to 13 were required to work part time, or full time if day care was available. To ensure a job to principal earners of families with children, the Carter plan provided 1.4 million public service jobs.

Furthermore, the Carter plan emphasized private jobs. This emphasis was shown by the fact that earned income tax credits would apply only to earnings from private or nonsubsidized public jobs. Also, applicants for public service jobs would be required to engage in a five-week search for private employment before becoming eligible for a public service job. Even those who were placed in public service jobs would have to engage in a job search for private employment every 12 months.

Carter's plan, if enacted, would have provided adequate benefits for those considered unemployable; it would have provided benefits to working poor families along with a strong incentive measure; and it would have ensured a public work job at least to heads of households. However, with political pressure mounting in other areas—the state of the economy and the hostage problem in Iran—the Carter administration withdrew its attempt to reform welfare.

ISSUES AND PROBLEMS IN WELFARE REFORM

Why is welfare so hard to reform? What are the major problems in welfare? We shall discuss the issues and problems in welfare in a

more systematic manner here, although many of them have been alluded to earlier.

The Work Incentive

The concern about the work incentive[14] among welfare recipients
is pervasive in the United States, where the public's belief in work
ethics is high. Moral value is attached to the idea of work. But the
issue of the work incentive arises not for moral reasons alone. There
is also some economic theoretical foundation that leads us to worry
about disincentive effects of welfare programs. Let us see what economic theory tells us. But, first, let us examine the basic structure
of a welfare program.
   Most welfare programs now in operation in the United States
have three basic features: the basic guarantee, the benefit-loss rate
(or the implicit tax rate), and the break-even level. The basic guarantee is the amount of benefit provided by a welfare program to families
who do not have any other income. This is the maximum payment.
The benefit-loss rate—or the implicit tax rate—is the rate at which
the government reduces benefits as income of the recipient family
increases. For example, AFDC payments are reduced by 67¢ for
each $1 of earnings. Under SSI, after a disregard of $255 earnings a
quarter (or $195 a quarter if the recipient has unearned income for
which an additional disregard of $60 is allowed), benefits are reduced
by 50¢ for each $1 of earnings. The implicit marginal tax rate under
AFDC is 67 percent and 50 percent under SSI.
   The break-even level is related inversely to the benefit-loss
rate. For example, under AFDC with an implicit tax rate of 67 percent, it takes $3 of earnings to offset $2 of benefits; therefore the
break-even level equals one and one-half times the basic guarantee
plus disregarded earnings. When the benefit-loss rate is 25 percent,
the break-even level is four times the basic guarantee plus the disregarded earnings. Thus the lower the benefit-loss rate, the higher the
break-even level.
   The basic guarantee, the benefit-loss rate, and the break-even
level are mathematically interrelated. Thus when two are known, the
other can be automatically calculated.
   Economists divide a person's time into work for pay, work at
home, and leisure. They theorize that people divide their time to maximize their sense of utility. They also say that leisure is one of the
commodities that people "buy" by not working. Leisure, in other
words, has a price. The decision to buy more leisure depends on the
price that a person is willing to pay for it.[15]
   What economists are worried about is that, when families receive

welfare, they tend to "buy" leisure by not working. How does this happen? When individuals receive nonwage income (or income for doing nothing) such as welfare payments, they usually reduce work effort because they can afford not to work. Put another way, they can now afford to buy leisure. Because someone gave them money for doing nothing, suddenly leisure becomes cheaper to acquire. Economists call such an effect the income effect.

When a welfare program reduces benefits as recipients earn more, the value of work goes down. For example, when a program reduces benefits by 67 percent of earned income, such as under AFDC, work at $3 per hour brings only $1 net income for each additional hour worked. Thus the value of work diminishes considerably. When this occurs, the workers sense that leisure (or not working) becomes cheaper to acquire because they would lose only $1 per hour for not working compared with $3 when not on the welfare program. It is quite probable that a rational person would opt for leisure under such circumstances. This is called the substitution effect.

However, the benefit-loss rate in a welfare program may cause an opposite effect. When a welfare program reduces benefits because the recipient earns more, that recipient may decide to work more to make up for the loss in benefits. Here, another type of income effect is at work, but in the opposite direction.

Because the effect of reducing welfare payments as the recipient earns more operates in two opposite directions—the substitution effect and the income effect—the question of how this feature of welfare may influence the work behavior of the recipient can be answered only through an empirical study. This was a major reason for OEO to fund the New Jersey Income Maintenance Experiment mentioned earlier. Which factor—the income effect of the basic guarantee or the substitution effect of the benefit-loss rate—discourages more the work effort of the recipient? There is little empirical evidence that enables one to estimate the net effect of these two disincentive effects. An "informed opinion" among economists seems to hold that the level of the basic guarantee is a less important factor than the benefit-loss rate in discouraging work effort among welfare recipients. [16] At any rate, the income effect involving the basic guarantee and the substitution effect involving the benefit-loss rate make informed citizens suspect that welfare programs create work disincentives among recipients.

Although the literature mainly focuses on the disincentive effect of welfare on families who participate in the program, there is some reason to worry that welfare programs may create the disincentive effect on nonparticipants as well. How can this be? Suppose Nixon's original FAP had been enacted. A family of four without any other income would have received $133 a month. If this family's head had obtained a part-time job and worked 50 hours a month at the hourly rate of $3, the monthly benefit would have been reduced to $88, thus making the total family income to be $238 a month.

How does a working family that is almost as poor as the foregoing family but is not on welfare compare its own economic condition? Suppose the head of this family worked full time at $4 per hour. This family might evaluate the situation of both families on the basis of the total family income and hours of work. On the basis of these two measures, the nonrecipient family might conclude that the family on welfare worked only 50 hours a month but received an income of $238, making the "effective" hourly wage rate $4.76. This compares with the rate of $4 for the nonrecipient family. Furthermore, the nonrecipient family might have to pay taxes to support FAP and other welfare programs. This is a simple and possibly unfair way to compare the economic condition of welfare and nonwelfare families. But it is entirely plausible to expect that near-poor families who do not receive welfare might assess the situation in such simple terms and point out the inequity involved.

What is important here is that, in the eyes of nonrecipient families, benefits from a welfare program change the ranking of income levels in relation to work effort. Somehow, families near the poverty line who sustain themselves without receiving welfare may feel threatened by the relatively diminished value of their work effort. Why, they may complain, should they work if little or no work can bring a relatively high income? They may as well decide to quit work and get on welfare. If many nonrecipient families should decide to quit work and join the rank of welfare recipients, the cost of welfare programs could explode beyond imagination.

Welfare programs (they are all income-tested) thus seem worse than a zero-sum game as far as the issue of the work incentive is concerned. There seem to be no winners but rather losers on both sides. Welfare programs may create disincentive effects on both those who receive welfare benefits and some of those who pay for them.

Cumulative Benefit-Loss Rates

There is concern enough about the probable disincentive effect of any welfare program. Concern is heightened when a family participates in several welfare programs simultaneously. Take, for example, a female-headed family with three children in Chicago, who participated in AFDC in 1971. Suppose that this family also participated in food stamp, public housing, and Medicaid programs at the same time. After work expenses and $30 were deducted from monthly earnings, the AFDC program reduced its payment by 67¢ for each $1 of earnings. Both the food stamp program and the public housing program reduced their benefits by a percentage of earnings. Medicaid was provided as long as the family was on AFDC. Because all of the programs except Medicaid reduced benefits simultaneously as earnings increased, in essence these programs together "taxed away" earnings at a cumulative implicit tax rate of great magnitude. On top of all this, the family had to pay 5.2 percent social security taxes on all earnings and income taxes on earnings in excess of $4,000 a year, making the cumulative tax rate even higher. A study by Leonard Hausman shows that when this family earned between $4,300 and $8,600 a year, the cumulative tax rate was as high as 76 percent. This meant that extra work effort worth $1 brought a net increase of only 24¢ in the total net family income. Put another way, for a family in this earnings bracket, a job paying $3 per hour really meant a job that paid only 72¢ an hour. When this family increased its annual earnings to $8,700 a year, an even more serious problem would have confronted it. The family would have lost Medicaid benefits (valued at $888) altogether, creating a notch problem. [17]

Subsequent attempts at welfare reform would not have noticeably improved the situation. For example, under H.R. 1, which cashed out food stamps and included their value in cash payments, the same Chicago family would have been subjected to an 87 percent cumulative tax rate if it earned between $720 and $4,320 and a rate of 107 percent if it earned between $4,320 and $6,000. The tax rate of 107 percent meant that each time the family earned an extra dollar, the net family income in fact declined. In essence, work would have been penalized.[18] Carter's proposal cashed out the value of food stamps and reduced the benefit-loss rate to 50 percent, improving the situation somewhat. (The comparable rate was 65 percent under FAP and 67 percent under H.R. 1.) However, as long as some families participate in multiple programs, the problem of cumulative tax rates would remain.

Not all families participate in multiple welfare programs, of course. It is estimated that the likelihood that AFDC families will participate in Medicaid is 99 percent, 60 percent in the food stamp program, and 14 percent in the public housing program.[19] When they do participate in multiple programs, combined benefits have a competitive edge on prevailing wages. The competitive edge steadily increases as the family size becomes larger.

What we are observing here is the compounding of the income effect associated with a high basic guarantee (combined benefits provided to nonworking families) and the substitution effect associated with a high cumulative tax rate that families are subjected to if they decide to work. On both grounds, the work disincentive effect accelerates as families participate in more and more welfare programs.

Concern for Program Costs and Target Efficiency

Nixon introduced his proposal on FAP with a double-edged slogan: "welfare is getting out of control" and "the nation needs workfare rather than welfare." With these rhetorical words, he sent a message to the nation that it should control welfare expenditures. But the nation still seemed to be compassionate enough to provide adequately for the "truly needy." (The same dual concern is being restated by the Reagan administration.) Because of the dual concern for controlling expenditures and for helping the truly needy, the idea of target efficiency became popular as an academic subject to pursue.[20] How realistic is this idea in light of what we have already discussed regarding the issue of the work incentive?

Target efficiency implies that benefits must be targeted to the poor and therefore must be withdrawn as quickly as possible when recipient families start earning income. The higher the rate of benefit withdrawal, the greater the target efficiency. For example, a welfare program that provides a basic guarantee of poverty-line income can successfully target its benefits to the poor if the program reduces benefits by $1 for each $1 of earnings. The target efficiency is perfect. There are no spillover benefits to the nonpoor. But, on the other hand, the work incentive is completely undermined. Suppose we try to improve the work incentive by withdrawing only 50¢ worth of benefit for each $1 earned and maintain the level of the basic guarantee at the poverty line. Then, the break-even level—or the point at which families get off a welfare program—becomes twice as large as the poverty-line income. Many nonpoor families become eligible for benefits as well. Thus target efficiency is undermined in this model in order to preserve the work incentive. Suppose, next, we attempt to target benefits to the poor and preserve the work incentive (providing, for example, a 50 percent benefit-loss rate) at the same time. Then the basic guarantee must be cut in half. In this model, the policy goal of "providing adequately for the truly needy" is undermined.

The point being made here is that the goal of target efficiency (and therefore the control of expenditures) cannot be attained without sacrificing either the policy goal of enhancing the work incentive or the policy goal of providing adequately for the truly needy. Therefore Nixon's aim to do something about welfare expenditures and at the same time to transform welfare into workfare is difficult to attain, indeed. Unless other factors—such as economic, social, and demographic conditions—change, these two goals can be attained only if the nation is willing to cut down on the basic guarantee provided to families who do not have any other income.

Is there any way out of this three-sided policy dilemma that involves the conflicting policy goals of adequacy, the work incentive, and target efficiency (or cost control)? Carter's proposal in part dealt with this problem. The proposal attempted to provide adequately for families who were not expected to work and at the same time to preserve the work incentive among families who were expected to work. And on top of these policy goals, the proposal attempted to control the overall costs of the plan. It tried to achieve all these goals by establishing separate income support schemes for working and nonworking families. Nonworking families were provided for generously; that is, they were provided with a relatively high basic guarantee. But benefits would be reduced as soon as recipients start earning. Working families were provided with a lesser basic guarantee but were allowed to keep the maximum payment (or the basic guarantee) until their earnings reached a certain level, at which point benefits would start being reduced. The separate treatment of working and nonworking poor was first advocated by Robert Lampman and Christopher Green in the mid-1960s.[21] The Carter plan implemented the schemes that Lampman and Green developed to disentangle the policy dilemma involved in welfare programs.

Different treatment of working and nonworking families solves old problems but creates new ones. Carter's proposal identified families that are presumably unemployable on the basis of either age (65 and over), preschool children at home, or disability. The first two criteria are clear enough. But what about disability? How disabled did a person have to be in order to benefit from the Carter plan for nonworking families? Many disabilities, especially in cases of mental illness, are relative. Research findings indicate that there is a positive relationship between a high unemployment rate and a high incidence of applications for SSI or disability benefits under social security.[22] For example, during recessions, some economically marginal persons become "disabled" and apply for these benefits. It is expected, therefore, that many disabled individuals will be borderline cases, and it will be difficult to assign them to either of the two schemes in the Carter plan.

Because persons with borderline disabilities benefit more under the scheme for the unemployable, they would have an incentive to be officially designated as "disabled" and therefore unemployable. If this occurred, the Carter plan would have created another type of work disincentive, incurring additional costs for implementing the plan.

Differential treatment of working and nonworking families also raises the issue of equity. Is it fair that presumably unemployable families receive more than presumably employable families, even though both have exactly the same amount of earnings? As a matter of fact, the issue of equity has been a strong driving force behind the welfare reform movement.

The Issue of Equity

There are two kinds of equity. Horizontal equity requires that families of the same size who have the same degree of economic deprivation should receive the same income assistance payments. Vertical equity requires that, even though families are of the same size, those having a greater income need should receive a larger assistance payment. In the case of social insurance, vertical equity requires that those who earned more during their working lives should receive larger benefits when they face a risk identified under the law. The issue of horizontal equity has been debated and discussed more intensely than that of vertical equity. Therefore we shall concentrate our discussion on horizontal equity.

The issue of equity can be discussed in many forms. One is equity involving families who benefit from welfare programs and those who do not. Because welfare programs in the United States have been developed with a categorical approach, some groups of families, by design, are excluded from such programs. Working families with children headed by a male are conspicuously excluded from many programs. In 1977, the majority (60 percent) of the male heads of poor families worked—48 percent of whom had full-time year-round jobs—but they still could not bring their families out of poverty.[23] One can argue that male-headed working families with children—and those families tend to be intact with both parents at home—are discriminated against in the welfare system. They are not eligible for many types of welfare benefits, although they may be just as needy as other families. Do they have to be penalized for keeping their families intact and for doing their best to earn a livelihood?

Horizontal inequity abounds as well in the treatment of families who participate in the same program. For example, there is wide interstate variation in AFDC payments, with the differential in payments far exceeding the differential in living costs among states. Consequently, families of the same size with the same degree of income need receive different amounts of assistance payments, depending on where they live. As of June 1980, the maximum annual payment (equivalent to the basic guarantee) for a family of four ranged from $1,440 in Mississippi to $6,828 in Oregon.[24] Findings from the author's study show that three independent variables associated with the state characteristics mainly account for the difference in state maximum payments. These variables are, in the order of their importance for explaining the proportion of variance in maximum payments, as follows: the percentage of nonwhite population, per capita personal income, and tax effort. Combined, these three variables explain 64 percent of the variance in state maximum AFDC payments.[25] Variation in payment levels according to the level of the state's per capita income may not evoke the question of equity, as per capita income reflects to a certain degree the state's ability to pay. But the issue of equity can be raised with regard to variation in payments according to racial composition or the tax effort in the state. Is it fair for children in different states to be treated differently just because certain states have a larger percentage of nonwhites than others or just because certain states are willing to tax themselves more than others?

Another type of horizontal inequity involves the treatment of families who participate in different types of welfare programs. For example, families on general assistance generally receive less than those on AFDC, who in turn may receive less than those on SSI. Similar horizontal inequity occurs when some families participate in more than one welfare program and others participate in only one or none at all.

Past attempts at reform addressed in part these types of horizontal inequities. Nixon's FAP covered intact families with children, whether or not adults worked. Coverage and standards were nationwide. The Carter plan went farther. It included all poor individuals and families, with no exclusion and with national standards regarding benefits.

What are the consequences of implementing horizontal equity? What price to pay? Suppose the policymaker wishes to make the benefit level uniform across states. If no one is to suffer from such a move, then the highest state standard must become the national standard. Such a move would create an enormous increase in program expenditures. Furthermore, a national standard so established might be too high in some states in relation to their living standards. Consequently, a compromise has to be made, setting the national standard somewhere around the median state standard. In fact, SSI and the proposals for welfare reform by Nixon and Carter took this approach and required high-paying states to supplement the federal payments. If such a compromise measure was put into effect, the between-state variation would lessen but would not vanish altogether.

Suppose the policymaker attempts to improve equity in the treatment of families who participate in few or no programs versus families who participate in many programs. Again, because multiple-program recipients cannot be sacrificed, the policymaker is likely to let other families participate in the same package of multiple programs as other families who have been doing so all along. If such a policy decision is made, the equity situation would improve, but now the policymaker has to do something about the greater work disincentive associated with a higher cumulative tax rate resulting from the receipt of multiple benefits for a larger number of families. In order to rectify this new problem, the policymaker may attempt to cash out benefits of other programs, include their value in cash payments, and establish an acceptable benefit-loss rate—say 50 percent—as Carter did.

The result would again be an enormous increase in welfare expenditures. The increase in this case is caused by many factors. First, opening up various programs to families who had not previously participated would cause greater expenditures. Second, cashing out the benefit from other programs, including their value in a cash assistance program, and then imposing a lower implicit tax rate than created by the combination of separate programs would always result in greater expenditures. This is true because the break-even level would increase and consequently families could stay on the program even though they earned more than they did before such a policy change. Furthermore, at a given level of earnings, a family would receive larger benefits under the new scheme. Last, because the break-even level had increased, many families who were not eligible for benefits before, on account of available financial resources, now become eligible for benefits and hence may participate in the program. All these effects of the policy change would contribute toward increasing expenditures.

Even if the policymaker succeeds in cashing out all existing welfare programs and comes up with one national negative income tax program, the story does not end here. If American legislative history is a guide, there will always be legislators who will make it their business to carry on a crusade to legislate some sort of in-kind program for one category of beneficiaries or another. The cycle then will start all over again.

What about the inclusion of working poor families in a welfare program? Advocates of equity in the welfare system have been particularly concerned with this question. It is believed that working and nonworking families deserve equal treatment under a welfare program. The idea of equity always sounds desirable in a democratic society. However, what are the consequences of implementing equity in this instance?

One probable consequence of including working poor families, or the employable, in a welfare program is heightened concern for the work incentive. In the past proposals for welfare reform and in many income-tested programs enacted in the 1960s and early 1970s, a benefit-loss rate of less than 100 percent was provided, and the work incentive became a focal point of the benefit formula. As a result target efficiency had to be compromised, incurring greater expenditures than otherwise. Greater expenditures resulted not only because a higher level of benefit was provided at a given level of earnings but also because more families became eligible for benefits.

Another form that policy concern for the work incentive took as a result of including working families in a welfare program was an explicit provision to require the heads of families to receive manpower training, or to sign up for a job at the local employment office, or both. If welfare recipients benefit from multiple programs they would simultaneously be subjected to such requirements under separate programs. Of course those heads of families who are already working would not need to worry about such requirements. But they would if they became unemployed.

All this means that as the government runs more and more income-tested programs, a larger number of families becomes subjected to governmental regulations in the conduct of their daily lives. They would be subject to reporting income under separate codes from those provided under the federal income tax law—codes that would require more frequent reporting and more rigid rules in regard to the definitions of filing units and taxable income. Furthermore, if they were out of work, they would be subject to questioning as to why they were out of work, why they are unwilling to take a job offered by the employment office, and so on. Does all this lead to governmental coercion and harassment for an increasing number of families? Is it a fair price to pay for advocating equity and including working families in welfare programs?

Another probable consequence of including working poor families in welfare programs is that work and welfare merge for many intact families with two parents at home. The line between the world of work and the world of welfare becomes blurred. Working poor families would have a higher level of income than the heads of such families could earn. But, at the same time, the value of the earnings by the breadwinner (probably the husband) might become less appreciated by the spouse (probably the wife). There is some evidence to indicate that this occurs. Findings from the Seattle-Denver Income Maintenance Experiments indicate that families in the experimental group experienced a higher rate of divorce than those in the control group. [26] Researchers speculate that at certain benefit levels the wives of working husbands are influenced more by the independence effect than by the income effect of transfer payments. The income effect makes the family better off while it remains together. But the independence effect lets wives feel more independent, which makes a divorce less economically painful. Apparently some wives in the experimental group chose to go through a divorce rather than to stay with their husbands, with transfer payments facilitating such a decision. The finding that families receiving negative income taxes under the experiment had a higher rate of divorce than did the control group is ironic indeed in light of the widely shared belief that AFDC (which mainly benefits female-headed families) breaks up families. This belief about AFDC led many academics to advocate a negative income tax program to benefit all families.

Another probable consequence of including working poor families in welfare programs may be that family heads who are used to being deemed unemployable may become subjected too, at least implicitly, to manpower training and work requirements. They may not actually participate in such programs while unemployable, but they will at least have to live in the environment that such a policy creates. Once subjected to such requirements, social expectations might change, making them open to closer scrutiny. Increasing expectations about AFDC mothers' work is a case in point.

As a result of changing expectations about work, AFDC mothers have increasingly been subjected to empirical studies. Irwin Garfinkel and Larry Orr report that a drastic change in the benefit formula of AFDC would not result in the change of a sizable percentage of working mothers who receive AFDC. They note that in order to increase the employment rate among AFDC mothers by 5 percent, either the basic guarantee has to be decreased by 40 percent, the tax rate decreased by 35 percentage points, the levels of set-aside and deductions increased by $50, the percentage of the caseload receiving rehabilitation services increased by 20 percent, a work test imposed in all states, or the aggregate unemployment rate decreased by 1.5 percentage points. [27] Such an unfavorable research finding resulted from the fact that so few AFDC mothers were potential workers. The mean employment rate of AFDC mothers among states was only 18 percent to start with at the time of the Garfinkel-Orr study (1967). Therefore, each hypothetical policy change brought about only a small absolute change in the employment rate of AFDC mothers, although it resulted in a statistically significant change in it. Obviously, the implication for policymakers is that the increase in expenditures from implementing such a policy change would be more than the savings accrued from greater aggregate earnings by AFDC mothers. With a wider gap between heightened expectations and actual performance, the welfare system would invite additional social tension.

Philosophically speaking, what does equity mean here? Equity as used in the present discussion of the coverage of families means equal treatment of families under the equal income conditions. Equity, however, often means more than equal treatment. It means fair treatment of families with due consideration given to different circumstances that families are placed under. For example, families traditionally eligible for welfare benefits—female-headed families with children and aged, disabled, or blind individuals—have less opportunity to earn income in the labor market than intact families headed by working persons. They may, therefore, deserve preferential treatment. Furthermore, if a female head of a family attempts to work, high expenses for child care and parental responsibilities make earning an income more difficult than is the case for the head of an intact family. Such factors, therefore, may have to be taken into account. A noncategorical program such as the negative income tax provides equal benefits to families with equal monetary needs and equal incomes. A political choice for such a program is reasonable from the standpoint of equality of result, but not from the standpoint of equality of opportunity.[28] Put another way, equal treatment of families on the basis of an income criterion alone may not constitute what society conceives to be fair and just. A program such as the negative income tax may miss the whole point of equity as society understands it.

The Issue of Stigma

Because receiving welfare contravenes the Protestant work ethic, which has long been cherished in this country, and because the idea of work is the cornerstone of this society that binds the people together, the United States developed elaborate incentive systems so that the choice between work and nonwork is invariably made in favor of work except in the most extreme situations. Society acknowledges full social membership for those who work and imposes social stigma on those who do not. Social stigma thus seems a part of the reward-punishment system aimed at the preservation of the labor force, which is essential for societal survival.

Not everybody who receives welfare is stigmatized, however. The degree of stigmatization seems in direct relationship with the current or future employability of those who receive welfare. Stigmatizing welfare recipients who have a prospect of employability seems to prevent the availability of assistance from becoming a threat to the production of goods and services by dissuading workers from thinking they can stop working with impunity. Because society seems to have eliminated the consideration of employability in the case of the aged, blind, and disabled, it is no longer necessary to attach stigma to a welfare program for these individuals.

Indeed various studies seem to indicate that the public shows different levels of acceptance for welfare programs, depending on the clientele for which the programs are designed. Even for programs benefiting AFDC families, the public tends to support governmental spending for specific items such as job training, employment services, rehabilitation, and health care. Therefore, one needs to be cautious in interpreting research findings in regard to the public's attitudes toward welfare in general. When the public speaks of welfare in negative tones, it may have in mind a certain category of welfare clientele or specific programs.

What do past studies tell us about stigma? A survey by Michael Schiltz of public opinion polls over a 30-year period reveals the

American public's strong negative attitudes toward welfare and indicates that people make unfavorable generalizations about welfare recipients.[29] A poll conducted in 1964 found that 65 percent of those who had an opinion about welfare said they would not support increases in governmental expenditures in this area.

People's attitudes toward those receiving welfare are associated psychologically with the idea of welfare itself, and the public therefore tends to develop a distorted perception of welfare recipients. A study by Joe Feagin in 1969 reveals such a phenomenon. For example, the overwhelming majority of respondents (84 percent) believed that "there are too many people receiving welfare money who should be working."[30] However, a study conducted in 1967 by the U.S. Department of Health, Education, and Welfare found that only 1 percent of the nation's welfare recipients were employable.[31] Feagin encountered stereotyped images of welfare recipients with respect to other issues as well. For instance, people held an exaggerated view of the dishonesty of recipients, the high frequency of illegitimate children among families on welfare, and the proportion of taxpayers' money spent on welfare.[32]

The public's stereotyped attitudes toward welfare in general and welfare recipients in particular help indoctrinate recipients themselves, so that their self-image becomes more negative and their sense of self-worth diminishes. In a rare study of the views of welfare recipients, conducted in 1965 by Scott Briar, a majority of the recipients interviewed believed that about a quarter of those receiving welfare cheated the welfare department.[33] Briar speculated that such self-denigration results in the recipients' willingness to give up the right to privacy ordinarily enjoyed by citizens. Sixty-six percent of those surveyed by Briar conceded that the welfare department had a right to know how recipients spent the money they received; 63 percent believed that the department should make night visits to check on those receiving aid. A subsequent study by Joel Handler and Ellen Hollingsworth reported a similar finding: Approximately half the AFDC mothers in the Milwaukee area did not object to unannounced visits by caseworkers.[34]

In general, those who behave in a way contrary to their community's expected norms are stigmatized. In the United States receiving welfare is considered a deviant behavior. Psychological warfare between taxpayers and welfare recipients is part of the process by which a deep sense of degradation is instilled in those on welfare. This sense is the price the community extracts from the individuals for receiving welfare. Handler and Hollingsworth found that about half (49 percent) the welfare mothers they surveyed felt embarrassed in their dealings with people who were not on welfare, and 38 percent felt that the community was either indifferent or hostile toward AFDC recipients. The sense of being stigmatized isolates and alienates welfare recipients from the rest of the community. Handler and Hollingsworth reported that more often than not those who felt stigmatized experienced difficulties in the community because they were on welfare.[35]

However, the findings from the foregoing studies generally relate only to recipients of AFDC or general assistance, who are apparently regarded by many people as the "undeserving poor." The public almost reverses its attitude concerning welfare programs for the so-called deserving poor, who include the aged, the blind, and the disabled. Many people believe that being poor is beyond the control of these individuals and that they are thus worthy of public support. Schiltz found that the old-age assistance program had enjoyed a high degree of public support since the 1930s and that this support had increased over the years.[36]

The findings of a survey conducted in 1961 by the Survey Research Center of the University of Michigan clearly indicate that the public's attitudes toward welfare programs for the aged are different from its feeling about programs for others in need.[37] Nearly 70 percent of the respondents, across all income classes, supported more governmental spending for the aged poor. However, a much smaller proportion supported such spending for "needy people," with middle-class and upper-class respondents being less supportive of programs for the needy than lower-income respondents. Moreover, the difference in public attitude toward welfare programs for those regarded as the deserving poor as opposed to the undeserving poor is apparently greater in a conservative than in a liberal community. In a study making use of a 1964 Gallup poll, Ernest Wohlenberg indicated that compared to the amount paid to AFDC recipients, the aged poor were eligible for disproportionately higher public assistance payments in a conservative region than they were in a less conservative region.[38] In a comparative study involving SSI recipients in Mississippi and California, and, using the 1973-1974 data from the Survey of the Low Income Aged and Disabled, this author made a similar finding. SSI payments in Mississippi were larger in relation to AFDC payments there than were SSI payments in California in relation to California's AFDC payments. Furthermore, SSI recipients in Mississippi showed a greater degree of contentment about the program and about themselves.[39]

Indeed, there does not seem to be any more stigma left in the eyes of SSI recipients across the country. In another study by this author, it was found that the aged and the disabled (including the blind) on SSI in 1974 had virtually no feeling of stigma about receiving SSI payments: 80.3 percent were not bothered by the fact that they accepted help from SSI; 88.5 percent did not feel embarrassed about telling their friends that they were receiving SSI; and 86.8 percent did not think that people in their community had less respect for them because they needed and used SSI.[40]

Although stigmatization acts as a means of social control for keeping the labor force in line, it also has a devastating effect on those stigmatized. As shown earlier, AFDC mothers so often cast themselves as second-class citizens that they are willing to give up their right to privacy. Such negative self-identity on the part of mothers obviously affects their children adversely. Therefore minimizing the stigma effect becomes an important policy concern.

The income testing involved in welfare programs is believed to impose social stigma.[41] Income testing forces welfare applicants to prove they are needy. In this society, a person who is poor and who asks for welfare is considered a deviant. Stigmatization validates the abnormality of such a person so that society can draw a boundary around what constitutes normality.[42] But some argue that income testing per se is not at issue but, rather, the manner in which income testing is performed.[43] Income testing through face-to-face, case-by-case investigation may be stigmatizing, but income testing submerged within income tax returns may not be. If this sounds logical, it is plausible to argue that less stigma may be attached to a welfare program administered by the federal government because federal administration may facilitate a more impersonal businesslike handling of applicants for such a welfare program. A study by this author shows that the degree of stigma perceived by the elderly and disabled (including the blind) significantly declined after they were transferred from state public assistance programs to SSI.[44]

How does the issue of stigma influence the policymaker in attempts at welfare reform? What might be the impact of launching a nationwide income support program such as negative income tax? It is quite probable that, if a negative income tax program was launched, the level of stigma attached to such a program would be lower than that attached to the current AFDC program. However, it might still be more stigmatized than SSI. If such a prediction is correct, families on AFDC would benefit but the aged, the blind, and the disabled would suffer.

State legislatures may not be ready for such a drastic move anyway. True, over the years, the federal government has come to assume greater responsibility for financing and administering various cash and in-kind welfare programs. But, according to Handler, states tend to retain their power over income maintenance programs as long as such programs deal not only with the financial need of recipients but also with the community's need to control recipients' social behavior.[45] According to this theory, the public needs to keep a close eye on recipients when it wishes to impose its values on them. Handing over financial and administrative responsibility to the federal government would make the political process that imposes the community's values on recipients more difficult, if not impossible. States gave up their prerogative over cash assistance programs for the aged, blind, and disabled poor, perhaps because the program had already become purely an instrument for the redistribution of income. However, AFDC is still considered, in part, as a means of social control and, in part, as a program for the redistribution of income. It may not be a coincidence that Nixon's FAP and Carter's Program for Better Jobs and Income—both of which took a varied form of a nationwide negative income tax—were not adopted by Congress.

Linkage Between SSI and Social Security

In recent years, the number of families who benefit simultaneously from SSI and social security has increased.[46] Currently one of every two SSI recipients benefit also from social security; and among the elderly seven out of every ten do so.[47] Because SSI and social security programs were developed from distinctly different philosophical foundations and program principles, it is important for the policymaker to understand the relationship between the two programs and to chart the proper roles that each should play in the income maintenance system in the United States. Many of the points made on the relationship between SSI and social security apply to the relationship between welfare and social insurance in general.

SSI currently guarantees about three quarters of poverty-line income to the aged and disabled poor. (It paid a basic guarantee of $238 for individuals and $357 for couples as of July 1980.) Thus SSI has become a powerful antipoverty instrument for the aged and disabled. The National Commission on Social Security recommends that the assets test be eliminated altogether and that SSI payments boosted immediately by 25 percent. Both this commission and the 1979 Advisory Council on Social Security recommend that the basic guarantee be eventually increased to the poverty line.[48] Obviously both the commission and the council believe that SSI should become a major instrument for the redistribution of income to ensure an adequate minimum for the aged, the blind, and the disabled and that this in turn would enable social security to become strictly a program for replacement of earnings. As a result, they believe, social security would be relieved of its welfare objective. Such a policy direction was reflected also when Congress in 1977 froze the minimum social security benefit at $122. Furthermore, the 97th Congress repealed the minimum benefit for future retired workers.

Undoubtedly the policy choice of letting SSI take an increasingly important role in providing an adequate minimum income to the aged, the blind, and the disabled is based on the objective of target efficiency. Because many nonpoor social security beneficiaries receive the minimum benefit or near minimum benefits—for example, federal civil service employees who retire after they have worked the minimum time in covered employment to become eligible for social security benefits—it would be difficult to increase social security benefits so that they would primarily benefit low-income elderly and disabled persons. An attempt to benefit low-income retirees would also benefit relatively well-off retirees who receive the minimum or near minimum benefits, causing target inefficiency in the use of social security funds. Inefficiency is compounded by the customary percentage increases in social security benefits. Each time the benefits are increased proportionately, high-income beneficiaries receive a larger increase in benefits in absolute terms. Therefore the consideration of target efficiency dictates the policy choice by the decision maker.

However, social policy is developed not for consideration of target efficiency for a particular program alone. The policymaker needs to pay attention to the spillover effects of such a policy choice on the beneficiaries of both SSI and social security and on current workers who are potential beneficiaries of both programs in the future.

The effects of focusing on SSI to prevent poverty would be rather overwhelming. Recipients of benefits—that is, benefits from both SSI and social security—would find that their social security benefits became almost worthless because, with a disregard of only $60 per quarter (or a monthly equivalent of $20), each $1 of social security benefits would be offset against SSI payments. For such beneficiaries their lifetime contributions to social security would bring them only $20 more per month than the benefits provided to persons who never contributed.

If recipients of dual benefits decide to work, the benefit formula of SSI overrides the benefit formula of social security. That is, whereas social security beneficiaries aged 65 or older can earn up to $5,500 a year (as of 1981) without having their benefits reduced, recipients of dual benefits would find that benefits were reduced as soon as their earnings exceeded $195 per quarter (or an annual equivalent of $780). Over the years, the exempt amount has increased greatly under social security, but not at all under SSI. This means that for recipients of dual benefits—who tend to be the poorest of all social security beneficiaries—the liberalization of the earnings tests (or the retirement test) under social security would be ineffective. As a matter of fact, due to inflation, the provision of a fixed amount of exemption ($195 per quarter) has resulted in the erosion of the work incentive. The National Commission on Social Security recommends that the exempt amount under SSI be increased annually by the same percentage as wage rise. However, as long as there is a difference in exempt amounts under social security and under SSI, with social security providing a larger exempt amount, the problem discussed here will remain.

The way SSI is linked with social security also creates an incentive for workers to retire early. Workers who expect their social security benefits to be lower than SSI benefits plus $20 a month would find it advantageous to retire as early as 62, receive reduced benefits for three years, and have SSI supplement their meager social security benefits starting at age 65. After benefiting from social security for three years—albeit at a reduced rate—they would find that their ultimate combined benefits beginning at age 65 would be the same whether or not they worked during these three years. In terms of lifetime combined benefits, they would come out ahead if they did retire early.

If this linkage between SSI and social security became public knowledge, it might influence middle-age workers and others approaching retirement either to plan an early retirement, or to evade the payment of social security taxes, or both. If they knew that their ultimate monthly retirement benefits would be the same as SSI payments plus $20, they might find it worthwhile to pursue such a course. If they were suffering from unemployment or from ill health, they would have an added incentive to do so.

The way SSI and social security are linked would have an intangible effect as well. As SSI payment levels become high in relation to social security benefits, a greater number of retired workers and their spouses would benefit from both programs. As a result, the value of social security as a social insurance program would be diminished. If current workers indeed perceive social security this way, they might lose faith in it. Furthermore, low-wage workers who eventually would have to depend on SSI might feel demoralized to work toward building their "own retirement accounts" under social security. This sense of demoralization might influence their day-to-day work behavior. In keeping with their own self-image, they would be branded as "welfare recipients" long before they retired. It may well be that a sizable minority of the elderly population will have financial security in old age primarily through SSI and the rest of the elderly through social security. Is such a demarcation really necessary?

The way SSI is linked to social security also seems to affect the current recipients of dual benefits. When they apply for SSI and social security, they are ushered to different windows in the social security office. They go through application processes handled by different governmental officials. At the social security window, they are called "beneficiaries." They are to receive "benefits." They are told they are "entitled" to them. At the SSI window, they are called "recipients" who receive "assistance payments" if they are found "eligible."

Finally, when everything is found in order, they receive "green checks" for social security benefits and "yellow checks" for SSI payments. Although there is evidence that their attitudes toward SSI are vastly improving, they are nonetheless treated differently by those handling the two programs. There still is a difference between the public's attitudes toward SSI and social security.

In addition to the double image that they get from the government, beneficiaries are treated with the contrasting ideologies of the two programs. The ideology of social security states that beneficiaries are entitled to social security benefits that they have earned through contributions. Therefore, a means test is irrelevant for those getting social security. They can depend on social security benefits as a supplement to their own private savings. This ideology further states that because social security is insurance for replacing earnings lost during retirement, workers have to prove the fact of retirement before they can receive benefits; for the same reason, the resumption of earnings income in excess of the stipulated ceiling will make their social security benefits subject to reduction. On the other hand, the ideology of welfare states that because assistance payments are paid by general revenue, recipients have to prove through a means test that their financial condition, both in terms of assets and income, is below standards of eligibility. Recipients who have a large amount of savings, for example, have to reduce them to a level at which they can be eligible for welfare. On the other hand, so the ideology goes on to state, recipients are encouraged or even morally obligated to earn income through work in order to save taxpayers' money. In short, under social security, savings are encouraged and work is not obligatory; but the reverse is true under SSI. To compound the whole situation, SSI allows recipients to earn only $195 a quarter before their payments are reduced, but social security allows beneficiaries to earn an equivalent of $1,375 a quarter (or $5,500 a year) under the same circumstances.

These contrasting ideologies are clearly understood by policy-makers in Washington and by taxpayers who foot the bill for SSI. As long as these programs are considered separately, such different ideologies may be understood and justified. However, when a person benefits simultaneously from the two programs, that person may face ideological confusion and identity crisis indeed. Workers have hitherto been encouraged to save and have been expecting to supplement their private resources with social security benefits. But they are now told that individuals cannot receive SSI payments if they have been thrifty enough to have accountable resources in excess of $1,500 ($2,250 for a couple), even though they may be eligible for SSI on the basis of the amount of their income.

LESSONS FROM THE PAST

The foregoing discussion underscores the point that the welfare system in the United States is complex and difficult to reform. The system is full of conflicting policy goals, fragmentation, inadequacies, and inequities. Furthermore, the system seems to have a built-in compulsion to become larger and larger each time an attempt at reform is made, and such attempts ironically have the never changing objective of "bringing welfare expenditures under control." Why this paradox?

The paradoxical problem of expanding welfare in the face of attempts to control it seems to have roots in the overemphasis that policymakers have placed on income-tested programs in order to provide an income floor. The problem was not so pronounced at first when recipient families were by and large unemployable—for instance, female-headed families, the aged, and the disabled. But as welfare programs extended the coverage to other families with real or potential earning capability, the issue of the work incentive became a paramount concern. The situation became even more acute when one income-tested program after another was enacted during the 1960s and 1970s and more and more families came to benefit from multiple programs. Concerned with the acute situation of work disincentives associated with cumulative tax rates, policymakers further attempted to solve the problem by consolidating programs and imposing an implicit tax rate lower than it might have been if the programs had operated separately. The result was to increase the pool of eligible families even further. Although all this was attempted in the name of "bringing welfare under control," its effect proved to be just the opposite—further expansion of welfare.

In a broader sense, the paradoxical problem was created because policymakers failed to put welfare programs in their place as part of the broader income maintenance system and put each part of that system in hierarchical order; and this nation has failed to recognize the discrepancy between how the breadwinner is paid through work and how welfare payments are calculated on the basis of family needs.

Welfare in Context

The income maintenance system consists of three layers of income provision. At the top lie earnings from work. Most families in the United States earn their income through work. When work becomes impossible either because of the worker's incapacity to work or the inability of the economy to provide jobs, then afflicted families first resort to social insurance programs to obtain income. Benefits from these programs constitute the second layer of income provision. If persons are ineligible for social insurance benefits or if their benefits are inadequate, then they have to resort to income-tested welfare programs. Welfare payments constitute the third layer of income provision.

The only way to minimize the number of families who have to resort to welfare is to maximize employment opportunities to the greatest number of families possible and to make social insurance programs more effective in meeting income needs of families. Unfortunately, proposals for welfare reform in the past were made in a vacuum. Policymakers failed to place welfare programs within the broader context of the income maintenance system in the United States. They did not deal with the deteriorating conditions of the labor market. They did not pay attention to the fact that the share of earnings among low-income families had been declining for some time. A study by Peter Henle shows that the share of the bottom fifth of all male workers decreased from 2.75 percent in 1959 to 2.15 percent in 1970. In contrast, the share of the top fifth of all male workers increased from 42.80 to 44.95 percent during the same period.[49]

Nor did policymakers attempt to expand or innovate social insurance programs with the antipoverty objective in mind as fast as welfare programs expanded. These welfare programs were called upon to deal with economic problems of too many families of too diverse backgrounds. When welfare programs are overburdened in relation to social insurance programs and in relation to wage levels, they tend to provide assistance to too large a number of families whose heads are either working or deemed employable, thus creating a disproportionate amount of political passion and hostility. The smaller the scope of welfare programs, the less political controversy will be associated with them. That is, welfare programs are politically most acceptable when they are truly residual. However, past experience shows that welfare programs have become more than residual.

To compound the situation, past attempts at welfare reform focused on consolidation and nationalization of various programs with the ultimate aim of enacting a federal program of a negative income tax for all poor families. Enactment of SSI to take over state programs of OAA, APTD, and AB was a sign of such policy direction. Nixon's proposal to nationalize AFDC and transform it into FAP and Carter's proposal to consolidate SSI, AFDC, and food stamps further reflected such a policy choice. A negative income tax, if enacted, would deal with the problem of poverty for all types of families. It is a complex problem with a range of causes that includes large family size, unemployment, old age, disability, mental illness, separation, divorce, and illegitimacy. When poor families are lumped together in one program, it is next to impossible to sort out the difficulties and deal with them effectively.

Worse yet, when families are placed within the context of "welfare," this society tends to use helping professionals such as social workers, psychologists, and psychiatrists to deal with diverse problems in that context. The context traditionally has been full of stereotypes and prejudice about the characteristics, the lifestyles, and the motivations of the poor. It should be recognized that some families are poor simply because they have a large number of children to support; some families are poor because of the loss of a job, caused by structural changes in the labor market. But no matter. These helping professionals are called upon to treat the symptoms of poverty as if they were caused primarily by personal inadequacy. Such treatment may be correct if families on welfare are a truly residual group who cannot be dealt with by improving job opportunities and maximizing the role of social insurance. But the fact of the matter is that many poor families are labeled and treated inappropriately by helping professionals. There is, then, the grave consequence that they are blaming persons who are the victims of the economic system and of inadequate social insurance programs.

By and large, what the government has done or has attempted to do for these blameless victims has been to place the problem of poverty in the welfare context rather than in the broader context of employment and employment-related benefit programs (that is, social insurance programs). In the process of doing this, the government has symbolically transformed poverty from an economic problem to a mental health problem and has used helping professionals to deal with poverty in that transformed context.

In short, the past policy thrust has been amiss because policymakers have been looking at the income maintenance system in an upside-down fashion. They have sought solutions to the problem of poverty primarily through the bottom layer of income security measures (that is, welfare programs). Instead, they should have paid attention first to the employment situation, then to social insurance programs, and last to welfare programs.

Gap Between Wages and Family Needs

Even if opportunities for employment are maximized and social insurance programs improved, welfare programs will not escape social tension as long as welfare benefits are calculated on the basis of family need and wages and social insurance benefits are not. In a free enterprise economy, wages are paid on the basis of the productivity of workers. Workers with the same productivity are paid the same level of wages no matter what the family size. Thus wages are insensitive to family size. Social insurance benefits, which are wage related, cannot provide for a large number of dependents without creating work disincentives and without distorting the ranking of total family benefits in relation to previous earnings. Thus social insurance benefits too are, in the main, insensitive to family size.

Welfare programs, on the other hand, have increasingly come to provide assistance on the basis of family need (or family size). Many years ago, public assistance payments were made on the basis of the doctrine of "less eligibility," which meant that families on welfare should never be provided with assistance greater than what the lowest wage earner was paid in the community. But the situation has changed over the years. Because welfare provides assistance according to family size, many welfare families in high-paying states often receive assistance payments that are larger than working families can earn. This has created much tension and hostility between those who receive benefits and those who do not. Therefore, as long as there is a gap between what the breadwinner is paid on the basis of individual productivity and what is provided to welfare recipients on the basis of family need, there will always be tension in the system of income maintenance in the United States. One item on policymakers' agenda for the future is to find a way to close that gap or counteract its effects.

NOTES

1. Robert J. Lampman, Ends and Means of Reducing Income Poverty (Chicago: Markham, 1971), p. 10.

2. Robert D. Plotnick and Felicity Skidmore, Progress Against Poverty: A Review of the 1964-1974 Decade (New York: Academic Press, 1975), pp. 53, 55.

3. For detailed discussion, see Robert J. Lampman, "What Does It Do for the Poor? A New Test for National Policy," Public Interest 34 (Winter 1974): 66-82.

4. Alma W. McMillan and Ann Kallman Bixby, "Social Welfare Expenditures, Fiscal Year 1978," Social Security Bulletin 43 (May 1980): 8, 10.

5. Social Security Bulletin: Annual Statistical Supplement, 1977-79 (Washington, D.C.: U.S. Department of Health and Human Services, Social Security Administration, 1980), p. 248.

6. U.S. Bureau of the Census, Statistical Abstract of the United States: 1979, 100th ed. (Washington, D.C.: U.S. Government Printing Office, 1979), Table 62, p. 47.

7. See, for detailed discussion of the development of social services in recent years, Neil Gilbert, "The Transformation of Social Services," Social Service Review 51 (December 1977): 624-41.

8. Social Security Bulletin: Annual Statistical Supplement, 1969 (Washington, D.C.: U.S. Department of Health, Education, and Welfare, Social Security Administration, 1969), p. 134.

9. Raymond Munts and Irwin Garfinkel, The Work Disincentive Effects of Unemployment Insurance (Kalamazoo, Mich.: W. E. Upjohn Institute for Employment Research, 1974), p. 25; and Harold W. Watts and Albert Rees, eds., The New Jersey Income-Maintenance Experiment: Volume II, Labor-Supply Responses (New York: Academic Press, 1977).

10. For an excellent review of chronological events surrounding the family assistance plan, see Vincent J. Burke and Vee Burke, Nixon's Good Deed: Welfare Reform (New York: Columbia University Press, 1974). See also Theodore R. Marmor and Martin Rein, "Reforming 'the Welfare Mess': The Fate of the Family Assistance Plan, 1969-72," in Policy and Politics in America: Six Case Studies, ed. Allen P. Sindler (New York: Little, Brown, 1973), pp. 3-28; and Martha N. Ozawa, "Four More Years of Welfare Nightmare?" Public Welfare 31 (Spring 1973): 6-11.

11. D. Lee Bawden, Glen G. Cain, and Leonard J. Hausman, "The Family Assistance Plan: Analysis and Evaluation," Public Policy 19 (Spring 1971): 323-24.

12. Burke and Burke, op. cit., pp. 153-54.

13. For a detailed analysis of President Carter's proposal on welfare reform, see Sheldon Danziger, Robert Haveman, and Eugene Smolensky, "The Program for Better Jobs and Income—A Guide and a Critique," study prepared for the use of the Joint Economic Committee, U.S. Congress (Washington, D.C.: U.S. Government Printing Office, 1977); and Martha N. Ozawa, "Anatomy of President Carter's Welfare Reform Proposal," Social Casework 58 (December 1977): 615-20.

14. For an excellent review of studies on the work incentive, see Munts and Garfinkel, op. cit.

15. See Jack Hirschleifer, Price Theory and Applications (Englewood Cliffs, N.J.: Prentice-Hall, 1976), pp. 373-410.

16. Bawden, Cain, and Hausman, op. cit., p. 331. See, for some empirical evidence, Nicholas Barr and Robert Hall, "The Probability of Dependence on Public Assistance," Economica 48 (May 1981): 109-23; and Frank Levey, "The Labor Supply of Female Household Heads, or AFDC Work Incentives Don't Work Too Well," Journal of Human Resources 14 (Winter 1979): 76-97.

17. Leonard J. Hausman, "Cumulative Tax Rates in Alternative Income Maintenance Systems," in Integrating Income Maintenance Programs, ed. Irene Lurie (New York: Academic Press, 1975), p. 44.

18. Ibid., pp. 56-57.

19. Vee Burke and Alair A. Townsend, "Public Welfare and

Work Incentives: Theory and Practice," Studies in Public Welfare, Paper no. 14, U.S. Congress, Joint Economic Committee, Subcommittee on Fiscal Policy, 93d Congr., 2d Sess. (Washington, D.C.: U.S. Government Printing Office, 1974), p. 12.

20. Martha N. Ozawa, "Income Redistribution and Social Security," Social Service Review 50 (June 1976): 209-23.

21. Robert J. Lampman and Christopher Green, "Schemes for Transferring Income to the Poor," Industrial Relations 6 (February 1967): 122-37.

22. Mordechai E. Lando, "The Effect of Unemployment on Applications for Disability Insurance," 1974 Business and Economic Section Proceedings of the American Statistical Association (Washington, D.C.: American Statistical Association, 1975), pp. 438-42; Mordechai E. Lando, Malcolm B. Coate, and Ruth Kraus, "Disability Benefit Applications and the Economy," Social Security Bulletin 42 (October 1979): 3-17; Martha N. Ozawa and Duncan Lindsey, "Is SSI Too Supportive of the Mentally Ill?" Public Welfare 35 (Fall 1977): 48-52; and Duncan Lindsey and Martha N. Ozawa, "Schizophrenia and SSI: Implications and Problems," Social Work 24 (March 1979): 120-26.

23. U.S. Bureau of the Census, Statistical Abstract of the United States: 1979, Table 768, p. 467.

24. AFDC Standards for Basic Needs, July 1980 (Washington, D.C.: Social Security Administration, Office of Research and Statistics, March 1981), Table 5, p. 10.

25. Martha N. Ozawa, "An Exploration into States' Commitment to AFDC," Journal of Social Service Research 3 (Spring 1978): 245-59.

26. Michael T. Hannan, Nancy Brandon Tuma, and Lyle P. Groeneveld, "Income Maintenance and Marriage: An Overview of Results from the Seattle-Denver Income Maintenance Experiments," paper (Stanford, Calif.: Center for Advanced Study in the Behavioral Sciences, Stanford University, January 25, 1978), and John Bishop, "Jobs, Cash Transfers, and Marital Instability: A Review of the Evidence," Institute for Research on Poverty Special Report Series no. 19 (Institute for Research on Poverty, University of Wisconsin, October 14, 1977).

27. Irwin Garfinkel and Larry L. Orr, "Welfare Policy and the Employment Rate of AFDC Mothers," National Tax Journal 27 (June 1974): 275-84.

28. Robert I. Lerman, "JOIN: A Jobs and Income Program for American Families," in Public Employment and Wage Subsidies, Studies in Public Welfare, Paper no. 19, U.S. Congress, Joint Economic Committee, Subcommittee on Fiscal Policy (Washington, D.C.: U.S. Government Printing Office, 1974), pp. 3-67.

29. Michael E. Schiltz, Public Attitudes Toward Social Security,

1932-65, Research Report no. 33, Social Security Administration, Office of Research and Statistics (Washington, D.C.: U.S. Government Printing Office, 1969), pp. 151-74.

30. Joe R. Feagin, "America's Welfare Stereotypes," Social Science Quarterly 52 (March 1974): 923.

31. U.S. Department of Health, Education, and Welfare, Estimated Employability for Recipients of Public Assistance Money Payments, July 1968 (Washington, D.C.: U.S. Government Printing Office, 1969).

32. Feagin, op. cit., p. 923.

33. Scott Briar, "Welfare from Below: Recipients' View of the Public Welfare System," California Law Review 54 (May 1966): 370-85.

34. Joel F. Handler and Ellen Jane Hollingsworth, "Stigma, Privacy, and Other Attitudes of Welfare Recipients," Stanford Law Review 22 (November 1969): 4.

35. Ibid., pp. 4-5.

36. Schiltz, op. cit., p. 170.

37. Eva Mueller, "Public Attitudes Toward Fiscal Programs," Quarterly Journal of Economics 77 (May 1963): 210-35.

38. Ernest H. Wholenberg, "A Regional Approach to Public Attitudes and Public Assistance," Social Service Review 50 (September 1967): 491-505.

39. Martha N. Ozawa, "SSI Recipients in Mississippi and California: A Comparative Study," Journal of Social Science Research (forthcoming).

40. Martha N. Ozawa, "Impact of SSI on the Aged and Disabled Poor," Social Work Research and Abstracts 14 (Fall 1978): 3-10.

41. See James Tobin, "The Case for an Income Guarantee," Public Interest, no. 4 (Summer 1966): 31-41; Alvin L. Schorr, "Against Negative Income Tax," Public Interest, no. 5 (Fall 1966): 110-19; and Evelin M. Burns, "Social Security in Evolution: Toward What?" Social Service Review 39 (June 1965): 129-40.

42. See, for an excellent discussion on stigma and income-tested programs, Lee Rainwater, "Stigma in Income-Tested Programs," a paper presented at the Conference on Universal Versus Income-Tested Transfer Programs, Institute for Research on Poverty, University of Wisconsin, Madison, March 15-16, 1979.

43. Lewis Meriam, Relief and Social Security (Washington, D.C.: Brookings Institution, 1946), p. 841.

44. Ozawa, "Impact of SSI on the Aged and Disabled Poor."

45. Joel F. Handler, Reforming the Poor: Welfare Policy, Federalism, and Morality (New York: Basic Books, 1972), pp. 58-71.

46. For a detailed discussion on this, see Martha N. Ozawa, "SSI: Progress or Retreat?" Public Welfare 32 (Spring 1974): 33-40.

47. Social Security Bulletin: Annual Statistical Supplement, 1977-79, Table 195, p. 237.

48. U.S. Congress, Advisory Council on Social Security, Social Security Financing and Benefits: Reports of the 1979 Advisory Council on Social Security (Washington, D.C.: U.S. Government Printing Office, 1980); and U.S. Congress, National Commission on Social Security, Social Security in America's Future (Washington, D.C.: U.S. Government Printing Office, 1981).

49. Peter Henle, "Exploring the Distribution of Earned Income," Monthly Labor Review 95 (December 1972): 20.

6

POLICY ISSUES IN
SOCIAL SECURITY REFORM

Social security, although not designed to help the poor exclusively, is
an important part of the income maintenance system in the United
States, which aims to ensure a decent minimum of income to eligible
individuals and families. Consequently, social security is a strong
weapon in preventing poverty for many individuals, especially the
elderly. At the same time, however, social security is a social insurance program with another important objective: replacing part of
the earnings lost because of retirement, disability, or death of the
breadwinner. Thus the challenge to the decision maker is to envision
a scheme of social security that can be an effective antipoverty instrument and at the same time adhere to the program's basic principle,
which is social insurance. However, before a new scheme can be con-
ceptualized, one needs to understand the current policy issues and
problems involved in social security. Only by sorting out these vital
issues and problems can a new scheme be envisioned.

EMERGING PROBLEMS

When the Social Security Act was passed in 1935, President Franklin D.
Roosevelt understood social security as a conservative pension system.
Under this system, working people were asked to contribute to the Old-
Age Insurance Fund so that their contributions would accumulate and
help secure their income upon retirement in old age. Under this scheme,
workers were supposed to ensure against the loss of earnings upon
retirement by contributing a fraction of their earnings to the fund. It
was an insurance model. The principle of individual equity was paramount. Individual equity meant that benefits were an actuarial equiv-

alent of contributions; that is, each insured worker would receive benefits that had been "paid for" by his own contributions.

The original scheme was quickly modified in 1939, when Congress changed the basic plan of social security on many fronts. In that year, survivors of insured workers and certain groups of dependents (wives and children) of insured workers were brought under coverage for benefits. Furthermore, a minimum benefit was instituted, which constituted a larger amount than the benefits derived from the regular benefit formula. Also, the year in which initial benefits were to be paid was shifted forward from 1942 to 1940.

What was behind this political move? Put another way, why did the Roosevelt administration push for enactment of social security more or less as a program of forced savings for retirement and thereafter increasingly incorporate the social adequacy principle in social security? The answer, it seems, was that Roosevelt and his administration wished to bail out financially vulnerable segments of the population from the financial distress caused by the Great Depression of the 1930s through a dignified, acceptable scheme of social security. The administration needed to channel financial resources to elderly persons and other financially distressed groups of families and individuals through a program that would be not only effective in redistributing income but also acceptable to the whole nation. To compound the situation, policymakers were under great pressure caused by the Townsend movement. Dr. Francis E. Townsend, the leader of the movement, advocated the provision of $200 per month for each elderly individual aged 60 and older, to be financed by sales taxes. Obviously, such a pension plan was too sweeping—or socialist at that time. On the other hand, relying solely on public assistance to help the elderly was not acceptable either.

Under these circumstances, the policymakers struck a brilliant political compromise. They originally developed a social security scheme that heavily leaned toward the insurance principle. This ensured passage of the Social Security Act of 1935. After the enactment, they proceeded to modify the original act through a series of amendments so that a redistributive objective could be attained. In short, redistribution of income was sought implicitly through social security, which nevertheless the public viewed as an insurance program.

Of course there is nothing wrong with the pursuit of redistribution of income through social security. Students of social insurance know that social security should do exactly that, if social security is to be a social insurance program. All social insurance programs have a social mission to accomplish as well as the insurance objective. Thus a question that should be raised now is not whether social security should redistribute income from one segment of society to another but rather in which directions social security should redistribute

income. The directions of redistribution that have been steered over
the years might have been appropriate to meet the political objectives
of bygone times. However, they may not be appropriate to meet
emerging problems. As the financial situation of social security becomes increasingly tight, the question of the directions of redistribution of income through social security becomes a serious one to
pursue.

At any rate, initiated by the Roosevelt administration, Congress
continued to make social security an instrument for redistributing income as well as a means of providing insurance benefits. The redistributive component of social security is generally termed social
adequacy. Under the principle of social adequacy, social security
attempts to channel financial resources to certain groups in order to
ensure an adequate minimum of income for beneficiaries.

Trends toward establishing social adequacy as an objective of
social security have accelerated since then, and new categories of
dependents have been added—for example, disabled dependents whose
disability originated in childhood (1956), children aged 18 to 21 who
attend school (1965), dependent husbands (1950), divorced wives
(1965), grandchildren under certain circumstances (1972), and so on.
In terms of the coverage or risks, disability of the insured worker
was added in 1956. In regard to financing, the idea of developing a
fully funded reserve was abandoned quite early in the history of social
security, and the principle of pay-as-you-go financing was adopted
instead. Under this principle, revenues raised through payroll taxes
were to be used to pay current beneficiaries, and there would be only
a small contingency fund—normally an amount large enough to pay
benefits for less than one year in the absence of the inflow of revenues.

The level of benefits has always been higher than warranted by
individual equity; that is, no cohort of beneficiaries has ever paid
into the system enough for its own income security in old age. Furthermore, benefit levels have steadily increased over the years. For example, in 1960, an average worker in manufacturing could expect to
receive social security benefits that were 31 percent of what was
earned just before retirement, but that worker's counterpart in 1976
could expect a 40 percent replacement rate.[1] Throughout the history
of social security, the benefit formula has been developed so as to
provide low-wage workers with larger benefits than high-wage workers
in relation to lost wages.

These redistributional measures were thought necessary by
policymakers in order to provide adequate levels of benefits to social
security beneficiaries. If social security provided, at early stages of
its development, benefits strictly on the basis of past contributions
by retired workers, few beneficiaries would have received adequate
benefits. Furthermore, during the early stages of social security, the

program had enough funds to distribute relatively high levels of benefits because there was only a small number of beneficiaries in relation to the contributing population. Another policy objective in those days was to make retired workers eligible for benefits with a relatively short duration of covered employment. The reason for such a policy choice was to increase social security beneficiaries as fast as possible so as to decrease the extent of reliance on welfare. It was only in 1950 that the number of elderly persons on social security exceeded those on public assistance for the aged (OAA). Thus, unless eligibility requirements for social security benefits were liberalized, more elderly persons would have had to resort to OAA to meet financial need. Nonetheless, it is also true that the current financial problems of social security stem in part from the legislative actions taken in the past.

From these illustrations of past development, it is clear that social security has truly become a powerful mechanism for redistributing income to beneficiary individuals and families, with greater intensity to some groups than to others. Redistribution of income has been taking place in the following directions:

- From the working to the retired population
- From single to family beneficiaries
- From two-earner to one-earner families
- From high-wage to low-wage beneficiaries

The first type if called intergenerational redistribution; the second and third types, horizontal redistribution; and the fourth, vertical redistribution.

Because redistribution of income through social security is taking place in several directions, it is hard to discern exactly whom social security is really helping beyond what individual equity warrants. Are low-income beneficiaries really helped more by social security than high-income beneficiaries, as is conventionally believed? It is hard to tell because, through horizontal redistribution, income is directed to high-wage beneficiaries with dependents as well as to low-wage beneficiaries with dependents. Furthermore, through intergenerational redistribution, the working population is asked to subsidize all beneficiary units, individuals and families, across all wage levels. In this process, current workers in relatively low-wage brackets are carrying a heavy burden because they are paying regressive payroll taxes. Indeed, two factors combined—the patterns for the redistribution of income through social security and the way social security is financed—are making concerned citizens confused and frustrated as to exactly what social security has come to be. There is no clear consensus as to what social security is all about.

Another source of frustration and puzzlement for the public is that, despite enormous and persistent increases in social security taxes, beneficiaries never seem to be adequately provided for. A discrepancy is apparently perceived between what taxpayers are asked to contribute to social security and what beneficiaries think they are getting from social security. Currently, more than one fourth of the federal revenue is raised through social security, and for about two thirds of taxpayers social security is now the largest tax.[2] Social security taxes are too high, but benefits always seem too low.

Why this perplexing situation? There are at least two reasons. First, categories of beneficiaries have expanded. Second, because of social security's pay-as-you-go financing, each generation of taxpayers has been asked to pay the benefits for all these groups of beneficiaries (including added categories of dependents and the workers who contributed to the system only for a short period of time) as the beneficiaries come on board by legislative fiat. Thus each generation of taxpayers has not only been paying for higher benefits to beneficiaries but also for growing numbers of beneficiaries. And the number of beneficiaries has increased faster than the taxpaying population.

The trend will get worse in the future, not so much because of new categories of beneficiaries being added, but because of the declining birthrate following the baby boom. As a result, in 2030 each 100 workers will have to support 45 beneficiaries; currently, the ratio is 100 to 30.[3]

To compound the situation, the Social Security Administration is still publicizing the old image of social security as an insurance, whereas, in reality, that is far from the program's real nature. A pamphlet called Your Social Security available to local social security offices states:

> The basic idea of social security is a simple one: during working years employees, their employers, and self-employed people pay social security contributions into special trust funds. When earnings stop or are reduced because the worker retires, dies, or becomes disabled, monthly cash benefits are paid to replace part of the earnings the family has lost.[4]

What is unrealistic about this statement is that it implies the existence of a fund reserved in the name of each insured worker. The truth is that there is no such fund. All social security has is a small contingency fund to deal with temporary imbalance between the inflow and the outgo of funds. Other than that, current revenues are used to pay for current benefits. The SSA statement also implies that workers' benefits are financed by their own contributions out of pooled trust funds. This has been untrue throughout the history of social security and is expected to be untrue in the future. The fact is that there has always been intergenerational redistribution of income—and all other types of redistribution, as mentioned earlier. Closer to the truth is that beneficiaries so far have never paid enough for their own benefits; some have paid much less; others, somewhat less.

All this does not imply that redistribution of income through social security is a bad idea. As discussed earlier, the implementation of social adequacy, which inevitably requires redistribution of income, is an integral part of social security objectives. The only problem here is that the public has not been told sufficiently about the redistributive component of social security, let alone the magnitude and directions of redistribution of income through social security. If social security is to be reformed structurally, the public should first be made aware of the magnitude and directions of redistribution of income involved in the current social security system. Only when these are known can policymakers receive public support for reforming social security.

However untrue the SSA characterization of social security, many citizens still believe in it. Because of belief in the publicized version of the nature of social security, the public has tolerated the form of financing social security has taken. It is financed by a payroll tax that hits low-income families relatively hard. In paying this tax, workers are paying for their own benefits, so they are told.

But one solution creates another problem. To the extent that the public has been educated to understand that social security is more or less a program for forced savings, it cannot understand why insured workers cannot collect social security benefits at age 65, whether or not they work thereafter. Here the public is questioning the validity of the earnings test (or the retirement test). If benefits are paid for by the workers' own contributions, why do they have to curtail their work substantially in order to receive benefits? To this question, a government official might respond by saying that social security is a program for replacing earnings lost because of retirement. Therefore workers must withdraw sufficiently from the labor force in order to benefit from the program. But still the social security pamphlet projects something else: an annuity program. However, the government justifies the earnings test on the grounds that social security is an insurance program for replacing lost earnings, not an annuity.

As social security has expanded its role to implement social adequacy, this trend ironically has been in a collision course with the trend of participation in the labor force by women. This is creating another source of stress in social security. As more and more women join the labor force and establish their own insured status as current or future beneficiaries, dependent benefits are increasingly perceived as a source of inequity in the treatment of women. The corollary to this is that married working women have often considered their social security contributions to be redundant taxes, which do not bring commensurately added benefits.

Three groups of women are under social security: married women who never work outside the home, married women who work outside the home, and single female workers. Single female workers feel they are discriminated against in comparison with other women. Working married women feel they are discriminated against in comparison with married women who never work outside the home, who in turn feel they are receiving dependent benefits justly due to them. In short, there is a three-way war among these three groups, each feeling discriminated against in relation to the others.

The injustice that many women feel about social security stems from cross-cutting trends. One is the trend in social security that has added more categories of dependents. The other is the trend for more and more women to move out of a dependent role and establish their own financial security for old age. When the Social Security Act was passed in 1935, the prototype of women was homemakers who did not work outside the home. But conditions have changed drastically since then. For instance, in 1940 one in four women was actively engaged in paid work. In that year only 3 out of 20 households had both the husband and wife working at the same time. But in 1980 over half of all women were in the labor force, and over half of all households had both the husband and wife working at the same time.[5] Implied in the cross-cutting trends in social security and in participation in the labor force by women may be the fact that changes in the world of work are requiring greater emphasis on equity in social security, based either on individuals or on households, while social security increasingly has taken on the mission of implementing social adequacy.

From the foregoing discussion, one can discern that social security has several major problems. Probably the most important one is the issue of redistribution of income through social security. Who currently receives subsidies through social security, and how much? Whose benefits, in the future, should be subsidized, and how much? The magnitude and directions of income redistribution need to be made more explicit. What new benefit scheme should social security pursue to achieve future goals? If social security benefits are to be distributed differently from the way they are distributed currently in order to achieve stated redistributive objectives, what changes should be made in financing the program? A second issue is the validity of the earnings test. Should it be repealed? Under what circumstances can it justifiably be repealed? What is the relationship between the earnings test and work behavior among the retired? Another issue confronting social security is the treatment of women under the program. How should social security be reformed to accommodate the emerging role of women as workers in the labor force?

Considering income maintenance programs that had existed before the Social Security Act was enacted in 1935, and also considering the political climate of the 1930s, social security represented a truly progressive and innovative idea. Subsequent administrations, both Democratic and Republican, tried to improve the program according to their policy objectives. Just as the policymakers of the past tried to improve the system, it seems incumbent upon the present policymakers to modify and change the system so that the program can address the emerging problems and thus become more compatible with the evolving sense of justice and fairness. These three major issues and the related questions raised above need to be addressed in order to reform social security.

INCOME REDISTRIBUTION THROUGH SOCIAL SECURITY: WHICH WAY?

Rates of Replacement

How are benefits distributed to current beneficiaries? And how should current patterns of redistribution be evaluated in terms of individual equity and social adequacy?

One widely used way to study patterns of the distribution of benefits is to calculate replacement rates, that is, the percentage of lost earnings replaced by benefits. Table 6.1 shows that a single maximum earner who retires in 1982 at age 65 can expect to receive a monthly benefit of $705. This replaces 28 percent of the gross monthly earnings made immediately prior to retirement. But a worker who is married and has a dependent spouse to support can expect a larger benefit, as social security provides 50 percent of the worker's benefit to a dependent spouse. Thus the maximum earner with a dependent spouse can expect in this case to receive a monthly benefit of $1,058, which would replace 43 percent of gross monthly earnings in 1981.

Replacement rates for workers with low earnings are greater than those for workers with high earnings. For example, workers who have always earned minimum wages throughout their working career can expect social security to replace 64 percent of lost earnings, if single; 96 percent, if married. High replacement rates for beneficiaries with a record of low earnings are a direct result of the way benefits are calculated. As mentioned in Chapter 2, in 1982 the first $230 of average indexed monthly earnings is subject to a 90 percent replacement, the next $1,158 to a 32 percent replacement, and

TABLE 6.1

Social Security Benefits as a Percentage of Gross Earnings in Year Before Retirement, by Levels of Earnings and Marital Status, for Hypothetical Workers Retiring at Age 65 in 1982

| | Maximum Earnings | | Average Earnings | | Earnings at Minimum Wage Level | |
	Single	With a Dependent	Single	With a Dependent	Single	With a Dependent
Gross monthly earnings in 1981	$2,475	$2,475	$1,144	$1,144	$581	$581
Monthly benefit in 1982	705	1,058	555	832	371	557
Replacement ratio: benefit/gross earnings	28%	43%	49%	73%	64%	96%

Note: Figures based on intermediate assumptions (alternative II-B) in 1981 Social Security Trustees Report. Benefits are computed under the wage-indexed system, without regard to the transitional provision.

Source: Data supplied by the Social Security Administration.

143

earnings in excess of $1,388 to a 15 percent replacement. At the low end of earnings, a worker's basic benefit is at least $122. However, this minimum benefit of $122 no longer applies to future retired workers.

Most government officials and experts in the field who look at these differential rates of replacement tend to conclude that income redistribution is taking place to help beneficiaries with a record of low earnings.[6] In philosophical terms, they say, social adequacy is implemented to help beneficiaries with a record of low earnings at the expense of beneficiaries with a record of high earnings. In the process, the individual equity of high-wage earners is compromised, so they say.

What is interesting about the logic behind this conclusion is the way individual equity is tested in numerical terms. When equity is evaluated on the basis of replacement rates, the individual equity of high-wage earners is considered as being eroded from the ideal state as long as the replacement rate of high-wage earners is lower than that of low-wage earners, because the ideal state of individual equity is a uniform replacement rate across earnings brackets. Thus as long as the benefit formula replaces a higher percentage of lost earnings for low-wage earners, high-wage earners will suffer from eroded individual equity. As long as this logic prevails, there will never be a sense of fulfillment in regard to individual equity for beneficiaries with a record of high earnings. A high-wage earner can be defined as anyone who earns more than the average earnings. Thus, if one evaluates individual equity this way, by definition half of the social security beneficiaries are considered to suffer from eroded individual equity.

But there is a lack of evenhandedness in the foregoing line of argument. One cause of this is that whereas individual equity is defined as benefits directly related to contributions, individual equity is evaluated by differential rates of replacements. Also, past contributions (or taxes) and average indexed monthly earnings (the basis on which benefits are calculated) are neither identical nor closely related to each other. However, the 1979 Advisory Council on Social Security treats those concepts as though they were closely related. It states:

> Maintaining a reasonable <u>relationship between taxes and benefits</u> has been described as the goal of individual equity. Assuring a basic level of income has been called the goal of adequacy. . . . The individual equity goal is clearly reflected in the fact that social security <u>benefits are related to the earnings</u> on which social security taxes are paid.[7] [Italics added]

Just a few features of social security can show that past contributions are not directly related to average indexed monthly earnings. First, in arriving at the average indexed monthly earnings, the computation period is obtained by counting the number of years elapsed since 1951 (or age 21, whichever is later) to the 62nd birthday. Such a computation period may be shorter than actual working life for many workers. Thus average indexed monthly earnings do not closely reflect lifetime contributions, although this situation will improve in the future. Second, the tax rate has not been uniform throughout the history of social security but has increased greatly over the years; for example, it was 3 percent in 1960 as compared to 5.35 percent in 1981 (both excluding contributions to hospital insurance). This means that those who earned greatly during the early part of their working life paid into the social security system less than those who earned relatively more during the latter part of their working life, other things being equal. A comparison can be made between a lumberjack whose earnings capability peaks at age 30 and a college professor whose earnings capability continues to increase until retirement. Other things being equal, the lumberjack contributes less to the system than the college professor, even though they may have had the same level of average indexed monthly earnings and thus receive the same amount of benefits.

To make the situation more complicated, under the current system there is no way to distinguish between those who have earned low wages throughout a long working life and those who have earned high wages for a short period of time.[8] Both the long-term low-wage earner and the short-term high-wage earner gain from the current benefit formula, which replaces a high percentage of lost earnings for both types of workers. On the other hand, the current formula replaces a low percentage of earnings for long-term high-wage earners. An example of a short-term high-wage earner is a federal civil service employee who, after retiring from a job with the federal government, works in covered employment for the shortest possible period required to qualify for social security benefits. Other examples are the self-employed in business or agriculture or other fields, military service personnel, and self-employed physicians—all of whom joined the program many years after the collection of social security taxes started.[9] All these short-term high-wage earners will gain from the benefit formula, which is slanted in favor of workers with a low level of average indexed monthly earnings. Thus vertical redistribution of income is taking place in favor of these types of high-wage workers as well as long-term low-wage workers.

When assessing, on the basis of differential replacement rates, the degree and direction of income redistribution through social security (and hence the social adequacy component of social security), a more serious problem is involved: A massive intergenerational redistribution of income is taking place from the working to the retired population. To compound the situation, social security provides horizontal redistribution of income from single to married beneficiaries with dependents. Thus, for example, due to intergenerational and horizontal effects of redistribution, both high-wage and low-wage retirees with dependent spouses are heavily subsidized compared with their counterparts without dependent spouses. Because these types of redistribution, as well as the vertical type, are taking place simultaneously, it is dangerous to conclude, on the basis of replacement rates, that social adequacy for low-wage earners is implemented by compromising individual equity for high-wage earners. Therefore, in order to make a more realistic assessment of income redistribution through social security, these different types of income redistribution—intergenerational, horizontal, and vertical—need to be disaggregated.

Such an exercise is a formidable task. But one might at least set a model and disaggregate benefits into some components for a group of workers who will retire soon. Therefore, the monthly benefits expected (according to the current formula) for workers who will retire at age 65 in 1982 have been disaggregated into two components: the part of benefits that represents the annuity value of past contributions plus interest, and that part of benefits that represents intergenerational subsidies (income redistributed from the working to the retired population). The first component can be tied to benefits representing individual equity; the second, to social adequacy. Of course, none of the past contributions or interest thereof has been physically accumulated on behalf of each retiring worker. However, disaggregation of benefits according to this model facilitates the assessment of the degree and the direction of income redistribution taking place under social security.

Subsidies Through Social Security

Table 6.2 presents monthly benefits that are then disaggregated into two components of benefits—an annuity based on past contributions and interest and subsidies—for workers who will retire at age 65 in 1982. It highlights the magnitude of intergenerational subsidies, depending on level of earnings, sex, and marital status. The table was developed by the author on the basis of the benefit/contribution ratios calculated by the Office of the Actuary of the Social Security Administration. The office used the interest rate of 2.5 percent over and above the inflation rate in order to arrive at the current value of past contributions to the OAI component of the OASDI fund and the current value of future benefits.[10] To calculate lifetime benefits, the office used current probabilities of surviving each successive year beyond

TABLE 6.2

Disaggregation of Social Security Benefits into Annuity Benefits and Subsidy
for Hypothetical Workers Retiring at Age 65 in 1982

Type of Worker	Monthly Benefits	Benefit/ Contribution Ratio	Annuity Based on Contribution	Subsidy	Subsidy as Percentage of Monthly Benefits
Single male, maximum earner	$705	2.485	$284	$421	59.7
Single male, average earner	555	2.755	201	354	63.8
Single male, minimum wage earner	371	3.535	105	266	71.7
Single female, maximum earner	705	3.105	227	478	67.8
Single female, average earner	555	3.440	161	394	71.0
Single female, minimum wage earner	371	4.410	84	287	77.4
Married male worker with dependent spouse, maximum wage earner	1,058	4.595	230	828	78.3
Married male worker with dependent spouse, average earner	832	5.090	163	669	80.4
Married male worker with dependent spouse, minimum wage earner	557	6.530	85	472	84.7

Note: Figures based on intermediate assumptions (alternative II-B) in 1981
Social Security Trustees Report. Benefits are computed under the wage-indexed
system, without regard to the transitional provision.

*In calculating the ratio, contributions by employers are credited to
employees.

Source: Data provided by the Social Security Administration; and U.S. Congress,
Advisory Council on Social Security, Social Security Financing and Benefits: Reports
of the 1979 Advisory Council on Social Security (Washington, D.C.: U.S. Government Printing Office, 1979), Table 3, p. 65.

age 65. The table is also based on the following assumptions: that workers contributed to OAI from the time of the program's inception in 1937, and that contributions made by employers belong to employees.

In the preparation of Table 6.2, the ratio of the discounted value of lifetime benefits to the compounded value of lifetime contributions to OAI was superimposed onto the ratio of actual monthly benefits to the monthly benefits that past contributions plus interest might have bought in terms of an annuity. The table, then, shows monthly benefits broken down into two additive components; one is directly related to past contributions plus interest, and the other is directly related to the amount in excess of contribution-based annuity benefits (in other words, the amount of the subsidies). This breakdown is done first by dividing the benefit/contribution ratio into two parts: that segment of the ratio that represents contributions plus interest and that which represents the remainder, or subsidies. By definition of the ratio, the segment representing contributions plus interest is always 1. Taking as an example the ratio of 2.485 (applicable to single, male, maximum earners), the portion in excess of 1—that is, 1.485—is attributable to subsidies. One can then break down the monthly benefits of $705 into two parts so that their ratio will stay the same: 1:1.485. One thus arrives at $284 as the amount attributable to contributions plus interest and $421 as the amount attributable to subsidies.

From Table 6.2, we observe several interesting facts:

- All workers retiring at age 65 in 1982 will receive all they have invested through the payment of social security taxes and much more as well.
- Proportionately speaking, workers with a record of low earnings will receive larger subsidies than workers with a record of high earnings. This can be observed by looking at either the amount of the subsidies expressed as a percentage of monthly benefits or simply at the benefit/contribution ratios.
- In absolute terms, however, workers with a record of high earnings will receive larger subsidies than workers with a record of low earnings.
- At the same level of earnings, female workers will receive larger subsidies than male workers, both absolutely and proportionately. The amount of the subsidies for female workers is greater because women have a longer life expectancy at age 65 than men do. [11]
- At the same level of earnings, married workers will receive larger subsidies than single workers, both absolutely and proportionately.

So who receives subsidies—or intergenerational income redistribution—through social security, and how much? The question of who receives subsidies has already been answered: Everyone who receives benefits receives subsidies. But the question as to how much are the subsidies that currently retired workers are receiving, depending on their backgrounds, is more complex to answer. If one measures subsidies in relation to the investment value of past contributions (that is, contributions plus interest), one tends to conclude that social security subsidizes low-wage earners more than high-wage earners. But if one measures subsidies in absolute terms, one tends to conclude that social security subsidizes high-wage earners more than low-wage earners.

The same problem exists in assessing intergenerational income redistribution to married workers with dependent spouses. Low-wage workers with dependent spouses receive greater subsidies in proportionate terms but less in absolute terms than do high-wage workers with dependent spouses. Thus the evaluation of subsidies for workers with dependent spouses involves the same judgment as in the case of single workers. The comparison between subsidies for single workers and for married workers with dependent spouses is easier to make. Whether in absolute terms or in proportionate terms, married workers with dependent spouses are provided with a greater income, which is redistributed from the current taxpaying population.

In comparing subsidies for low-wage and high-wage workers, which way—in absolute or proportionate terms—is more appropriate for measuring subsidies? Suppose one takes the proportionate approach. Such a policy creates the impression that the government helps retirees on the basis of how well they fared in their past work histories. This may sound fair enough for the moment. But subsidies, as defined earlier, are windfall benefits—the excess amount over and above the annuity value of past contributions plus interest. When one considers that income redistribution through social security is generally justified on the ground of social adequacy (meaning ensurance of a decent minimum benefit), one begins to question the wisdom of measuring subsidies in proportion to the past productivity of retired workers. It is the opinion of this author that, as a public policy, it is more appropriate to measure subsidies in absolute terms than in proportionate terms because if the proportionate measurement is used, high-wage earners would be assessed as undersubsidized even though in reality they are receiving larger subsidies in dollar terms than low-wage earners.

But this preference to assess intergenerational subsidies in absolute terms is a minority view in the field of social security. Why is that the case? One reason is that most experts in the field—who are, in the main, highly trained economists—conceptualize individual equity in the image of private insurance and overemphasize that image when evaluating social security. They tend to argue that if social security is to be strictly based on individual equity, it should provide the same rate of return on past contributions regardless of the level of earnings. Any deviation from this, they say, should be considered as implementing social adequacy to help low-wage retirees. If this conception of individual equity were carried out, benefits would be in strict proportion to past contributions plus interest, thus making the benefit/contribution ratio exactly the same across all levels of earnings. The tendency of many experts to tie individual equity to an equal rate of return on past contributions is parallel to their tendency to relate individual equity to a uniform rate of replacement of lost earnings, discussed earlier. In both cases, they tend to overplay the concept of proportionality in the distribution of total benefits. As a result, in both cases they tend to conclude that the individual equity of high-wage earners is compromised to accommodate the social adequacy of low-wage earners.

If social security benefits were provided on the basis of individual equity conceived in this way, benefits for high-wage retirees would have to be subsidized even more than at present, or else benefits for low-wage retirees would have to be subsidized less. On the basis of such reasoning, some justify decreasing, over time, the benefits for low-wage retirees and letting the Supplemental Security Income program take a larger role than at present in meeting their needs.[12] The trend in this direction seems to have already started. It was evident when Congress, through the 1977 amendments to the Social Security Act, froze the minimum benefit at $122, regardless of the rise in wage levels in subsequent years. Furthermore, the 97th Congress repealed the minimum benefit for future retired workers.

The problem concerning this model, however, is that social security has been, and still is, providing a much higher rate of return on past contributions than normal private annuity programs might have provided. Thus the result of imposing the private insurance approach on social security is the prescription of proportional subsidies, because the principle of proportional equality is applied not only to contribution-based benefits (which already include compounded interest) but also to subsidized benefits. In other words, the problem arises because the concept of individual equity is not applied to the level of benefits that a reasonable return on contributions would provide. Rather, the concept is applied to actual social security benefits, and the actual benefits happen to be much greater in amount than the reasonable return. Proportional equality is overplayed to operationalize the concept of individual equity.

It is the judgment of this author that subsidies in social security can best be evaluated on their own, quite independent of past contributions or level of earnings. After all, subsidies are subsidies. The government is not obligated to provide subsidies in relation to the worker's past performance. In short, the principle of individual equity should be applied only to a reasonable return on past contributions, or an annuity value. Beyond that, the principle of social adequacy should take over. There should be no overlap between these two concepts. They are not in adversary relationship, as generally thought.[13] They are additive components.

If this view of individual equity prevails, then one tends to recognize, on the basis of the figures in Table 6.2, that social security is providing larger subsidies (or redistributing more income) to high-wage earners than to low-wage earners. Examples in Table 6.2 are hypothetical cases that assume other variables of beneficiaries to be equal. In reality, the degree and the direction of redistribution of income may be even more acutely felt. Henry Aaron presents the following reasons why hypothetical cases such as those used in the table do not reflect but understate what goes on in reality:

- Persons in high-income classes typically start working at a later age and so will tend to pay taxes for a shorter period.
- Persons in high-income classes have a higher life expectancy and so will tend to receive benefits for a longer period.
- The employer tax is excluded from the personal tax base, which is of much greater advantage to persons in high-income classes.
- Even more important, social security is not subject to the personal income tax, which again is a greater advantage to persons in high-income classes.
- The self-employed pay a lower tax rate, and although some are in low-income groups, many, particularly professionals, are in high-income groups.[14]

It is safe to conclude, therefore, that redistribution of income from the young to the old is occurring in favor of high-wage rather than low-wage beneficiaries, as commonly believed. Some may question the validity of my argument when it is applied to future beneficiaries—those who receive benefits after the program has matured and those who are just entering the labor force and starting to contribute to the social security system. If program maturation is defined as the period during which a worker 21 years old in 1937 has contributed to the system until reaching age 65, then the program has practically matured. Thus, as far as those hypothetical cases in Table 6.2 are concerned, redistribution of income is taking place, not because the individuals have not worked long enough but because there is a sizable amount of income that is redistributed from the young to the old.

But for those entering the labor force now, the situation seems quite different. A study by the Office of the Actuary indicates that new entrants will fare relatively poorly in receiving intergenerational income transfers, or subsidies, if the benefit formula now in effect is not structurally changed. According to this study, single workers with a record of high earnings, for example, will not receive benefits that are large enough to get back the investment value of contributions by them and their employers, although they will get back the investment value of their own contributions.[15] If this gloomy prediction holds true, single high-wage earners may not receive any subsidies when they retire, whereas single low-wage earners and married workers with dependent spouses across all wage brackets may receive subsidies.

In social security, however, business has never been done as usual. True, since 1975, benefits have been adjusted automatically according to cost-of-living increases, and the taxable base has increased according to the rise in average wages. But these developments are recent. Before 1975, benefits were increased and new categories of dependents added without any consideration for establishing actuarial equivalence between contributions and benefits for each cohort of beneficiaries. These changes were made primarily because of political pressures, or legislators' whims, or both.[16] The point is that massive income redistribution is taking place now in the magnitude and directions described earlier and, with even greater intensity, in absolute terms, than in the past.

How does the foregoing discussion square with the discussion in Chapter 4, where it was argued that social insurance programs—and social security in particular—redistribute income effectively from the rich to the poor? The apparent confusion can be cleared by the following explanation. The retired population as a whole is financially worse off than the working population as a whole. Thus income is redistributed from a well-off segment (the working population) of society to a less well-off segment (the retired population) of society. Put more precisely, greater proportions of aggregate social security benefits go to lower-income classes, in which retired families predominate. But in the process of distributing income through social security in this way, more dollars are redistributed to relatively high-wage beneficiaries than to low-wage beneficiaries.

THE EARNINGS TEST AND THE PROBLEM OF THE INCENTIVE

When the Social Security Act was passed in 1935, the nation was in the midst of the Great Depression. Social security was designed to provide income support to workers who retired. It was meant to be an earnings-replacement program, not an annuity, although the idea of forced savings was entertained for a few years after the enactment. This was an important reason for incorporating the earnings test (or retirement test).

A secondary objective was to open opportunities for employment to younger workers. The Social Security Act established 65 as the official retirement age. Many employers followed suit in their pension programs. The 1956 amendments to the Social Security Act lowered the minimum retirement age for women to 62 with actuarially reduced benefits; the 1961 amendments lowered the minimum retirement age for men.

The rate of participation in the labor force by men 65 and over declined from 45.8 percent in 1950 to 20.1 percent in 1977; that for women 65 and over declined from 9.7 to 8.1 percent.[17] In 1965 only 31.7 percent of retired workers were receiving reduced benefits because of early retirement; by 1977, the proportion reached 59.3 percent.[18] Thus the elderly have been behaving as the original legislation intended that they behave.

Quite suddenly, however, Congress and the public have seen a potential problem in the declining participation in the labor force by the elderly and are aware of an impending crisis in financing social security for a proportionately greater number of retirees in the next century. Because of the declining birthrate following the baby boom, each 100 workers in 2030 will have to support 45 beneficiaries; currently, the ratio is 100 to 30.[19]

The 1974 Quadrennial Advisory Council on Social Security reported that 65 percent of the estimated future deficit could be attributed to the demographic shift. One third of the deficit would be due to a flaw in the 1972 amendments that allowed future benefits to be adjusted not only for the cost-of-living increase in the benefit formula but also for the increase in taxable wages.[20] The 1977 amendments corrected this double adjustment. Thus the bulk of future deficits will be attributable almost solely to the demographic shift. How much will payroll taxes have to be raised if the present system of financing OASDI is continued in the next century? Projected expenditures during the period 2027-51 will require payroll taxes at 16.69 percent, whereas under the 1977 amendments projected taxes during this period will be only 12.40 percent of taxable payroll, creating a deficit of 4.29 percent.[21]

Faced with the growing problem of financing, it is reasonable to expect that policymakers will wish to change the policy in regard to retirement. In the past, retirement was encouraged. But now, the policy goal seems reversed. Policymakers wish to find a way to discourage rather than encourage retirement. Studies indicate that the earnings test strongly affects the issue of encouraging or not encouraging the elderly to retire. Furthermore, the earnings test is interrelated with economic conditions and society's economic need for the elderly to stay in the labor force.

Legislative Developments

The 1937 amendments to the Social Security Act included the first provision for the earnings test, which allowed retired beneficiaries to earn no more than $14.99 per month without losing benefits; earnings in excess of $14.99 subjected the beneficiary to the entire loss of that month's benefits. The 1960 amendments provided, for the first time, an implicit tax rate on a certain range of earnings, in excess of an annual exempt amount, thus correcting the all-or-nothing situation. Legislative efforts since 1939 have focused on either increasing the annual exempt amount or lowering the implicit tax rate on earnings. The 1977 amendments provided that the amount would rise from $3,000 to $4,000 in 1978 and by $500 each year until 1981 and thereafter in accordance with the rise in wage levels.[22] (A lower amount—$4,080—applies to younger beneficiaries.) Thus, currently (1981) retired beneficiaries can earn up to $5,500 a year without reducing their benefits. Excess earnings are subject to a 50 percent implicit tax rate; that is an additional $1 earned beyond $5,500 a year reduces benefits by 50¢.

The implicit tax rate of 50 percent still acts as a disincentive to work. Not only do working retirees lose benefits but they also have to pay social security and income taxes. A certain range of earnings is therefore subject to an implicit cumulative tax rate that may be even higher than 70 percent. If retirees also receive SSI, the implicit cumulative tax rate could be even higher.

The 1977 amendments made two other related changes. These amendments eliminated the monthly measure of earnings, except during the first year in which a beneficiary is entitled to benefits, in calculating reduced benefits. Thus any reduction in benefits is now calculated solely on the basis of annual earnings. The new provision eliminates the unfair advantage previously enjoyed by retirees who could earn a sizable income during a part of the year and still draw full monthly benefits during the rest of the year. Also, the age at which the earnings test no longer applies will be lowered in 1982 from 72 to 70. This was postponed for one year under the Omnibus Budget Reconciliation Act of 1981.

The Earnings Test and Retirement Incentives

The decision to retire is a complex one. Some workers have to retire because of poor health, compulsory retirement policies, or other reasons. Some respond to incentives built into the social security program and private pension programs. For some, compulsory retirement policies or poor health may interact with retirement incentives.[23]

William Bowen and T. Aldrich Finegan investigated factors associated with the marked difference in the rate of labor force participation between men aged 64 and 67—a difference of 33 percent.[24] Their multiple regression analysis indicates that, controlling for other variables, over one-third of this difference can be attributed to the level of "other income"—that is, income other than earnings. Social security benefits constitute the largest portion of "other income" for the majority of the elderly.[25] Therefore, one can conclude that social security benefits are strongly associated with the decision to retire. However, social security benefits depend on the degree of withdrawal from the labor force or the level of earnings. Also, many firms link compulsory retirement to the eligibility for pensions (another type of "other income"). Therefore, it is wrong to say that the decision to retire is influenced solely by the effect of other income.[26]

The effects of the earnings test and the benefit level on the probability of the worker's retirement were the focus of a study by Michael Boskin.[27] It used net earnings as a proxy independent variable for the earnings test. Net earnings refer to earnings after the deduction of the earnings-tested loss in social security benefits. Boskin found that net earnings and social security benefits were the two most statistically significant predictors for the probability of retirement. He estimated that an increase of $1,000 in annual net earnings reduced the probability of retirement by about 60 percent. He also found that, at the mean, increasing annual social security benefits by $1,000 increased the probability of retirement by 40 percent. Furthermore, he estimated that revising the earnings test by reducing the implicit tax rate from 50 to 33 percent could reduce the annual probability of retirement by 60 percent.[28]

A 1963 study by the Social Security Administration indicated that the rates of labor force participation among those aged 63 to 72 noticeably declined when earnings exceeded the exempt amount.[29] The implicit tax rate at this point increases from 0 to 50 percent. However, the study found that no sudden decline in the rates of labor force participation occurred when the implicit tax rate increased to 100 percent.[30] Another study by the administration indicated that about half of the men who received benefits in 1969 and worked at the same time kept their earnings within the annual exempt amount of $1,680.[31]

Recently, some researchers have focused on the effects of asset value of social security benefits on retirement decision. The asset value of benefits means the amount of lifetime benefits that are discounted to the present value. Richard Burkhauser, for example, reports that, at the mean, increasing the asset value of social security benefits by \$3,000 raises the probability of retirement at age 62 by 0.027 (from 0.212 to 0.239).[32] This finding implies that when the worker anticipates adequate benefits in his retirement life, he is more likely to retire. This finding also implies that the worker may have an incentive to retire early in order to maximize the asset value of lifetime benefits.

These empirical studies show that the earnings test and the level of income available after retirement are two strong incentives for workers to retire. Retirement income makes leisure a less expensive commodity. This is especially true when the replacement ratio of retirement income to preretirement income is high. Then retirement becomes less economically painful.

In addition to these built-in incentives, the way in which the benefit formula is designed discourages postponing retirement. Although a worker who retires between 62 and 64 years of age receives actuarially reduced benefits, postponing retirement beyond age 65 does not provide benefits that are as much as actuarial calculation warrants. Under the 1977 amendments, the benefits for persons retiring at an age later than 65 will be increased by 3 percent for each year of postponed retirement. This appears to be a measurable improvement over a 1 percent increase provided previously, but not much in actual terms. The provision of 3 percent increase in benefits for each year of postponed retirement was enacted to make up partially for a loss in benefits for late retirees that was caused by the indexing of earnings initiated under the 1977 amendments. That is, before the indexing of earnings was put into effect, workers who postponed retirement gained greatly by substituting earnings credited in early years with earnings credited in years past age 65. But because earnings came to be indexed under the 1977 amendments, the substitution of earnings in this way has not benefited such workers as much as when earnings were not indexed. Thus the provision of a 3 percent increase in benefits (instead of a 1 percent increase in benefits previously) for each year of postponed retirement was in part to make up for such a loss incurred by late retirees. At any rate, the increment of benefits by 3 percent for each year of postponed retirement is significantly short of an actuarially warranted increase, which is about 10 percent.[33]

Indeed, the interaction of taxes, social security benefits, and the earnings test operates in such a way as to encourage workers to take an early retirement. An Urban Institute study indicates that in 1979 a worker who earned \$10,000 could receive 79 percent of preretirement net income by retiring at age 62 and working part time to earn up to the exempt amount, which was \$3,720. This meant that even though the worker reduced work effort by as much as 63 percent, this worker could maintain 79 percent of preretirement net income.[34]

Thus it is clear that, in concert, the earnings test, social security benefits, and the benefit formula are strong economic incentives for a worker to retire, possibly earlier than age 65, and not to postpone retirement beyond 65. Downgrading benefit levels probably would not be politically feasible unless the benefit structure was radically changed. However, a policy change in the earnings test to boost work incentives and a policy change in the benefit formula to encourage late retirement would seem to be acceptable to the majority of the public and the policymakers in Washington. These changes would greatly ameliorate the financing of social security in the next century.

The Earnings Test: Pro and Con

Because the earnings test is linked with incentives to retire early, the way seems open for considering repeal. However, policy issues related to repeal involve much more than the work disincentive. Proponents of the earnings test argue that retirees who forego total social security benefits are highly paid professionals, as shown by a study by the Social Security Administration.[35] Probably the strongest argument for retaining the test is that highly paid workers would receive windfall benefits if it were abolished.[36] A part of this argument is that repeal would increase social security expenditures by approximately $6 to $7 billion a year.[37] Another argument for the test is that retirement opens up opportunities for younger workers. However, available data seem to indicate that the rate of unemployment is not related to the rate of retirement.[38]

Still another important argument for the test concerns the basic objective of social security as a partial replacement of earnings lost because of retirement. Also, it has been pointed out that a sizable portion of social security benefits was not paid for by the retired population but is being financed by the working population; this portion represents intergenerational subsidies, as shown earlier. These two factors together provide convincing evidence that social security is not an annuity duly paid for by the retiree. This argument inevitably goes on to say that repeal of the test would accentuate social security's component of intergenerational subsidy. Increasing that component would seem unfair to the nonaged working population, especially low-wage earners. Social security taxes are regressive and hit low-wage earners hard.

In the main, arguments against the test emphasize its adverse economic and social effects on the elderly themselves and its adverse impact on the economy.

It is said that, while keeping the cost of social security down by a few billion dollars and also keeping off the benefit rolls the few high earners among the elderly, the earnings test is forcing a sizable portion of the elderly to retire or curtail their work effort substantially against their will.[39] Furthermore, those who work less because of the test tend to be low-wage retirees.[40] They typically are the persons who need to supplement their meager social security benefits.[41] Research findings indicate that earnings are a decisive factor in lifting elderly persons out of poverty.[42] Staying longer in the labor force would also ensure in the future that the income level of the elderly would not lag as far behind that of the general population as it does at present.[43] Moreover, work helps the elderly to maintain social contacts and the involvement that they need to keep their sense of self-esteem and self-identity as members of the community.

Another argument against the test points out the inequity involved in the way earned income and unearned income are treated. Retirees— typically high-income retirees—who do not work but derive income from such sources as rent, interest, and dividends are not affected by the earnings test, but those who work are affected. It seems unfair. However, the issue involved here goes right back to the basic objective of social security: a partial replacement of earnings lost because of retirement.

Some argue that imposed retirement, reduced work, or both are bad for the economy. Keeping as many people as possible off social security could, they say, channel financial resources to other uses— to capital formation, for instance, or to stimulation of industries that produce hard commodities. The elderly, too, would continue to participate in producing goods and services. On the other hand, workers forced out of the labor market become full-time consumers, mainly of soft commodities such as social services and medical care, and thus the production of these types of services will be stimulated.[44] Impact on economic growth is less favorable than it would be if the elderly were allowed to stay in the labor force as long as possible.

Policy Options

How should policy on the earnings test be changed in order to mitigate the problem of retirement incentives? That question is difficult to answer. If, for example, we are asking for ways both to remove work disincentives among middle-wage and low-wage earners and to prevent high-wage earners from receiving windfall benefits, then we should improve the earnings test but not eliminate it altogether. If we are to keep the basic structure and maintain the objective of partially replacing lost earnings, we have to resort to an incremental approach. On the other hand, if social security were radically trans-

formed into an annuity, repeal of the test would be justified. If this
change were made, all of those reaching age 65 would simply get back,
in the form of benefits, the investment (or annuity) value of their past
contributions.

If an incremental approach were taken, the earnings test could
be improved to lower the implicit tax rate on excess earnings. Because
the annual exempt amount has kept up with the rise in wages, as a result of the 1977 amendments, additional action along that line seems
unnecessary now. But the implicit tax rate could be further liberalized. Currently, earnings in excess of $5,500 are implicitly taxed at
a 50 percent rate. The policymaker might adopt the recommendation
made by the 1974 Quadrennial Advisory Council on Social Security:
Apply a 33 percent tax rate to earnings in excess of the annual exempt
amount but less than twice this amount and apply a 50 percent tax rate
on earnings in excess of twice the exempt amount.[45]

What would be the effect of upgrading the annual exempt amount
and lowering the implicit tax rate on a lower range of excess earnings?
First, the break-even point, at which the beneficiary ceases to receive
social security benefits, would be higher than at present. Liberalizing
the earnings test according to the council recommendation would also
mean that a relatively low level of excess would be subject to the
lowered implicit tax rate of 33 percent. This would boost work incentives of low-wage and middle-wage earners who are now adversely
affected by the earnings test. In addition, the policymaker could boost
the work incentive by providing actuarially increased benefits to those
who retire after age 65. This would correct the built-in bias that favors early retirement.

The policymaker might also look into the exemption of workers
aged 65 and over from payroll taxes for social security, as proposed
by Joseph Pechman et al.[46] This would mitigate the problem of the
high cumulative implicit tax rates imposed on earnings above the
exempt amount. It would also make the hiring of elderly workers
more attractive economically, as employers as well as workers would
be exempt from payroll taxes for social security. And what about the
equity of the situation? Is it fair, on the one hand, to tax the aged who
continue to work and do not receive social security benefits and, on
the other hand, not to tax the aged who stop working and receive their
benefits? It seems not.

A radical approach could be taken and the earnings test could be
repealed altogether. But such a radical change in policy could be justified only if social security was transformed into an annuity program.
Such a policy change would be interrelated with issues concerning the
redistribution of income through social security—especially the issue
of individual equity versus social adequacy—and with the issue of how
best to deal with the emerging role of many women as workers. Thus

such a change cannot be made in isolation. Later we shall attempt to tie these issues together and come up with a coherent direction that the social security program might take.

THE CHANGING ROLE OF WOMEN AND ALTERNATIVE
GOVERNMENT PLANS ON SOCIAL SECURITY

When the scheme of social security was developed nearly half a century ago, the female prototype was the homemaker, and the program treated women as homemakers. But the conditions of women are quite different now. As mentioned earlier, the rate of participation in the labor force by women has increased enormously, resulting in a sizable proportion of families with both husbands and wives working. Because a greater number of women work, inequity in social security in dealing with single working women, married working women, and married nonworking women is becoming more visible.

Another source of the problems that face social security and that involve many women is the increasing rate of divorce. In the early 1970s, the divorce rate surpassed the record high that occurred right after World War II. Currently, one out of every two marriages is expected to end in divorce. It is becoming increasingly difficult to consider marriage as a permanent bond for partners, as conceived by the founders of social security. Frequent changes in marriage partners mean that social security benefits for dependent spouses somehow must be made portable—just as pension benefits are now portable under many programs when workers change employers. Social security, as it currently operates, is not flexible enough to handle problems involving divorce and remarriage.

Social security has inflexibility of this kind in one sense. But it tends to be overly generous in redistributing income to divorced spouses. Yet the divorced spouses who receive dependent benefits do not have an appreciation commensurate with the amount involved. This paradox can be briefly explained as follows: Dependent benefits for divorced spouses are based on the worker's lifetime earnings even though the marriage may have lasted much less time. Furthermore, social security provides benefits to all qualified divorced dependent spouses who were married to the worker for at least ten years at different times. However, the benefits provided to each divorced dependent spouse—which are based on 50 percent of the worker's benefit—seem inadequate for supporting a person living alone. Dependent benefits were originally designed to support dependents who live with the worker. All this illustrates that social security subsidizes, possibly to an unreasonable degree, workers who marry and divorce frequently within the confines of the program regulations, and yet does not manage to provide an adequate level of income to individual divorced dependent spouses.

To deal with these major concerns regarding women, together with the impending crisis in financing social security, Joseph A. Califano, Jr., former secretary of Health and Human Services (HHS), sent a report to the Congress on February 15, 1979.[47] This report was mandated by the social security amendments of 1977 and constituted a vital step in the nation's effort to address important issues that involve the future of social security. The report was intended to open public debate on the future direction that social security should take. It included two alternative plans for restructuring social security benefits: the "earnings sharing plan" and the "double-decker plan."

The Two Alternative Plans

The Earnings Sharing Plan

Under the earnings sharing plan, annual earnings by a husband and a wife would be combined into earnings for the couple, with half of each year's combined earnings credited to the account of each spouse. The combined earnings would continue to be divided until one spouse reached age 62. If the couple were divorced, each spouse would take half of the combined earnings credits for each year of the marriage. At retirement, benefits for each spouse would be based on the earnings of each while unmarried, half of their annual earnings while married, plus the earnings of each after the division of earnings terminated. Slight deviations are made from the basic model to meet the needs of surviving families and families with disabled workers.

When one spouse dies, the surviving spouse would be credited with 80 percent of the couple's total earnings during their marriage or with 100 percent of the earnings of the spouse having higher pay, whichever figure is greater. This would constitute inheritance of earnings credits by the surviving spouse.

For purposes of benefits for young survivors—children and young surviving spouses caring for children—earnings would not be transferred between the spouses with regard to a marriage in effect at the time of death. Benefits for young survivors would be based on any earnings credits the deceased person had from paid work (while unmarried or during a current marriage), plus any credits acquired as a result of a prior marriage terminated by death or divorce.

For purposes of disability benefits, earnings would not be shared in regard to a marriage still in effect at the time of disability. Disability benefits would be based simply on any earnings credits the disabled person had from paid work (while unmarried or during the current marriage), plus any credits the disabled person acquired from a prior marriage.

In addition to the drastic changes in the treatment of taxable earnings (which would be the base for calculating ultimate benefits), the plan incorporates changes that recognize the changing patterns of work among women. The earnings sharing plan would not pay surviving spouses under age 65 who have children for as long a time as the current system does. Under this new plan, such spouses would receive benefits only until the youngest child reached aged 7, rather than 18 as under the current system. Their benefits, even while received, would be only 50 percent of the worker's basic benefits instead of 75 percent as under the current system. However, the first surviving child would receive 100 percent of the worker's basic benefits, instead of 75 percent under the present system, and each additional child would receive 50 percent, subject to family maximum. Surviving spouses without children would have to wait until age 62 to be eligible for survivors benefits instead of age 60 as under the present system. To make up partially for the loss in the benefits for nonaged and aged survivors, an adjustment benefit equal to 100 percent of the deceased worker's benefits would be paid for one year following the death of the worker. This benefit would be paid regardless of whether there are children in the family eligible for benefits. HHS discusses these policy changes related to nonaged surviving spouses with children and aged survivors without children as an economy measure.

The Double-Decker Plan

Under the double-decker plan, each U.S. resident would be provided with a flat-amount benefit of $122 a month upon attaining age 65 (a reduced amount payable at age 62), becoming widowed before age 65 with children in their care, or becoming disabled. Each child of a retired, disabled, or deceased worker also receives this flat-amount benefit, subject to family maximum. This provision would constitute a universal first-tier flat-amount old-age, survivors, and disability benefit. On top of this first-tier benefit, the beneficiary would receive a second-tier benefit based on the worker's earnings in employment covered by social security. The second-tier benefit would be equal to 30 percent of the worker's average indexed monthly earnings.

Except for the provision of the flat-amount benefits, most other features of the double-decker plan are similar to those discussed under the earnings sharing plan. That is, a couple's combined earnings would be divided equally at the time of divorce; the surviving spouse would inherit the earnings credit of the deceased spouse; surviving spouses under age 65 who have children would receive benefits for a shorter period than under the present system; and so on.

One important difference between the two plans is that under the double-decker plan earnings credits would be shared only for the purpose of getting a divorce. Thus earnings credits would not be shared when calculating retirement benefits for each spouse as they would be under the earnings sharing plan. The benefits of each would be the first-tier flat-amount benefits plus the second-tier benefits based on each one's own earnings.

Basic features of the two alternative plans studied by HHS are summarized in Table 6.3. The present system is also described for comparative purposes.

Analysis of the Two Alternative Plans

The two alternative plans are analyzed here in terms of how they relate directly or indirectly to retirement benefits. Neither survivors benefits for aged spouses or for spouses under age 65 who have children nor benefits for the disabled will be specifically discussed. The basic rationale for both the earnings sharing plan and the double-decker plan involves strengthening the relationship between contributions and benefits; recognizing implicitly that women's work at home is "paid work" and letting their husbands pay for it; and applying the community property principle to earnings credits.

Strengthening the Relationship Between Contributions and Benefits

The current system of social security favors one-earner couples over two-earner couples, who in turn are favored over single workers. The comparisons that follow will help to clarify and explain the inequities. In comparing a one-earner couple with a two-earner couple having the same amount of total taxable family earnings, the one-earner couple is favored under social security over the two-earner couple because the one-earner couple in fact receives a larger monthly benefit than the two-earner couple. The following example under the 1979 decoupled benefit formula illustrates the inequity:

	Average Indexed Monthly Earnings	Family Monthly Benefits
One-earner couple	$12,000	$703
Two-earner couple	$6,000 $6,000	$593

The inequity results from the fact that one and one-half times the worker's benefit (PIA) at the $12,000 earnings level is larger than the

TABLE 6.3

Comparison of Major Provisions Under Present Law and Comprehensive Options

Provisions	Present Law	Earnings Sharing	Double-Decker
Eligibility for retirement benefits	Person must have worked in covered job long enough to be insured for benefits or be a dependent of such a person.	At least one spouse must be insured as under present law.	No insured status requirement for tier I or tier II.
Earnings credits	Person gets earnings credits based only on his or her own work in covered employment.	Total earnings of married couple divided equally between them for each year of the marriage and credited to their individual earnings records. Surviving spouse credited with 80 percent of earnings credits of couple (or 100 percent of higher earner's credits).	For tier II, earnings credits based on person's own work in covered employment. Earnings credits of married couples (while married) divided equally at divorce. Surviving spouse credited with 80 percent of earnings credits of couple (or 100 percent of higher earner's credits).
Benefits			
A. Retired worker (married, separated, or divorced)	Gets weighted benefits based on own earnings credits.	Gets weighted benefit based on half of couple's earnings credits while married and own earnings credits while	Gets tier I benefit of $122 plus tier II benefit equal to 30 percent of own average earnings credits acquired

164

		single, plus any credits acquired as a result of a prior marriage.	as a result of divorce or death of a spouse.
B. Aged homemaker (married, separated, or divorced)	Dependent spouse's benefit equal to 50 percent of retired worker's benefit.	No dependent spouse's benefits; gets benefits based on any earnings credits acquired through work or marriage.	No dependent spouse's benefits; gets tier I. Gets tier II if has any earnings credits acquired through work or as a result of a prior marriage.
C. Aged widow(er)	Dependent's benefit equal to 100 percent of deceased worker's benefit.	No dependent surviving spouse's benefit; gets benefit based on earnings record as described above (including credits inherited when spouse died).	No dependent surviving spouse's benefit; gets tier I. Also, tier II if has any earnings credits as described above (including credits inherited when spouse died).
D. Child	Benefit equal to 50 percent of worker's benefit paid to child of retired or disabled worker (75 percent for child of deceased worker) until child reaches age 18 (or 22, if a student). Where several children eligible family maximum applies.	Same as present law for child of retired or disabled worker. For surviving child, first child gets 100 percent of worker's benefit; 50 percent for each additional child. Total allocated equally among children and subject to family maximum.	Tier I benefit payable to child of retired, disabled, or deceased worker, subject to maximum of 250 percent of tier I benefit. In addition, in survivor cases, one tier II benefit equal to 100 percent of worker's benefit payable; benefit divided equally among children.

(continued)

TABLE 6.3 (continued)

Provisions	Present Law	Earnings Sharing	Double-Decker
E. Young mother's or father's benefits	50 percent benefit (75 percent in death cases) payable to young parent caring for child under age 18 (or disabled).	50 percent of the worker's benefit payable if there is an entitled child under age 7 in his or her care. (Not paid for any month an adjustment benefit payable.)	Tier I benefit payable if there is an entitled child under age 7 in his or her care.
F. Adjustment benefit for widow	No comparable benefit. (Lump sum of $255 payable on death of worker.)	100 percent of deceased spouse's benefit payable for 1 year.	100 percent of deceased spouse's tier II benefit payable for 1 year.
G. Disabled person	Disabled worker who meets recency-of-work test gets benefit based on own earnings credits. Surviving spouse who meets restricted definition of disability can get a reduced dependent's benefit if aged 50 or older.	Insured person gets benefits same as present law based on earnings credits as described above, excluding credits acquired as a result of the present marriage.	Tier I payable. Also gets tier II if has any earnings credits acquired as described above. Where recency-of-work requirement is not met, a more strict definition of disability must be met.

Source: U.S. Department of Health, Education, and Welfare, Social Security Administration, "Men and Women: Changing Roles and Social Security," Social Security Bulletin 42 (May 1979): 31.

sum of two workers' benefits, each at the $6,000 earnings level. Indeed, an empirical study by Burkhauser confirms the effect of the benefit formula on the amount of intergenerational subsidies—or "pure transfers," as he calls them—that different types of families receive. His findings indicate that, other things being equal, one-earner households receive larger intergenerational subsidies (that is, windfall benefits over and above what their contributions might have bought in terms of annuity) than two-earner households receive. Furthermore, the disparity becomes greater as the level of earnings increases.[48]

Comparing single workers with one-earner or two-earner couples shows clearly that the present system favors couples. A single worker may pay as much as a one-earner couple to the social security system, but may receive less in benefits. When comparing a single worker with a two-earner couple, it is highly probable that a two-earner couple will receive greater social security benefits in relation to what was contributed because (1) the working wife may be entitled to a higher benefit as a dependent spouse based on her husband's earnings, and (2) the weighted benefit formula works to provide higher total benefits to two workers (regardless of whether or not they are married) than to a third worker whose earnings are equal to the combined earnings of the first two workers. When few women worked such inequities were not so visible to the public. But now that about 50 percent of women are working, such inequitable features of social security arouse public controversy. The inequities in the treatment of women under social security create a sense of unfairness in the minds of many beneficiary families who are adversely affected. The two plans studied in the HHS report attempt to reduce the inequities in the treatment of households that differ in marital status and work history.

The plans try to establish a better connection between family contributions and eventual benefits by eliminating dependent benefits for spouses. Under the earnings sharing plan, each spouse's benefits would be based on earnings while unmarried plus half the total earnings of both while married. If divorce occurs, each spouse takes along an equal share of the earnings credits accumulated during the marriage. Under the double-decker plan, earnings credits are not shared at retirement but are shared should divorce occur. These plans attempt to individualize both benefits and contributions and to bring about a higher degree of equity than does the current system. At present, the relationship between contributions and benefits is not evenhanded: Contributions are tied to individuals, and benefits tend to cater to the needs of households.

A closer relationship between the contributions and the benefits of retired families brought about by individualizing both what is contributed and what is received would result in more equitable treatment of beneficiary families. Under either plan, there would no longer be the suspicion that one group of beneficiary families has contributed more to the system and yet received less in benefits than some other group of beneficiary families with different marital status and work history. The plans, for instance, would eliminate the present unfair situation that often provides greater benefits to wives who never worked than to single women with a long work history. In the absence of benefits for dependent spouses, all benefits for nonworking wives would be "paid for" by sharing the husbands' earnings credits under the earnings sharing plan. In essence, this would make the husbands' benefits lower when they are married to nonworking wives. Under the double-decker plan, nonworking wives would receive the first-tier benefits, like everyone else, but no more than that. Thus, other things being equal, greater earnings acquired collectively as a couple or individually as a single worker would always bring greater benefits, regardless of marital status.

Implicit Recognition of Women's Work at Home as Paid Work

Sharing earnings credits equally between spouses means that nonworking women, while they are at home taking care of their families, would be credited with half of the earnings their husbands made in each year of their marriage. Accrued earnings would become the base for the wives' own benefits, no matter what happens to their marriage. The plans thus recognize that the production, and hence the earnings, of husbands are in part due to what their wives contribute while managing their homes. Implicitly, then, the plans place a monetary value on the homemaking activities of nonworking wives or of working wives who do not usually earn as much as their husbands earn, as many of them have interrupted careers or work part time.

Under the present system, women who do not work outside the home must indeed count on having a marriage that lasts. If marriages fail before their tenth anniversary, women lose the benefits from all the work they have devoted to the family's well-being. A divorced wife who did not stay married for more than ten years and did not work during her marriage would have to start from scratch to accumulate her own taxable earnings and work long enough to be eligible for benefits. The only other option open to such a woman is to marry a man with an earnings record as good as that of her previous husband.

Even if divorced wives work during their marriage, they are still at a disadvantage under the present system. If, like most working wives, they withdrew from the labor force when their children were small, their years of nonwork would count against them in calculating their benefits.

Application of the Principle of Community Property

The idea of splitting combined earnings equally between spouses originated from state community-property laws that entitle spouses to an equal share of what both earn after marriage.[49] The community property principle—commonly known as a principle set forth in the Napoleonic Code--prevails in eight western states that have a background of French or Spanish colonization.[50] The 1948 federal tax law incorporated the principle of community property and permitted income splitting in joint income tax returns for married couples.

It appears that, under the plans, social security would also incorporate the principle of community property in crediting taxable earnings to spouses. Any and all of the spouses' earnings after marriage would belong to each of them equally. In case of divorce, each spouse would be entitled to half the taxable earnings credits accumulated during marriage. Under the present system, the nonworking wife who gets a divorce could expect nothing from social security unless she was married ten years or more. Even then, she would receive "dependent benefits," not benefits she would be entitled to in her own right.

To the extent that both the earnings sharing plan and the double-decker plan provide for the splitting of earnings credits between the spouses when divorce occurs (or for the purpose of calculating retirement benefits under the earnings sharing plan), social security in the future would recognize that marriage constitutes a partnership between man and woman, in which each could claim equal right to, and obligation for, income security in old age. The term obligation is emphasized because under the plans, income security of both divorced spouses is provided by redistributing earnings credits and the associated benefit rights between them. In contrast, under the present system, society is obligated to finance the benefits for dependent spouses, both divorced and nondivorced. By changing from the current system to either of the plans, nonworking spouses who are divorced (and also the nondivorced under the earnings sharing plan) would be better provided for at the expense of the working spouse than under the current system, at the same time costing less to society. Thus, if either plan—but particularly the earnings sharing plan—was adopted, two vital social policy goals could be achieved: economy in the financing of social security and the provision of more adequate benefits for dependent spouses.

Differences Between the Earnings Sharing Plan and the Double-Decker Plan

What are the differences between the two plans? And what are the implications of these differences? The essential difference is that

FIGURE 6.1

The Earnings Sharing Plan

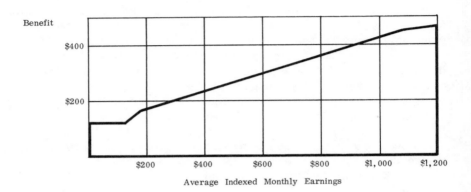

FIGURE 6.2

The Double-Decker Plan

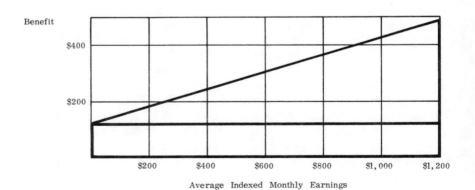

the double-decker plan attempts to ensure a basic minimum benefit
to all elderly persons aged 65 and over (and reduced amounts as early
as 62), regardless of levels of earnings or previous employment, but
the earnings sharing plan does not do this. Figures 6.1 and 6.2 contrast the benefit formulas under the two plans. The figures are based
on the benefit formulas effective February 1979.

Under the double-decker plan, benefits are in two tiers: The
bottom tier represents a minimum benefit ($122) that society wishes
to ensure to all elderly individuals, and the second tier, a replacement of part of earnings lost because of retirement. Although second-
tier benefits replace past earnings proportionately, first-tier and
second-tier benefits combined replace a higher percentage of past
earnings as the level of earnings declines, thus forming a progressive
benefit structure as a whole. In contrast, the benefit formula for the
earnings sharing plan is basically the same as the one used under the
present system. Because of the minimum benefit of $122 and the tilts
in replacement rates, the benefit structure as a whole is progressive:
The lower the earnings level, the higher the rate of replacement.

One difference between the two plans is that the earnings sharing
plan inherits an unintended but undesirable feature of the current system, whereas the double-decker plan eliminates it. That is, the earnings sharing plan would disproportionately favor workers with a short
period of covered employment but with high annual earnings. Such an
inequity occurs because the earnings sharing plan, like the current
system, permits high-paid workers to draw out the full amount of the
weighting in the benefit formula over many fewer years than can low-
paid workers. The reason is that the weighting is scaled to total earnings credits rather than to length of covered employment.[51] The
double-decker plan terminates this more favorable treatment of high-
wage earners with a short period of covered employment because the
first-tier flat-amount benefit is paid to everyone regardless of earnings credits or length of covered employment and because there is no
tilt in replacement rates involving the second-tier benefit.

Because of the progressive benefit formula adopted by the earnings sharing plan (with replacement rates of 90 percent up to the
average indexed monthly earnings of $180, 32 percent between $180
and $1,085 and 15 percent for such earnings in excess of $1,085 in
1979), couples who manage to divide equally their combined earnings
credits so that the average indexed monthly earnings of each spouse
fall in a lower earnings bracket would have a higher replacement of
earnings in terms of benefits. On the other hand, if one considers the
difference between the benefits derived from such a progressive benefit formula and the benefits derived from a straight-percentage-
replacement formula (with a 32 percent replacement rate) as analogous
to the second-tier benefit under the double-decker plan, then couples

whose equally divided earnings fall in the bracket between $180 and
$1,085 would receive the largest absolute amount of such additional
benefits. At any rate, the earnings sharing plan cannot escape from
the inequities that are inherent in a progressive benefit formula. The
structure of formula adopted by the earnings sharing plan is identical
to that of the current benefit formula. However, the extent of inequity
discussed here is less than that under the current system, which provides dependent benefits for spouses. The double-decker plan, which
adopts a benefit formula that replaces a straight percentage of earnings, would not create inequity such as described here.

Another important difference between the two proposed plans is
that benefits for retired couples would be more nearly equalized between husbands and wives under the earnings sharing plan than under
the double-decker plan, assuming lifelong marriage. The sharing,
during marriage, of total earnings credits equally between the spouses
under the former plan is what equalizes benefits. The projection of
an HHS study indicates that if the earnings sharing plan were adopted,
the average benefits for retired married men would be 18 percent
lower in the year 2000 than they would be under the present system.
On the other hand, the average benefits for retired married women
would be 30 percent higher. However, if the double-decker plan were
adopted, such a shift in average benefits between retired married men
and retired married women would not occur.[52] These differences
mean that the earnings sharing plan more explicitly ensures economic
independence to retired women who are still married. The double-
decker plan, as well as the earnings sharing plan, ensures economic
independence for women in case they are divorced or widowed, even
though it does not do as much for those who are still married.

Which scheme favors the poor? Beyond the first-tier benefits
in the double-decker plan, replacement rates under both plans are
almost identical: 30 percent in the double-decker plan and 32 percent
in the earnings sharing plan for most levels of earnings. However,
beneficiary families with little or no earnings would benefit more from
the double-decker plan for two reasons: The double-decker plan provides every elderly person with the first-tier flat-amount benefits,
regardless of levels of earnings or employment experience; and benefits under the earnings sharing plan are tied to past earnings and minimum employment requirements (insurance coverage) on the part of
at least one of the spouses. Indeed, a study by Jennifer Warlick et al.
using a simulation model indicates that the double-decker plan would
particularly help disadvantaged groups of workers—black male workers and both black and white female workers compared to white male
workers.[53] However, their findings should be interpreted with caution
because the simulation model used the level of first-tier benefits that
is somewhat higher than that studied by HHS. The question of how well

these disadvantaged groups are treated under the double-decker plan is also related to how first-tier benefits are increased over time. First-tier benefits could be increased either according to the rise in prices or the increase in average wages. If the past economic trend can be a guide for the future, increasing first-tier benefits according to the increase in wages would help these groups more than if benefits were increased according to the rise in prices.

The policy choice between these two alternative plans will have an important effect on the future role of the SSI program. That is, the double-decker plan has the potential for minimizing or eliminating the SSI program altogether (if the level of first-tier benefits is allowed to go up as high as SSI payments), whereas the earnings sharing plan might increase its scope. Because of that potential, the social security outlay would probably be greater for the double-decker plan than for the earnings sharing plan. But the total government outlay for supporting the elderly population would not be radically different. The only important difference would be in the source of financing. Under the double-decker plan, payroll taxes would have to bear a greater share of support for the elderly than under the earnings sharing plan. However, if the earnings sharing plan were adopted, general revenue would continue to finance SSI at the same level as at present or perhaps with greater scope. Of course, the policymaker could, as the HHS report hints, choose to use general revenue to finance part of the double-decker plan—especially the first-tier flat-amount benefits. In that case, financing the double-decker plan would be less regressive than it would be if general revenues were not used.

Absorbing the SSI program into the social security system would be a significant step from both an ideological and a philosophical viewpoint. Under the double-decker plan, society acknowledges responsibility for providing a minimum floor of income to all persons who pass 65 years of age merely on the ground of their being elderly members of the society. There would no longer be differential treatment of elderly persons who are poor and those who are not. The effects that this universal treatment of the elderly would have on the elderly themselves and on society as a whole cannot be measured in dollars and cents.

Limitations in the Plans

From both a philosophical and a practical viewpoint, it seems clear that the double-decker plan is preferable to the earnings sharing plan as a policy option. The major grounds for this choice are these. First, the double-decker plan implements universal provision of a minimum income to the aged, the disabled, and the widowed with children in their care, regardless of earnings level or work experience, thus potentially minimizing the SSI program. If the first-tier benefits could be provided at the poverty-line level, not only all elderly persons would be ensured an adequate minimum of income but also SSI could be eliminated altogether. Second, the double-decker plan generally is more favorable to the poor. Third, it has a greater potential for securing general revenue to finance social security than does the earnings sharing plan. Against these advantages, the double-decker plan has the disadvantage of not being able to ensure the degree of economic independence to retired women who are still married that the earnings sharing plan does.

If policymakers choose either the double-decker plan or the earnings sharing plan in changing social security, they must recognize that neither will meet the basic challenge or resolve the controversy of intergenerational subsidies. Whether younger generations are willing to pay a part of the social security burden for the older generation, and if so, how much, must still be determined.

James N. Morgan of the Institute of Social Research at the University of Michigan maintains that no generation should be begging for its own income security in old age. He states:

> What is crucially important is equity between generations, which means that the system should be so organized that each generation pays its own way. We need an actuarially fair system where the payroll taxes and contributions of each age group or generation over its lifetime, plus interest at market interest rate, cover their own expected benefits. [54]

It takes considerable courage to agree with Morgan. If his proposal were implemented in the United States, current retirees would receive much smaller social security benefits, as Table 6.2 shows. To implement the principle of generational independence that Morgan advocates and still pay adequate social security benefits—adequate in terms of replacement rates and benefits related to the living standards of the general population—at least two conditions would have to be met. One is that the program must have matured, that is, that retiring workers have contributed to the system for their entire working life. The second is that the social security program must provide a large portion of the total money income of the elderly. The first consideration will be met in the near future. The second condition would not be met in the United States as long as the commitment to social security is as small as it is at present in spite of an enormous increase in social security expenditures in recent years. The 1979 Survey of Income of the Population, 55 and Over, carried out by the Social

Security Administration, indicated that in 1976 only 39 percent of the total money income of the elderly 65 and older came from social security.[55] This proportion is not expected to increase very much even when the social security program matures. Income of the retired that is derived from sources other than social security tends to be fixed and is therefore hard to defend against increases in cost of living. Even if prices do not increase and even if each generation saves enough by contributing to the social security system, it is still difficult to ensure its adequate living standards in old age that are comparable to those of younger populations, ironically in a society that has potential for economic growth. Thus, as long as per capita economic growth continues in the United States and as long as social security does not provide a large portion of the income of retirees, their relative economic condition is expected to drift downward as they become older. This is why some degree of intergenerational subsidies seems justified.

Even if one does not agree totally with Morgan, a lesson can be learned from his statement about the importance of responsibility of each generation to finance its own retirement. However, some degree of intergenerational subsidies is required to help beneficiaries maintain their living standards in a growing economy. Therefore the social security system in the future should be organized so that each generation of retirees at least knows exactly how much social security benefits it has paid for (the annuity value of its contributions and interest at the market interest rate) and how much it gets through subsidies paid by younger generations. Neither the earnings sharing plan nor the double-decker plan can quantify explicitly and precisely these two components of benefits. Modifications to the plans are needed in order to make redistributive components of benefits explicit and precise so that the system can be understood by all Americans. Whether under the plans studied by HHS or under the current system, redistribution of income through social security is done implicitly, making it difficult to implement the social adequacy principle according to the sense of fairness and justice that society aspires to at a given time in history.

A NEW DIRECTION IN SOCIAL SECURITY

How can a new scheme of social security be envisioned in light of the multiple policy issues that have been discussed? How can social security be reformed so that the following four policy objectives can be achieved simultaneously? Provide adequately for low-wage retirees. Encourage work efforts among elderly individuals. Reflect the principle of individual equity in benefit levels. Recognize the changing roles of women. It seems that the policy objectives cannot be met if social security is programmed in a single-decker fashion as it is currently. Only if some type of double-decker plan were adopted could these goals be achieved.

The current system cannot achieve these objectives for various reasons. First of all, the current benefit structure does not facilitate, in an explicit and precise manner, the division of benefits into two parts, one reflecting individual equity and the other social adequacy. Unless such division is done explicitly and precisely, it is difficult to implement simultaneously these two policy objectives without creating confusion between them. Under the current system, one can measure the degree of social adequacy in varied ways, depending on different definitions and assumptions used. Furthermore, because the objective of social adequacy is commingled with that of individual equity under the current system, it tends to give an erroneous impression that the pursuit of social adequacy is done at the expense of individual equity. Second, the current system cannot provide an adequate minimum floor of benefits without affecting the issue of the work incentive, because the system provides benefits only after the worker withdraws substantially from the labor force. In other words, the system operates so that workers retire in order to receive social security benefits; and the higher the minimum benefit, the greater the probability that low-wage workers will choose to retire. Last, the current system is not handling with a sense of coherence or justice the complex situations that women are placed in.

What social security is doing is carrying out a redistribution of income in multiple directions as discussed before, making the system inefficient in utilizing its resources to implement social adequacy to ensure an adequate minimum floor of income for the elderly. As already seen, massive amounts are redistributed to high-wage retired workers—those with dependent spouses particularly. Yet the view of social security presented to the public through the various media is that it is supposed to do just the opposite, that is, help low-wage individuals and families. Such unintended redistribution of income through social security has occurred since social security has come to support households rather than individuals, has permitted dependents to claim a percentage of the worker's basic benefit, and yet has not asked each cohort of beneficiary families to pay its own way. Contributions have been based on individuals, not households, and have been too small. Throughout the history of social security, intergenerational redistribution of income has been so massive that vertical redistribution through the progressive benefit formula is not strong enough to offset the effect of intergenerational transfers in favor of high earners. In order to correct this anomaly, individual equity needs to be more clearly defined and directly linked to the concept of actuarial equivalence between contributions and benefits; also, dependent benefits for spouses need to be abolished. Furthermore, social adequacy should be implemented independently of individual equity.

This author believes that the double-decker plan studied by HHS has a potential to strike all four of these policy goals, if it is modified. To achieve these goals and others (explained later), this author recomments that the double-decker plan be modified in the following way:

- Provide an annuity on the basis of past contributions to OAI, plus interest, as second-tier benefits to retirees and aged widows and widowers.
- Set the level of first-tier flat-amount benefits at the poverty line.
- Eliminate the earnings test in social security altogether.
- Eliminate dependent benefits for children altogether.
- Limit the duration of benefits for nonaged widow(er)s with children to three years.
- Allow the sharing of earnings credits (which are to be converted to contributions credits for the purposes of calculating benefits in old age) between spouses until one of the spouses reaches age 62. If the couple were divorced, each spouse would take half of the combined earnings credits for each year of the marriage. However, for the purposes of benefits for the disabled and nonaged survivors with children, earnings would not be shared with regard to a marriage still in effect at the time of disability or death of the worker, respectively.
- Finance first-tier flat-amount benefits through general revenue.

Impact on the Elderly

If the double-decker plan is modified this way, it would simultaneously achieve the four major policy goals in regard to the elderly. First, because the first-tier benefits at the poverty line would be provided to all individuals reaching 65 regardless of their past or present working status or level of earnings, the notion of an adequate floor of income for the elderly would be established. Furthermore, because first-tier benefits would not be subject to an income test or the earnings test, the issue of the work incentive would not be seriously questioned. Second, the second-tier benefits that take the annuity approach would explicitly implement individual equity. This would ensure maintaining the insurance principle. Third, because the second-tier benefits would be an annuity, the earnings test in social security could be repealed. Abolishing this test would enhance work incentives for the elderly across all wage levels. Fourth, having the spouses equally share earnings credits accumulated during marriage, for both divorce and retirement purposes, would help establish economic independence for women. Also, this model establishes the prototype of women as workers, not homemakers. This shift in women's image is compatible with the trends in their participation in the labor force. And yet the provision for inheritance of earnings credits as discussed by HHS (see Table 6.3) would ensure maintenance of living standards of women after their spouses die (more discussion later on inheritance of earnings credits by the surviving spouse).

The idea of a double-decker plan is not new. In a somewhat more conventional sense, the double-decker system is well known in many European countries and some other parts of the world. Such a system generally combines a contributory flat pension program and/or a noncontributory universal pension program with a contributory earnings-related pension program. A major objective of the double-decker system is to provide a basic floor of income to all beyond a certain age and simultaneously to provide retirement income based on previous work records.

As a way to cope with problems of income maintenance for the aged, disabled, and survivors, a few European countries followed the British tradition of poor laws. That is, they originally developed relief programs to provide for the needy aged through an income or means test. Some means-tested programs were later converted into universal noncontributory pension programs to eliminate the stigma attached to relief programs. In Britain, when a comprehensive social security system was developed during the 1940s, the flat amount of benefit became the basis for the contributory pension program. In countries with such programs, there has been a marked movement since the 1950s toward adding earnings-related benefits to pension programs. On the other hand, more European countries began with contributory earnings-related pension programs, patterned after the pioneering German law of 1889, which enacted Bismarck's social insurance program. To ensure an effective minimum floor of income to all pensioners, however, some countries later supplemented contributory earnings-related pension programs with contributory flat pension programs and/or noncontributory universal pension programs. In short, European social security systems have been moving from two different directions toward double-decker systems, supplemented by income-conditioned relief programs in some countries.[56]

The major difference between the modified double-decker plan proposed here and the plans in effect in most European countries—or between the modified plan and the double-decker plan studied by HHS— is that the modified plan provides an annuity for second-tier benefits and the other plans provide earnings-related benefits.

In addition to the four policy goals mentioned earlier, this modified double-decker plan would have several secondary positive effects. In the author's opinion, basing second-tier benefits strictly upon actuarial calculations would constitute an ideological and conceptual breakthrough in social security. Using such a benefit formula would clearly show both the retired population and the rest of society exactly how much past contributions of retired persons were worth in terms of annuity benefits. The two populations would no longer suspect that one group or the other was being cheated. When all generations know exactly how much retired persons have saved for themselves through social security, then society as a whole can determine how much it wants to support the retired population over and above what the retirees have done for themselves. Such societal support would be expressed in the first-tier flat-amount benefits financed by general revenue. Also, the public would better understand the principles of social adequacy and individual equity as applied to social security if social adequacy were tied to intergenerational transfers (first-tier flat-amount benefits) and individual equity to the benefits based on the annuity value of each worker's contributions plus interest (second-tier benefits).

Indeed, when earnings are the base for calculating second-tier benefits, it is difficult to calculate benefits so that they are actuarially justifiable. Earnings-related benefits would be either more or less than actuarially based benefits, depending on the rate at which earnings are replaced. (The replacement rate is now set at 30 percent in the double-decker plan studied by HHS.) When the replacement rate is higher than warranted by actuarial calculations, high-wage retirees would receive greater windfall benefits in absolute terms than would low-wage retirees. When the replacement rate is lower than actuarially warranted, the reverse is true. The current system is providing greater windfall benefits to high-wage retirees than to low-wage retirees, although the benefit formula is weighted in favor of low-wage retirees. This ironic situation occurs when the rate of replacement is greater than actuarially warranted, as is currently the case. Furthermore, there can be no assurance that each generation of the elderly has "paid for" its second-tier benefits, as long as second-tier benefits are tied to past earnings rather than to retirees' contributions plus interest.

Another secondary effect of the modified double-decker plan is the establishment of intertemporal equity. With intertemporal equity, retired workers would receive the same benefits regardless of when they worked as long as their contributions were the same. Second-tier benefits based on earnings could not establish this type of intertemporal equity. For example, two retirees having the same average indexed monthly earnings and thus the same social security benefits may have paid different amounts of social security taxes depending on when they worked, as tax rates have not been uniform but rather have increased over the years. But this would not occur if second-tier benefits amounted to an annuity. Because the second-tier benefits do constitute an annuity under the modified double-decker plan, the favorable treatment that short-term high-wage earners currently receive would disappear also.

The modified double-decker plan would create a built-in fiscal constraint. Each retiree's benefits would be an annuity based on that retiree's past contributions plus interest. Beyond that, benefits would depend on the willingness of society at large to finance the first-tier flat-amount benefits through general revenue. Under either of the plans studied by HHS or under the current system, no one knows how much retirees have paid for and how much they are helped by society. In the absence of clear quantification of the two components of benefits, social security benefits are increased by the sheer political power of the retired population.

When such an annuity is considered for second-tier benefits, it should be remembered that the modified double-decker plan would not create a full reserve fund to pay for future obligations, as is done under private annuity programs. Under the proposed plan, pay-as-you-go financing would continue; only the method of calculating benefits would change from the earnings replacement approach to the annuity approach.

In regard to first-tier flat-amount benefits, this author recommends that they not be subject to an income test. Why not? If the economy of the program is the overriding concern, they should be income-tested. However, from the point of view of preserving the work incentive among the elderly, first-tier benefits should not be income-tested. As mentioned earlier, the modified double-decker plan accomplishes the policy goal of maintaining the work efforts by eliminating the earnings test with regard to second-tier benefits. It would be counterproductive to introduce another type of income-testing.

When considering the economy issue in regard to providing first-tier flat-amount benefits, one should remember that larger subsidies are now provided to high-wage beneficiaries than to low-wage beneficiaries. Subsidies (the first-tier benefits) under the modified double-decker plan would be the same for all elderly individuals. Therefore, in financing subsidies greater economy might be attained under this modified double-decker plan than under the current system. However, this would depend on the level of first-tier benefits. The objective of economy could be achieved in other ways than by introducing an income test for first-tier benefits. For example, on the one hand, all social security benefits—both in the first tier and the second tier— could be subjected to income tax, and on the other hand, social security taxes could be deducted from income tax.

Although the modified double-decker plan proposed by this author could effectively deal with many policy concerns, a question can be raised as to how it would fare in the future when second-tier benefits eventually predominate. Because those currently working are paying social security taxes at a higher rate than did those who are currently retired, the annuity value of past contributions plus interest will be higher for future beneficiaries. This means that for many future retirees, second-tier benefits alone might be adequate for their support. When that stage arrives, the government could adjust downward the level of first-tier flat-amount benefits. Or if the policy goal is to maintain a proper range of benefits, the first-tier benefit level could be manipulated to achieve such a policy goal. For instance, the level of first-tier benefit could vary according to age of the elderly. As they get older, they might be provided a higher first-tier benefit. In short, the modified double-decker has a built-in flexibility in providing benefits according to the legislative intent of a given time.

Treatment of Nonaged Surviving Spouses with Children
and Disabled Workers

Providing an annuity as the second-tier benefits makes sense as far as the treatment of the elderly is concerned. However, the same method of calculating benefits for nonaged surviving spouses with children and disabled workers is not appropriate. This is the case because the nature of economic risk involved in losing the breadwinner due to death or disability is quite different from attaining old age. A more appropriate way to calculate the second-tier benefits for these groups of beneficiaries would be the adoption of group insurance—that is, the same approach adopted in the original double-decker plan. For this reason, this author recommends the original double-decker plan outlined in Table 6.3, as far as the treatment of nonaged surviving spouses with children or disabled workers is concerned. That is, the second-tier benefits for these groups of beneficiaries would be a percentage—not necessarily 30 percent, depending upon legislative intent—of the average indexed monthly earnings.

It is recommended, however, that the duration of benefits for nonaged surviving spouses with children be limited to a fixed number of years—say, three years—instead of the duration of time until the youngest child reaches age seven as discussed by HHS. However, survivors benefits should not be subject to the earnings test. A fixed duration of benefits for nonaged survivors seems justified because income security of children would be dealt with outside the domain of social security under the author's recommendation as discussed in Chapter 7. Therefore, the duration of benefits for nonaged surviving spouses does not need to correspond with the length of child dependency. Instead, the duration is linked to the length of time that might be needed for surviving spouses to adjust to the death of deceased spouses. During these three years, nonaged surviving spouses with children could count on social security benefits that would be provided whether or not they work, thus providing options for them to plan for life after the death of deceased spouses. They might save such benefits for meeting future costs of educating their children, or spend them for obtaining vocational training for themselves. Benefits not subject to the earnings test might result in preserving work incentives of nonaged surviving spouses as well as enhancing the principle of equity in social security. However, for an economy measure, survivors benefits—both in the first tier and the second tier—could be subject to income tax; this could be also said about disability benefits. Benefits for the disabled would stop upon recovery and after a trial period of gainful employment.

A question remains as to whether disabled workers and deceased workers must have worked a minimum duration of employment before disability benefits and survivors benefits could be provided. What would be the eligibility requirements for first-tier and second-tier benefits? The double-decker plan studied by HHS would require no prior work for disabled persons and survivors of workers to receive the first-tier flat-amount benefits. Second-tier benefits would be a percentage of the average indexed monthly earnings in covered employment, again requiring no minimum duration of employment before the onset of disability or death of the worker.

Adoption of such a policy would have a profound ramification. If first-tier flat-amount benefits were provided unconditionally to disabled persons and nonaged surviving spouses with children as well as to the aged, and if the amount is as high as the level of poverty-line income, as proposed by this author, then the adoption of such a policy would make SSI redundant and thus it could be abolished. Abolishment of SSI would have several beneficial effects, such as the elimination of one income-tested program from the system of income maintenance, a reduction in recipiency of multiple benefits, and a lessening of stigma. (As discussed in Chapter 5, receipt of social security benefits and SSI at the same time is strongly related to the issue of work disincentives.) Therefore, the adoption of such a policy of not requiring a minimum duration of employment is recommended.

Inheritance of Earnings Credits by the Surviving Spouse

What about the question of whether earnings credits (which are to be converted to contributions credits for the purposes of calculating benefits in old age) should be inherited by the surviving spouse in case of death of the other spouse? As mentioned earlier, the plans studied in the HHS report provided that when an elderly spouse died, the surviving spouse would be credited with 80 percent of the couple's total earnings credits during their marriage or with 100 percent of the earnings credits of the spouse having higher pay, whichever figure was greater. If such a policy were adopted, future benefits for the surviving spouse would be greater than when inheritance of earnings credits was not allowed.

The decision on whether or not to adopt such a policy on inheritance of earnings credits by the surviving spouse depends on the policymaker's judgment in regard to the unit of beneficiaries and in regard to protection of economic independence for women. For example, allowing inheritance of earnings credits by the aged surviving spouse would prevent such a spouse's living standards from declining as a result of the death of the other spouse, as especially happens when female spouses survive. When their husbands die before reaching age 65, their records of earnings credits (hence the eventual annuity value of past contributions to OAI) might be relatively low unless they are allowed to inherit earnings credits accumulated by the deceased husbands.

The policymaker, on the other hand, might decide not to allow earnings credits to be inherited by the surviving spouse on the ground that more and more women are establishing their own economic security both while they work and after they retire. Furthermore, at least in retirement, a sudden decline in living standards resulting from the death of a spouse could be prevented if beneficiary families, by reducing their benefits when both spouses are alive, were given the option of arranging benefits so that when one spouse dies the other would receive more than the amount of one person's benefit. Such an option was suggested by Burkhauser.[57] If these views prevail, inheritance of earnings credits by the surviving spouse would be unjustified. Moreover, inheritance of earnings credits would maintain the notion of households as beneficiary units, which the policymaker might object to. As long as records of earnings and contributions are kept in individual accounts, beneficiary units would also have to be individuals, not households, if the principle of individual equity is to be vigorously pursued. Furthermore, permitting inheritance of earnings credits by the surviving spouses implies that the objective of social adequacy is pursued through the second-tier benefits as well, whereas this author argues that the social adequacy objective should be pursued solely through the first-tier flat-amount benefits. The first-tier flat-amount benefits at the poverty line are provided, under the modified double-decker plan as recommended by this author, exactly for the purpose of meeting social adequacy needs of individuals who accumulate low earnings credits for whatever the reason, including death of their spouses. As more and more women work and earn more, the implementation of such a policy option would not create undue hardship. Therefore, as a long-range plan, this author recommends no inheritance of earnings credits by the surviving spouse.

But the picture is quite different, at least for now. The level of labor force participation among married women is lower than that among single women. Even when married women work full time, they tend to earn less than their spouses. Not providing for inheritance of earnings credits by the surviving spouse might make couples feel treated unfairly. Therefore, this author recommends the adoption of inheritance of earnings credits as a transitional measure.

Taking Children Out of the OASDI System

The same line of reasoning on maintaining individuals as both contributing units and beneficiary units applies to this author's recommendation to exclude children as dependents from social security altogether. As long as social security taxes are based on individuals, basing benefits on households introduces confusion and constraints in implementing individual equity and social adequacy. It would also result in inefficient utilization of fiscal resources. Social security cannot provide for an indefinite number of children in a beneficiary family, maintain a proper balance between individual equity and social adequacy, and preserve the work incentive at the same time. Therefore, it would be better to deal with income security of children outside the domain of social security. The problems in dealing with income security for children in the current welfare system were discussed in Chapter 5. Inequities involved in the treatment of children under social security will be touched upon in Chapter 7.

To recapitulate, the following are the major points of recommendations by this author:

- Each elderly person (being retired or a homemaker) would receive social security benefits that are the sum of universal flat-amount benefits (the first-tier benefits) and an annuity (the second-tier benefits). Annuity would be calculated on the basis of past contributions plus interest, derived from half of the couple's earnings credits while married and their own earnings credits while single, plus any credits acquired as a result of a prior marriage.
- Aged widow(er)s would receive social security benefits that are the sum of universal flat-amount benefits (the first-tier benefits) and an annuity (the second-tier benefits). Annuity would be calculated in the same way as for other elderly persons (see above), except that earnings credits would include credits inherited when the spouse died).
- Nonaged surviving spouses with children would receive social security

benefits that are the sum of universal flat-amount benefits (the first-tier benefits) and a percentage of the average indexed monthly earnings of the deceased worker (the second-tier benefits) for a period of three years. The second-tier benefits would be calculated on the basis of any earnings credits the deceased person had from paid work, plus any credits acquired as a result of a prior marriage terminated by death or divorce. Earnings would not be transferred between the spouses with regard to a marriage in effect at the time of death.

- The disabled worker would receive social security benefits that are the sum of universal flat-amount benefits (the first-tier benefits) and a percentage of the average indexed monthly earnings of the disabled worker. The second-tier benefits would be calculated on the basis of any earnings credits the disabled person had from paid work, plus any credits acquired from a prior marriage. Earnings would not be shared with regard to a marriage still in effect at the time of disability.
- The level of first-tier flat-amount benefits is set at the poverty-line income.
- Credits of earnings accumulated during marriage would be shared equally between spouses until one of the spouses reaches age 62. The exception to this rule would be made for the purpose of calculating benefits for the disabled and the nonaged surviving spouses with children, as indicated above. Divorce would terminate the sharing of earnings credits.
- Inheritance of earnings credits by the surviving spouse would be allowed as a transitional measure.
- General revenue would finance the first-tier flat-amount benefits; payroll taxes would finance the second-tier benefits.

Thus it can be seen that the modified double-decker plan can indeed achieve simultaneously the four policy goals set forth. This modified plan also deals effectively with a number of other problems in the social security system that have plagued policymakers: the earnings test, fair dealing for both short-term high-wage workers and long-term low-wage workers, benefits for divorced spouses, and differential treatment of various groups of beneficiaries—married and single workers, wives working and those not working outside the home, and the poor and the rich. Furthermore, this modified double-decker plan seems flexible enough to be adapted for use in the future, even when worker-retiree ratios, living costs, and other conditions radically change.

Of course, more questions remain to be answered. For example, how will the conversion of disability benefits to retirement benefits be done? If a worker is disabled for a long time, this person cannot accumulate enough earnings credits to ensure an adequate annuity for old age. Another important question is: What happens if only children survive the worker? In the absence of a spouse of the deceased worker, does at least one of the children in the family receive survivors benefits, taking the place of the spouse? Does this child receive such benefits in addition to children's allowances, which this author recommends (in Chapter 7) for all children under age 18? Finally, how can the current system be transformed into such a radically different system as recommended by this author? Further study is needed to answer these vital and difficult questions. At least the modified double-decker plan as recommended hopefully will stimulate discussion on the future of social security.

NOTES

1. Peter Henle, "Recent Trends in Retirement Benefits Related to Earnings," Monthly Labor Review 95 (June 1972): 12-20; and Alicia H. Munnell, The Future of Social Security (Washington, D.C.: Brookings Institution, 1977), Table 4-1, p. 64.

2. George F. Break, "Social Security as a Tax," in The Crisis in Social Security, ed. Michael J. Boskin. (San Francisco: Institute for Contemporary Studies, 1977), p. 108.

3. U.S. Congress, Advisory Council on Social Security, Reports of the Quadrennial Advisory Council on Social Security, 94th Congr., 1st sess. (Washington, D.C.: U.S. Government Printing Office, 1975), p. 49.

4. U.S. Department of Health, Education, and Welfare, Social Security Administration, Your Social Security, HEW Publication no. (SSA) 76-10035, June 1976.

5. Richard V. Burkhauser, "Earnings Sharing: Incremental and Fundamental Reform" paper delivered to the Conference on Social Security and the Changing Roles of Women, cosponsored by the Institute for Research on Poverty and the Women's Studies Research Center, University of Wisconsin, April 11-12, 1980.

6. See, for example, Munnell, op. cit.; Carl V. Patton, "The Politics of Social Security," in The Crisis in Social Security, ed. Michael J. Boskin (San Francisco: Institute for Contemporary Studies, 1977), p. 169; and 1979 Advisory Council on Social Security, Social Security Financing and Benefits (Washington, D.C.: U.S. Government Printing Office, 1979).

7. 1979 Advisory Council on Social Security, op. cit., p. 53.

8. For a detailed discussion of this problem, see Herman Grundmann, "Treatment of Short-Service Workers under OASDI Retirement Provisions," Policy Analysis with Social Security Research

File, proceedings of a workshop held on March 15-17, 1978, at Williamsburg, Va. (Washington, D.C.: U.S. Department of Health, Education, and Welfare, Social Security Administration, Office of Research and Statistics, 1978), pp. 489-517.

9. It was 1954 for the self-employed, 1956 for members of uniformed service personnel, and 1965 for self-employed physicians.

10. 1979 Advisory Council on Social Security, op. cit., pp. 58-68. The benefit-contribution ratio is applicable to workers retiring at age 65 in 1979. However, the use of the ratio to those retiring in 1982 seems acceptable, in the absence of other data, as the margin of error is small.

11. In 1977 life expectancy at age 65 was 13.9 years for white males and 18.4 for white females; it was 14 years for nonwhite males and 17.8 years for nonwhite females. See U.S. Bureau of the Census, Statistical Abstract of the United States: 1979 (Washington, D.C.: U.S. Government Printing Office, 1979), Table 102, p. 71.

12. See, for example, Munnell, op. cit., pp. 39, 140; and Richard J. Zeckhauser and W. Kip Viscusi, "The Role of Social Security in Income Maintenance," in The Crisis in Social Security, ed. Michael J. Boskin (San Francisco: Institute for Contemporary Studies, 1977), p. 50.

13. See, for example, Rita Ricardo Campbell, "The Problems of Fairness," in The Crisis in Social Security, ed. Michael J. Boskin (San Francisco: Institute for Contemporary Studies, 1977), p. 127.

14. Henry J. Aaron, "Demographic Effects of the Equity of Social Security Benefits," in Economics of Public Services, ed. Martin S. Feldstein and Robert I. Inman (New York: Macmillan, 1977), p. 152.

15. Orlo R. Nichols and Richard G. Schreitmueller, "Some Comparisons of the Value of a Worker's Social Security Taxes and the Benefits," Actuarial Note no. 95 (Washington, D.C.: U.S. Department of Health, Education, and Welfare, Social Security Administration, April 1978).

16. For an interesting discussion on this, see Martha Derthic, Policymaking for Social Security (Washington, D.C.: Brookings Institution, 1979).

17. Employment and Training Report of the President, 1978 (Washington, D.C.: U.S. Government Printing Office, 1978), Table A-4, p. 186.

18. Social Security Bulletin: Annual Statistical Supplement, 1977-1979 (Washington, D.C.: Department of Health and Human Services, Social Security Administration, 1980), Table 90, p. 151.

19. U.S. Congress, Advisory Council on Social Security, Reports of the Quadrennial Advisory Council on Social Security, op. cit., p. 49.

20. Ibid., p. 50.

21. A. Haeworth Robertson, "Financial Status of Social Security Program After the Social Security Amendments of 1977," Social Security Bulletin 41 (March 1978): 27.

22. The annual exempt amount for those aged 62 to 64 was set at $3,240 in 1978, and this amount would thereafter change automatically according to the rise in wages.

23. For research findings on the interaction between limitations in health and level of retirement income in the decision-making process, see Joseph F. Quinn, "The Early Retirement Decision: Evidence from the 1969 Retirement History," Staff Paper no. 29 (Washington, D.C.: Social Security Administration, Office of Research and Statistics, 1978).

24. William G. Bowen and T. Aldrich Finegan, The Economics of Labor Force Participation (Princeton, N.J.: Princeton University Press, 1969), p. 282.

25. For those who retired during January–June 1970, social security benefits constituted 40 and 48 percent of "other income," depending on marital status and sex. See Alan Fox, "Income of New Beneficiaries by Age at Entitlement to Benefits," in Reaching Retirement Age: Findings from a Survey of Newly Entitled Workers, 1968-70, Research Report no. 47, U.S. Department of Health, Education, and Welfare, Social Security Administration (Washington, D.C.: Social Security Administration, Office of Research and Statistics, 1976), Table 8.2, p. 99.

26. For detailed discussion, see Quinn, op. cit., pp. 2-5.

27. Michael J. Boskin, "Social Security and Retirement Decisions," Economic Inquiry 15 (January 1977): 1-25.

28. Ibid., p. 13.

29. Kenneth G. Sander, "The Retirement Test: Its Effect on Older Workers' Earnings," Social Security Bulletin 31 (June 1968): 3-6.

30. In 1963 when the data for this study were collected, benefits were reduced $1 for each $2 of earnings from $1,200 to $1,700 and $1 for each $1 of earnings in excess of $1,700.

31. Virginia Reno, "Retirement Patterns of Men," in Reaching Retirement Age: Findings from a Survey of Newly Entitled Workers, 1968-70, Research Report no. 47, U.S. Department of Health, Education, and Welfare, Social Security Administration (Washington, D.C.: Social Security Administration, Office of Research and Statistics, 1976), p. 32.

32. Richard V. Burkhauser, "The Early Acceptance of Social Security: An Asset Maximization Approach," Industrial Labor Relation Review 33 (July 1980): 484-92.

33. Munnell, op. cit., p. 79.

34. Gary Hendricks and James R. Storey, "Disincentives for Continued Work by Older Americans: Final Report," Working Paper 1394-03 (Washington, D.C.: Urban Institute, July 1980).

35. Reno, op. cit., Table 3.10, p. 35.

36. Rita Ricardo Campbell, Social Security: Promise and Reality (Stanford, Calif.: Stanford University, Hoover Institution, 1977), p. 210.

37. U.S. Congress, National Commission on Social Security, Social Security in America's Future (Washington, D.C.: U.S. Government Printing Office, 1981), p. 146.

38. Lloyd Saville, "Flexible Retirement," in Employment, Income, and Retirement Problems of the Aged, ed. Juanita M. Kreps (Durham, N.C.: Duke University Press, 1963), Table 1, p. 144.

39. Zeckhauser and Viscusi, op. cit., p. 59.

40. Reno, op. cit., Table 3.16, p. 38.

41. Virginia Reno and Carol Zuckert, "Income of New Beneficiaries by Size of Social Security Benefit," in Reaching Retirement Age: Findings from a Survey of Newly Entitled Workers, 1968-70, Research Report no. 47, U.S. Department of Health, Education, and Welfare, Social Security Administration (Washington, D.C.: Social Security Administration, Office of Research and Statistics, 1976), Table 9.7, p. 131.

42. For example, for the couples newly entitled to social security benefits during January-June 1970, only 8 percent of those who reported earnings had income below the poverty line, compared with 41 percent of the couples without earnings. See Fox, op. cit., Table 8.7, p. 105.

43. Joseph J. Spengler and Juanita M. Kreps, "Equity and Social Credit for the Retired," in Employment, Income, and Retirement Problems of the Aged, ed. Juanita M. Kreps (Durham, N.C.: Duke University Press, 1963), pp. 204-05.

44. Saville, op. cit., p. 163.

45. U.S. Congress, Advisory Council on Social Security, Reports of the Quadrennial Advisory Council on Social Security, pp. 22-23.

46. Joseph A. Pechman, Henry J. Aaron, and Michael K. Taussig, Social Security: Perspectives for Reform (Washington, D.C.: Brookings Institution, 1968), pp. 144-45.

47. U.S. Department of Health, Education, and Welfare, Social Security and the Changing Roles of Men and Women (Washington, D.C.: Department of Health, Education, and Welfare, 1979). An abbreviated version of this report was published in Social Security Bulletin 42 (May 1979): 25-33.

48. Richard V. Burkhauser, "Are Women Treated Fairly in Today's Social Security System?" Institute for Research on Poverty

Discussion Paper no. 530-78 (Madison: Institute for Research on Poverty, University of Wisconsin, 1978).

49. Harold M. Groves, Financing Government, 6th ed. (New York: Holt, Rinehart and Winston, 1965), pp. 223-25.

50. Robert J. Lampman and Maurice MacDonald, "Underlying Concepts and Institutions," paper presented at the Conference on Social Security and the Changing Roles of Women, cosponsored by the Institute for Research on Poverty and Women's Studies Research Center, University of Wisconsin, April 11-12, 1980.

51. For detailed discussion of the problem, see Grundmann, op. cit.

52. U.S. Department of Health, Education, and Welfare, Social Security and the Changing Roles of Men and Women, p. 94.

53. Jennifer Warlick, David Berry, and Irwin Garfinkel, "The Double Decker Alternative for Eliminating Dependency under Social Security," paper presented at the Conference on Social Security and the Changing Roles of Women, cosponsored by the Institute for Research on Poverty and the Women's Studies Research Center, University of Wisconsin, April 11-12, 1980.

54. IRS Newsletter, Spring 1979, p. 8.

55. Susan Grad and Karen Foster, "Income of the Population, 55 and Over, 1976," Staff Paper no. 35, U.S. Department of Health, Education, and Welfare, Social Security Administration, Office of Research and Statistics, SSA Pub. no. 13-11865, December 1979, Table 28, p. 46.

56. For more detailed discussion on the development of the double-decker system, see Margaret S. Gordon, "The Case for Earnings-Related Social Security Benefits, Restated," in U.S. Congress, Joint Economic Committee, Subcommittee on Fiscal Policy, Old Age Income Assurance, Part II: The Aged Population and Retirement Income Programs (Washington, D.C.: U.S. Government Printing Office, December 1967), pp. 312-39.

57. Burkhauser, "Earnings Sharing: Incremental and Fundamental Reform," op. cit.

7

A CHILDREN'S
ALLOWANCE PROGRAM
AS AN ALTERNATIVE

The development of a coherent system of income maintenance requires
a hierarchical order of various types of income maintenance programs.
But no matter how ideally we reorganize current programs according
to that hierarchical vision, there always will be tension in the system
as long as programs attempt to meet family needs and the labor market pays workers on the basis of individual productivity. What all this
boils down to is the problem of ways with which a nation attempts to
ensure income security for children. This is the case because children
are the major factor creating the gap between what the family needs
and what the breadwinner brings to the family through work.

Indeed, a concern for the income security of children has been
a focal point in developing many of the current income maintenance
programs. Such programs have intended to ensure income security
for children by filling the gap between the needs of families with children and the earnings, or lack of them, by the head of the household.
However, precisely because these programs have attempted to provide income security for children this way, we are in the present pre-
dicament of being trapped within an income maintenance system that
is unable to provide adequately for children and yet is criticized for
inequity in providing income and for its tendency to destroy the work
incentive among recipients of income transfers. In short, ironically,
the government's current ways of providing income support for children
are creating the major stumbling blocks to a systematic reform of the
income maintenance system.

A cause of the failure of current income maintenance programs
in providing adequately for children without creating concern for
diminishing work incentives of their parents is that income provision
for children is made contingent upon their parents' work status and

level of earnings. Precisely because the government provides income for children conditionally, depending upon the employment and financial conditions of their parents, the system has created built-in constraints of being unable to provide adequately for children.

LIMITATIONS OF CURRENT INCOME MAINTENANCE PROGRAMS IN PROVIDING INCOME FOR CHILDREN

Let us take an example of the social security programs as a means to provide income support for children and investigate their limitations in doing so.

Part A of Table 7.1 shows the 1977 average social security benefits for children under three different social security programs (OAI, DI, and SI). The average benefits are shown for all children, children whose families come under the rule of maximum family benefits, and children whose families are not affected by such a rule. As discussed in Chapter 6, the rule of maximum family benefits is imposed when the beneficiary family is too large. A family is too large when the sum of benefits of all eligible family members exceeds the maximum family benefit, which ranges from 1.5 to 1.88 times the PIA (the basic benefit for the worker without actuarial reduction), depending on the level of average indexed monthly earnings. (If not affected by the rule of maximum family benefits, each dependent of a retired or disabled worker is entitled to 50 percent of the PIA, and each survivor of a decreased worker, 75 percent of the PIA. When affected by the rule, each dependent or survivor receives a proportionately reduced benefit so that the sum of all benefits of family members equals the maximum family benefit.)

It is clear from Part A that children of families affected by the rule receive, on the average, smaller benefits than children of families not affected by the rule, both absolutely and in proportion to the PIA. For example, children covered under DI received on the average $136 a month if they were born to a family not affected by the rule, but only $74 if born to a family affected by the rule. The average benefit for children of large families—that is, those affected by the rule— amounted to only 25 percent of the PIA, whereas benefits for children of small families amounted to 50 percent of the PIA, which was a statutory entitlement.

Part B of the table indicates that the majority, 51 percent, of all families with children were affected by the rule of maximum family benefits. The situation is especially acute for families receiving disability insurance benefits. Eighty-three percent of families with children that received dependent benefits under DI in 1977 were affected by the rule.

TABLE 7.1

Estimates of Average Monthly Dependent Benefits per Child,* Expressed as Percentage of PIA; Number and Percentage Distribution of Families with Child Beneficiaries; and Number and Percentage Distribution of Child Beneficiaries; by the Effect of the Rule of Maximum Family Benefits and Type of Insurance, 1977

Part A		Average Monthly Dependent Benefit per Child				
	All Benefits		Benefits Not Affected by the Rule of Maximum Family Benefits		Benefits Affected by the Rule of Maximum Family Benefits	
Type of Insurance	Amount	Percent of PIA	Amount	Percent of PIA	Amount	Percent of PIA
Old-age insurance	$89	(37)	$122	(50)	$83	(34)
Disability insurance	78	(27)	136	(50)	74	(25)
Survivors insurance	166	(61)	199	(75)	138	(48)

Part B		Number (in 1,000s) and Percentage Distribution of Families with Child Beneficiaries				
	All Families		Families Not Affected by the Rule of Maximum Family Benefits		Families Affected by the Rule of Maximum Family Benefits	
Type of insurance	Number	Percent	Number	Percent	Number	Percent
Old-age insurance	463	(100)	159	(34)	304	(66)
Disability insurance	755	(100)	125	(17)	630	(83)
Survivors insurance	1,567	(100)	1,078	(69)	489	(31)
All insurance	2,785	(100)	1,362	(49)	1,423	(51)

Part C		Number (in 1,000s) and Percentage Distribution of Child Beneficiaries				
	All Children		Children Not Affected by the Rule of Maximum Family Benefits		Children Affected by the Rule of Maximum Family Benefits	
Type of insurance	Number	Percent	Number	Percent	Number	Percent
Old-age insurance	708	(100)	159	(22)	549	(78)
Disability insurance	1,527	(100)	125	(8)	1,402	(92)
Survivors insurance	2,793	(100)	1,302	(47)	1,491	(53)
All insurance	5,028	(100)	1,586	(32)	3,442	(68)

*Data include 404,000 disabled children age 18 and over and 865,000 students age 18 to 21.

Source: Social Security Bulletin: Annual Statistical Supplement, 1977-1979 (Washington, D.C.: Social Security Administration, 1980), Tables 65 and 105, pp. 117-28, 164-65.

Part C of the table indicates that a great majority of children on social security did not receive statutory percentages of the PIA as their benefits. In all, 68 percent of all children on social security received proportionately reduced benefits due to the ceiling on family benefits. Again the situation is the worst in the case of children under DI. An overwhelming majority of children, 92 percent, did not receive their statutory shares in benefits.

Children of disabled workers do not fare well in receiving adequate benefits compared to children of retired or deceased workers. The reasons are these: Disabled workers are younger than retired workers and consequently tend to have a larger number of children still eligible for dependent benefits. In comparison with children of deceased workers, children of disabled workers must face the fact that disabled workers themselves are beneficiaries. Thus, in comparison with children of retired or deceased workers, children of disabled workers have a greater probability that their families will be subjected to the rule of maximum family benefits. As a result, the probability is high that they receive not the statutory share as their benefits but proportionately reduced benefits.

It is clear from Table 7.1 that the question of whether a child is adequately provided for under social security is a function of family size—a factor totally beyond the control of the child. The larger the size of family, the lesser the income security for the child.

Black children on social security suffer not only from their being born to a large family but also from their parents' level of earnings, which tends to be lower than that of their white counterparts. To compound the situation, as mentioned in Chapter 2, the maximum family benefit is a smaller multiple of the PIA when earnings are low than when they are high—that is, 1.5 times the PIA at the lowest level of earnings and moving up to 1.88 times the PIA as earnings increase to the upper-middle level and tapering off to 1.75 times the PIA as earnings reach the maximum level. However, as PIAs for low-wage workers are a larger proportion of the average indexed monthly earnings, the disadvantage stemming from the maximum family benefits as a smaller multiple of the PIA is offset by the advantage stemming from how the PIA is calculated. Therefore, the factors that significantly disadvantage black children are a large family size and the low levels of earnings by their parents.

Table 7.2 shows average monthly benefits in 1976 for children categorized by race. These benefits are further expressed as a percentage of the average monthly benefits for workers in the case of OAI and DI and as a percentage of the PIA in the case of SI. The effects of the two factors mentioned above are also shown in the table. Lower levels of earnings among black workers are reflected in their lower average benefits (or the PIA in the case of SI). In addition, a larger

TABLE 7.2

Average Monthly Dependent Benefits per Child,* by Race and Type of
Insurance, Expressed as Percentage of Average Monthly Benefits of
Workers (PIA under SI), 1976

Type of Insurance	All	White	Black
Old-age insurance			
Benefits per worker	$224.86	$228.63	$183.16
Benefits per child	85.64	92.92	65.61
As percentage of the worker's benefit	(38)	(41)	(36)
Disability insurance			
Benefits per worker	245.17	251.10	213.75
Benefits per child	68.26	72.57	53.96
As percentage of the worker's benefit	(28)	(29)	(25)
Survivors insurance			
Average PIA of the worker	235.80	†	†
Benefits per child	151.94	162.20	117.94
As percentage of PIA	(64)	†	†

*Data include 382,000 disabled children age 18 and over and
835,000 students age 18 to 21.
†Data not available.
Source: Social Security Bulletin: Annual Statistical Supplement,
1976 (Washington, D.C.: Social Security Administration, 1976),
Tables 68 and 104, pp. 109-19, 149-50.

number of black dependents in a family are forced to share the maximum family benefits that are commensurately smaller than the maximum family benefits for white families. Thus these two factors—low
earnings of black workers and a large family size—together bring
about a decidedly low dependent benefit per black child. In 1976, black
children's average benefit was 71 percent of white children's under
OAI, 74 percent under DI, and 73 percent under SI. Dependent benefits
for black children thus were smaller not only absolutely but also in
relation to the worker's benefit, compared to dependent benefits for
white children.

Inability to ensure economic security for children also prevails
in other types of social insurance programs. Dependent benefits are
almost nonexistent under worker's compensation; only the programs

in Arizona and Vermont provide dependent benefits. The situation is a little better in the case of unemployment insurance, but not much; only ten states and the District of Columbia provide dependent benefits.[1] Lawmakers' hesitation to provide dependent benefits under all insurance programs stems from their belief that social insurance benefits should be earned—that is, benefits should be tied to the level of previous earnings, and furthermore, benefits so obtained should be no greater than what the worker earned before the onset of industrial or social hazards recognized under the law. Provision for children gets in the way of implementing these principles. Therefore, even social security—a social insurance program most dedicated to meeting family needs—cannot provide for an indefinite number of dependents; hence the rule of maximum family benefits.

Welfare programs of all types have been developed to cushion the inability of the economy to provide jobs, the inability of social insurance programs to provide adequate benefits, and the inability of heads of households to participate in the labor force or, if they do, to earn enough to support their dependents. But these programs too have built-in constraints to accomplished such an objective, stemming from the fact that the provision of welfare benefits for families with children is contingent upon the work status and the level of earnings of heads of households. Legislators are always torn between their wish to provide for needy dependents and their fear of destroying the work incentive of heads of households by providing for such dependents.

Legislators' ambivalence is understandable because, in a basically unplanned capitalistic society, those who do not participate in the economic development of a nation should not be provided for more adequately than those who have participated in the past and are currently benefiting from social insurance programs, who in turn should not be provided for more adequately than those who are currently working. Such sequential logic and hierarchical vision of income provision seem essential to keeping the industrial labor force at work without demoralizing the workers. When that vision is blurred and the order of income provision is broken, some segments of society may begin to complain or cease to work.

As a matter of fact, during the past 15 years of rapid development of welfare programs of all types, that vision indeed has been blurred and that order of how families ought to obtain income and how much they should obtain has been distorted. This has occurred because the combined benefits from various welfare programs often are greater in amount than what a full-time minimum-wage worker can earn, let alone what beneficiaries may receive from any social insurance program. Because such distortion has occurred, the incentive to work that would have come naturally from the maintenance of the hierarchical order of income provision has become harder and harder to come by. Or at least the public believes that this is the case.

When the public believes strongly in such a phenomenon, it becomes more real than inconclusive evidence from research findings can demonstrate to the contrary. The result of the perception of the diminishing work incentive stemming from the distorted order of income provision has been an explicit requirement by the government that recipients of welfare benefits either sign up for a manpower training program, accept a job offered by the local employment office, or both. Thus, in the end, the poor obtain welfare benefits that are often greater than what a minimum-wage worker can earn, but in turn they are subjected to governmental coercion to behave in ways the government says they ought to. Although there are signs that the blatant stigma traditionally imposed on welfare recipients is somewhat fading, explicit work requirements by the government are filling the void to accomplish the same purpose: coercing the poor to get out and work. Accepting coercion in a country where personal freedom is highly regarded amounts to accepting the status of a second-class citizen.

Another adverse effect of providing income support for children that is contingent upon the parents' employment status and level of earnings is that the initial intent of adequately aiding needy children soon becomes secondary in importance, and concern for the work behavior of their parents becomes paramount instead. This has occurred in the AFDC program. The initial intent of AFDC was to aid needy children. But during the past 15 years—notwithstanding the increasing rate of labor force participation among women—social legislation has mainly focused on encouraging AFDC mothers to work by such means as the WIN program and benefit formulas that incorporate work incentive measures. Through this process, the original intent of adequately providing for needy children has been undermined; and, instead, encouraging and often coercing AFDC mothers to go out and work have taken over as major policy objectives of the program. Concern for children has become secondary in importance.

One tends to conclude that the thrust of social policy in the past 15 years for ensuring income security to dependent children has been ambiguous. The more the government attempts to provide for dependent children, the more governmental concern there is over the work behavior of their parents. As a result, society is trapped in a dilemma: Helping children ends up with regulating and coercing their parents. One way out of this dilemma is to provide income support for children with no conditions attached to such provision—income support provided to all children in the nation whether or not their parents work and regardless of their level of earnings if they do work. The answer is to explore the idea of children's allowances for the United States.

ROLE OF CHILDREN'S ALLOWANCES IN THE
INCOME MAINTENANCE SYSTEM

Children's allowances are an integral part of the family allowances
that many nations in the world currently provide. Family allowances
may be defined as systematic payments made to families with dependent children, either by employers or by the government, for the
primary purpose of promoting the welfare of families with children.
With such an objective, some countries provide a comprehensive
package of benefits with an intent to enhance the well-being of families
with children. Such a package includes, for instance, in Bolivia, housing allowance, birth grant, nursing allowance, and burial allowance,
in addition to monthly cash payments for each child. Children's allowances refer to periodic cash payments specifically designated for
children as beneficiaries. Thus, in this book, we shall use the term
children's allowances in that sense. Although children's allowances
and family allowances are often used interchangeably, we shall use
them distinctly.

Children's allowances originated in France in the 1870s, when
several French administrative services and railways began paying
allocations familiales as an addition to the regular wages of workers
with families to support. The provision for children as family dependents, however, was made in substance even earlier. In 1795, the
British Speenhamland system, instead of raising wages, provided
"relief, in cases where there are a number of children, a matter of
right, and an honor instead of a ground for opprobrium and contempt."[2]
Thus children's allowances as we know them today have had a history
of continuous development for more than a century; they have been
adopted in some form by 69 nations. Among these are all 28 European
countries and 24 countries in Africa, most of which were formerly
French territories or colonies. There are two programs in Asia
(Japan and Kambuchea), two in Oceania (Australia and New Zealand),
three in the Middle East (Iran, Israel, and Lebanon), and ten in the
Americas (Argentina, Bolivia, Brazil, Chile, Colombia, Costa Rica,
Cuba, Paraguay, and Uruguay).[3]

Although the idea of children's allowances is relatively foreign
to the public in the United States, the adoption of such a program
would solve many problems in regard to the welfare mess discussed
earlier and would further enable this nation to free itself from the dilemma of aiding the children versus being concerned with the work
incentive of their parents.

Economic Impact of Children's Allowances on the Poor

A program of children's allowances does not cover all the poor, but it does cover the largest single group among the poor—poor families with children. In 1978, 77 percent of all poor families had one or more children. Of all poor families with children, 61 percent were headed by females and the rest, 39 percent, were headed by males. Seventy-two percent of such male heads worked some time during the year, of whom 89 percent worked full time the year around. Forty-two percent of such female heads with children had some work experience during the year, of whom 63 percent worked full time the year around.[4] Thus, while children's allowances are not targeted to the poor they benefit both nonworking and working poor families with children. Working poor families have traditionally been neglected by welfare programs in this country.

The Question of Work Incentive

There are two questions about the work incentive. The first asks, "Does a person who has been working choose to stop working or work less if given an outright grant?" The second asks, "Does a person stop working or work less when benefits are reduced as earnings increase?" The first question relates to the income effect that results in reducing work effort. The second question relates to both substitution and income effects. Here the substitution effect results in reducing work effort, but the income effect results in increasing work effort. These effects were discussed in Chapter 5. All income maintenance programs that provide outright grants are affected by the first question. A program of children's allowances is no exception. However, it is not affected by the second question. The current welfare programs that incorporate provisions to reduce benefits by a fraction of earnings are vulnerable to the second question as well. A program of children's allowances would provide allowances to all eligible children regardless of family income and thus would not impose a tax on the income of the poor. It would not be too closely involved in the first question about work incentive either, as allowances would not be enough to move the family out of poverty without income from other sources. Hence, it is expected that policymakers need not be as concerned about the question of the work incentive in regard to children's allowances as they would be in regard to benefits from income-tested transfer programs.

Another important point is that a program of children's allowances would move families out of poverty in most cases, if the heads were able to work—that is, were not sick and unemployable and if jobs were available to those who could work. Those families who would stay poor after a program of children's allowances was put into effect are the ones who are poor not because they do not have the incentive to work but because they cannot work. Other programs supplemental to a program of children's allowances could then be targeted primarily at the people who are poor for reasons of disability and unemployability, without much concern about the question of the work incentive.

Stigma and the Preservation of Human Dignity

An income maintenance program should not influence recipients' behavior or their perception of themselves and others in a negative way. Recipients should have the utmost freedom of choice in their lifestyle and the ways they spend transfer payments. One way to achieve this objective is to make the status of recipients independent of the status of poverty. For example, veterans' compensation and civil service pensions satisfy this criterion. On the contrary, welfare programs using eligibility based on need create a clear relationship between the status of the poor and the receipt of transfer payments, whatever administrative methods are used. They remain public programs to feed the poor, financed by the nonpoor, and some degree of stigma is bound to be attached to such programs. There is a polarization of the poor and the nonpoor, aggravated by racial problems here in the United States.

A program of children's allowances, in contrast to welfare programs, seems able to achieve these goals. Because allowances are provided to both rich and poor children, the program would not divide the community into groups of those who receive the allowances and those who pay for them. Another characteristic that distinguishes this program from welfare programs is that children's allowances are provided in a way that may prevent poverty from occurring, whereas welfare programs deal with the problem of income insecurity only after it has occurred. Because the government intervenes in a preventive manner through children's allowances, the public may consider the allowances as an investment in the human capital of future generations. In contrast, the public tends to feel negative and often helpless about providing for those who have "failed." When people associate a sense of hope for the future well-being of the nation with a program of children's allowances, they may in turn feel positive not only about the program itself but also about the recipients of the program's benefits.

Unlike current welfare programs, children's allowances would touch the lives of families at a crucial life stage of families. They benefit families at times when they need extra income to raise and educate children. The program would also help families with older children who might avoid having to leave school to go to work for purely economic reasons.[5] Helping otherwise poor children stay in school may be one means of breaking the intergenerational cycle of poverty.

Relationship with Other Programs

A program of children's allowances would increase the effectiveness of social insurance and minimum wage provisions in relation to the poor, whereas current welfare programs weaken them. Welfare benefits diminish the value of minimum wages and social insurance in relation to current or past work effort. On the other hand, it is impossible to convert minimum wages and earnings-related social insurance benefits to meet the needs of all sizes of families, as mentioned earlier. If they were adjusted to family size, the principles of earnings-related contributions and earnings-related benefits would be destroyed. A free economy is not expected to adjust minimum wages to family size, either. Therefore, children's allowances could free earnings-related social insurance and minimum wages from providing for an indefinite number of dependents. With children's allowances, social insurance could establish an adequate and equitable benefit schedule for the insured. Likewise, minimum wages could focus on providing for workers and their dependent spouses.

If children's allowances were introduced, current income-tested programs would remain supplemental programs but their scope would be greatly reduced. The especially controversial programs of AFDC and AFDC-UP would be almost eliminated upon enactment of a program of children's allowances as long as heads of households could earn enough to support themselves. Those who would still need governmental support as well as children's allowances would be families whose heads could not work—the disabled, the blind, the aged, and the single parents of preschool children. The question of work incentive is less important for these groups than for other groups of individuals.

Effects of Children's Allowances on the Near Poor

Past efforts to reform welfare emphasized economizing on a transfer program by targeting its benefits to the poor. But the public might have opposed the program precisely because the benefits went only to the poor. As the late Whitney M. Young, Jr., stated, a strong political resistance might come from lower-middle-class persons who think economic success is a product of their own effort and poverty is the fault of the poor.[6]

A classic study by Robert Lane of the political beliefs of blue-collar workers indicates that they do not have much sympathy for the poor. The study cites findings from a Gallup poll in 1964, which found that 54 percent of those blue-collar workers who responded said the cause of poverty was individual lack of effort, in comparison with 46 percent who said the cause was circumstances.[7] Various facts about people's attitudes toward welfare for the poor seem to indicate that a new program involving additional public funds must be attractive to the nonpoor if it is to gain their support. "A new program that offers increased benefits to the poor alone is likely to arouse strong and perhaps fatal opposition from lower-middle-income groups, whereas a program that benefits near poor in a manner palatable to them as well as the poor could gain wide support."[8]

Including the bulk of the near poor as beneficiaries of a new program is politically expedient and possibly could ensure improvement of the system. If a new income maintenance program is directed strictly at the poor, outside pressure must be developed each time it needs an improvement. The poor, a minority group, have had little political power. There is a clear relationship between a wide range of beneficiaries and constant improvement in social security programs. When, like the situation in social security, a great majority of the public both contribute to an income maintenance program and benefit from it some time in their lifetime, the program is expected to have strong public support for its maintenance and improvement.

A program of children's allowances seems to meet the requirements of these political realities: It benefits all families with children. It is financed by all taxpayers in a country. And it would have a sustained body of constituents for its preservation and enhancement.

Simple Administration

The administration of the program of children's allowances that would provide universal flat-rate allowances would be simpler than that of the income-tested programs now operating in the United States. For the administration of a program of children's allowances, all that is required is verification of the age of the children. Once eligibility has been established, benefits would be paid automatically until children reached the age at which they were no longer eligible.

Simple administration can prevent administrative errors in benefit calculation from occurring and frauds from being committed by recipients. The administrator of an income-tested program must be alert to enforce accurate reporting of income and to calculate benefits based on complex requirements for eligibility. A program administered under complex legal arrangements always produces some errors in the calculation of benefits. Also, it is easier for recipients to commit frauds and harder for the administrators to detect them when income support is provided under a complex set of legally defined circumstances. An Urban Institute study reports that administrative errors occur more often than frauds. For instance, in 1975-76, AFDC had a 21.5 percent rate of administrative error, compared to a 1.8 percent rate of fraud.[9] In any case, the complexity involved in current welfare programs creates inequity in income provision to eligible families, whether caused by administrative errors or frauds committed by recipients.

Under a program of children's allowances, the burden of making periodical payments would rest with the government; under welfare programs the burden of applying for assistance rests with the poor. Thus a program of children's allowances could ensure the equitable distribution of benefits to all eligible children. There are always a certain number of poor families who fail to apply and hence fail to benefit from a program that involves a means test or an income test.

Furthermore, as discussed earlier, complex requirements for eligibility and regulations associated with current welfare programs place poor families under constant pressure from the government to report, behave, and regulate their lives according to the legislative intent of welfare programs. A regulated lifestyle is imposed on recipients of many current welfare programs. In contrast, the simple administration that a program of children's allowances requires could eliminate such a superordinate-subordinate relationship between the government and beneficiary families. The energy that welfare recipients now use for posturing defensively against bureaucrats might be freed for the positive development of their lives, if they received children's allowances instead.

Large Expenditures Required

All these positive features of a program of children's allowances need to be weighed against the relatively large outlay required to provide them. Because allowances would be provided to all children under a certain age regardless of the income level of families, the program would be costlier than an income-tested program. Even if allowances were declared taxable, there still would be spillover benefits to nonpoor children. But precisely because allowances are provided to all children whether or not their parents work, the administration of the program would be simple and the work incentives of their parents could be preserved. The preventive approach that a program of chil-

dren's allowances takes and its simple administration are conducive
to the maintenance of human dignity. In short, like any other income
maintenance program, a program of children's allowances cannot
have it both ways. All the advantageous features of children's allowances would not come about if they were provided in a manner similar
to the way income-tested benefits are provided. This is an ultimate
trade-off that policymakers have to make. James McCamy, a political
scientist, asserts that Americans still prefer governmental responsiveness to efficiency. They want the government to do what they need
and want it to do. They count the cost second.[10] A program that makes
sense to the public is not necessarily an economical one.

ARGUMENTS ON CHILDREN'S ALLOWANCES

So the idea of a program of children's allowances sounds positive in
that it has the potential to solve many problems associated with the
ways in which income transfers are provided through current income
maintenance programs in the United States. But the idea is relatively
foreign to the public, possibly because of lack of experience with such
a program. Therefore, it is instructive to review and discuss arguments advanced in the past and in other countries about the program.

The sense of social equity seems strong behind the development
of children's allowances. Benefits are provided to equalize the burden
of child rearing. They are a deliberate way of achieving horizontal
redistribution and to some extent vertical redistribution of income
from childless families to those with children.

When the issue of social equity in sharing responsibility for
children was discussed by the Canadian Parliament in 1945—a year
before children's allowances were put into effect in that country—the
prime minister quoted statistics to show that 84 percent of the children
under age 16 were depending on 19 percent of the gainfully employed.[11]
In 1942 the Beveridge Report pointed out that one quarter to one sixth
of the poverty in England was the result of failure to relate earned
income to family size.[12]

In the United States, too, a disproportionately small number of
families bear an excessive burden in rearing children. In 1978, the
total 61 million children under age 18 were cared for by 54 percent of
the families. A relatively large number of children were concentrated
in a relatively small number of large-size families. For example,
45 percent of all children were in only 14 percent of all families who
had three or more children. The distribution of children was severely
skewed also among poor families: 63 percent of all poor children were
born to the 31 percent of all poor families who had three or more children. Putting statistics about poverty in a different perspective, poor

children constituted 16 percent of all children in the United States but were concentrated in 7 percent of all families.

The situation was bleak on the income front as related to family size. In 1978, the median family deficit (or the poverty gap) for families of three was $1,871 but for families of six, $2,854. These were the amounts necessary to bring the family income up to the poverty line. If a child was born to a family of six or more, that child's probability of being poor was 42 percent, in contrast to 10 percent for an only child. [13]

The idea of social equity and justice implies that all children, while growing up, should be provided with minimum welfare. Children's allowances purport to ease the handicap of children born to large families. They are offered to implement the

. . . ultimate right of every child irrespective of background, place of living, income of parents, and so on, to be welcomed, to have an economically and socially secure childhood and adolescence, with equal opportunities for a good start in life and equal access to educational opportunities in order to develop his full potentialities. [14]

What are the effects of children's allowances on a nation's general economy? [15] Keynesian economists believe that children's allowances help stabilize the economy and ensure stable employment in a basically unplanned capitalistic society. They further believe that full employment hinges on maintaining sufficiency in the effective aggregate demand. This in turn depends on the levels of consumption and investment. A program of children's allowances, if financed by progressive taxes, would help keep the consumption level higher than otherwise because it would facilitate vertical redistribution of income from rich families to poor families with children. The poor generally have a higher marginal propensity to consume than the well-to-do. They would be quite likely to spend their allowances promptly and wholly. According to the multiplier principle, this initial expenditure by the poor would bring about multiple economic transactions during the course of a year. Furthermore, according to the principle of acceleration, added expenditures for consumption would also result in more expenditures for investment. Thus a program of children's allowances is a good economic policy when the economy is in a recession. The reverse is true when the economy is in an upswing. In spite of the risk during an overheated economy, children's allowances— like any unseasonal transfer payments such as the old-age pensions provided in many countries—would help stabilize the economy. However, the effect of children's allowances in stabilizing the economy might be less than that of other types of income transfers, such as unemployment insurance benefits, which are known to have a built-in countercyclical force. That is, unlike children's allowances, unemployment insurance benefits are provided precisely at times of economic recession and tend to be withdrawn when the economy picks up. Unemployment insurance benefits have a countercyclical power to soften the blow of economic ups and downs, but children's allowances do not.

Not all economists are in favor of children's allowances—or any other type of transfer payments, for that matter. Advocates of orthodox economic principles oppose children's allowances for several reasons. First, children's allowances, like any governmental intervention in economic activities, would impede free competition and eventually result in uneconomic utilization of resources. Second, children's allowances would conflict with the basic principles of the capitalistic system, in which all are to be rewarded, not according to their needs but according to their contribution to the general economy. Third, children's allowances would create a powerful drive toward socialism. Fourth, if financed by progressive taxation, children's allowances would reduce the capacity and the incentive for the rich to save and invest. This in turn would discourage innovation and invention, which are real sources of economic progress, and consequently could adversely affect standards of living. Fifth, for advance in the economy, human beings should not have excessive security but a balance between reasonable security and reasonable exposure to the risks in life.

Indeed, to neoclassical economists, now called supply-side economists, children's allowances are an anathema, especially if they are financed by progressive taxes. In the minds of these neoclassicists, economic growth does not depend on effective consumption but rather on incentives to work, save, and invest. These incentives come precisely from lowered tax rates. Susan Lee expresses it this way:

> That is, reducing marginal rates lowers the relative price
> of work in the trade-off between work and leisure, and
> lowers the relative price of investment in the trade-off
> between investment and consumption. All of this is a long
> way to say that the more you can keep of the next dollar
> you earn, the more likely you are to go earn that dollar.[16]

The progressive income taxes for financing children's allowances suggest a threat to the whole foundation on which supply-side economics is based.

Keynesian economists believe that consumption by the poor that was financed by public income transfers salvaged this country from the depression of the 1930s. Supply-side economists now believe that savers and investors, not consumers, will help revitalize the economy.

But not all believers of supply-side economics are against children's allowances. For example, David A. Stockman, Director of the Office of Management and Budget, advocated what he called "the universal child payment system" in his 1978 article, "Welfare is the Problem," in the Journal of Institute for Socioeconomic Studies (3, Fall 1978: 39-50). Stockman believes that universal child payments do not create such adverse side effects as those associated with the current income-tested welfare programs. George Gilder, another believer of supply-side economics, advocates children's allowances in his recent book, Wealth and Poverty (New York: Basic Books, 1981). He, like Stockman, is appalled by work disincentives created by the current welfare programs and believes children's allowances to be superior to AFDC or AFDC-U in helping low-income families. More important, he believes, children's allowances could avoid the moral hazards of the war on poverty while giving support to the most welfare-prone families because they do not create an incentive to stay poor.

How do children's allowances stand in the political arena? Political leaders in countries that have instituted children's allowances have encountered opposition and doubt about the program—or, on the other hand, have gained support for it—because of various political issues. [17] One such issue is the effect on population. Will children's allowances cause an increase in population? This possibility is considered to be a serious deterring factor in countries with a high birthrate and a positive factor in countries with a declining birthrate. For instance, in the early 1930s France and Sweden discovered a so-called population crisis with steadily declining birthrates, and they wished to reverse the trend. [18] Germany and Italy also wished to increase their populations for military reasons. All four countries have introduced children's allowances. Among the countries desiring an increase in population, some are also concerned with the quality of child welfare. Sweden is a good example. The Swedish government publicly encourages voluntary birth control but believes that community resources should be available and utilized by children whose parents want and welcome them. Children thus born are ensured higher quality parental care, so it is believed. [19]

Although many nations have instituted children's allowances with the legislative intent that the program would contribute to an increase in population, there is no evidence that this has occurred. Paul Douglas's study in 1927 indicated that, in spite of expanded per capita children's allowances and wider coverage, the number of children per family in France remained unchanged, namely, 1.66. [20] Comparison of birthrates in Canada and the United States also seems to indicate that the rise and fall in birthrates is not connected with children's allowances. Although Canada adopted children's allowances in 1945 and the United States did not, statistics show that since 1925 the patterns of birthrates in the two countries have been strikingly similar. [21]

A more recent study shows that children's allowances are in fact inversely related to birthrates: The higher the allowance, the lower the birthrate. [22] Such a trend may be observed also from what has been happening in France lately. In spite of constant improvement in the level of benefits, the scope of the program, and the coverage for children and their families, France since 1975 has been experiencing a population decline. That nation is not reproducing enough to maintain the current level of population. [23]

Concern for a probable increase in rates of illegitimacy might be raised if the United States decided to launch a program of children's allowances, as the public has long suspected that AFDC encourages the breeding of illegitimate children. A study by Phillips Cutright indicates that there is no relationship between the levels of children's allowances and rates of illegitimacy in countries that provide the allowances. For example, in France in 1966 women aged 30 to 34 had a lower rate of illegitimacy than their counterparts in the United Kingdom, although women in France received much larger children's allowances (expressed as a percentage of wages) than did women in Great Britain. On the other hand, these French women had a higher rate of illegitimacy than their counterparts in the Netherlands, although women in France received larger children's allowances than those in the Netherlands. As a matter of fact, the rate of illegitimacy in the United States, which does not provide children's allowances, was higher than the rate in seven of the eight nations in the study that are providing the allowances. [24]

Despite the public's fear, rates of illegitimacy do not have much to do with the level of AFDC payments either. The Cutright study indicates that there is no relationship between rates of illegitimacy and levels of AFDC payments in states. Although black women tend to have a higher rate of illegitimacy, the rate is not related to the level of the AFDC payments they received in different states. [25] Another study by Cutright and John Scanzoni indicates that family breakups are not related to the level of AFDC payments in the state. The percentage of families with children with two parents at home was the same both in 1960 and 1970, regardless of the level of AFDC payments in the state. Of course, the percentage of such families declined during the ten-year period between 1960 and 1970, but this occurred across the country, quite independently of the difference in AFDC payments among states. [26]

Would men lose the incentive to work to support their families once a program of children's allowances was put into effect? An earlier discussion on the income effect and the substitution effect involved in income maintenance programs dealt with this question.

Expectedly, children's allowances are less detrimental to the preservation of the work incentive than current income-tested programs. But a similar question arose when a state endowment plan for mothers was proposed in Great Britain during the 1920s. One of the British critics who expressed anxiety about diminished parental responsibility for children was F. Y. Edgeworth, an economist. He stated: "It does not require much knowledge of human nature to justify the apprehension that in relieving the average house-father from the necessity of providing necessaries for his family, you would remove a great part of incentive to work."[27]

Later, Eleanor Rathbone, a strong advocate of children's allowances in Britain in the 1920s and 1930s, claimed that parents' need and love for children transcend economic responsibility for children. She said:

> Granted that poverty and dependency, like war, do often call out what is finest in human nature—its capacity for endurance and self-sacrifice, the triumph of the spiritual over the material—do they not also call out what is best? And are they necessary to the full manifestation of their finer things? Do not the unalterable facts of human life— the miracles of marriage and birth, the helplessness of infancy, sickness and old age, the infirmities of character which make us all such a trial to our nearest—do not these give to human nature ample room and occasion to rise to the full measure of its stature? It would be a poor look-out for the institution of the family if it were really held together by the bond of £.s.d. But it is held together by something much stronger—by the call of the blood; by the memory of experiences enjoyed or endured together; above all by Nature herself, who makes the man need the woman, the woman the man and both the child.[28]

Arguments advanced by Edgeworth and Rathbone give a glimpse of contrasting orientations in sexes in regard to understanding how parents may react to public income transfers on behalf of children. To Edgeworth, who is a male intellectual, having another child could be put in a simple economic equation. Having a child entitles the child's family to children's allowances, and that in turn influences the child's parents to slow down in work effort. If Edgeworth were alive today, he probably would argue that AFDC mothers would have another child just to obtain extra income from the program. A male, for whom child-bearing is not such a physically and emotionally significant, and sometimes traumatic, experience as it is for a female, may find it relatively easy to reason this way.

Rathbone, a female political activist, would have viewed the situation differently. For a woman, the decision to have another child may not be made from a narrow economic interest but in a broader, more complex perspective. For example, political uncertainty, a decaying economy, the fear of a nuclear war, or the fear of environmental pollution may be of much more concern to a woman in deciding whether to have another child. The idea that the government provides a certain minimum income for that child seems to be a rather peripheral issue for a woman. Of course, if a woman wants a child, children's allowances would help her go through the vicissitudes of bearing and raising it. However, it is unlikely for a woman to reverse her inclination not to have a child and to have one just because the government provides children's allowances. If women in fact did thus change their minds, many countries such as France that attempted to increase population through the provision of children's allowances would have long since succeeded in achieving their policy goal.

Another implied issue stemming from the arguments by Edgeworth and Rathbone is that Edgeworth assumed that parents see a certain fixed level of well-being for their children, whereas Rathbone assumed that parents aspire to an infinitely rising level of well-being for their children as more resources become available. According to Edgeworth, if the government subsidized the cost of raising children, parents could decrease their responsibility for raising children by that much. In contrast, Rathbone believed that parents would aspire to infinitely expanding possibilities for their children. If the government subsidized the cost of child rearing, such subsidies would not decrease but rather increase parents' wish to do more for their children.

These different orientations between Edgeworth and Rathbone in regard to parental responsibility for children in turn might lead to their different prognoses as to whether children's allowances would result in an increase in population. Because Edgeworth assumed a fixed level of well-being for children, he might have also assumed that parents would have a larger number of children if the government subsidized the cost of raising children. But Rathbone would have reached just the opposite conclusion. Because Rathbone assumed that parents tend to emphasize quality of life for their children as they become more secure economically, she would have concluded that children's allowances would influence parents to have fewer children, not more.

What have been the reactions of unions to children's allowances? Some unions in some countries have favored children's allowances and some have not. Catholic labor unions have usually been partial to them. For example, Catholic unions in Belgium approved of them, but for large families only. Union support in that instance was motivated more by the wish to ban birth control than the desire to ensure a minimum of well-being for all children. In the Netherlands, socialist unions opposed a program of children's allowances on the grounds that (1) it tends to keep wages low and is thus acceptable only to the employer; (2) it is an attempt, under the pretext of "payment according to needs," to avoid the introduction of an adequate standard of minimum wages; and (3) it weakens union solidarity between workers with large families and childless workers and hence undermines union collective bargaining efforts—and this, in turn, perpetuates existing inadequate wages.[29]

Union suspicions were not totally unwarranted. In France, for example, private establishments launched children's allowances after the First World War on either a regional or industrial basis, partly to avoid increases in wage levels and partly as a result of concern about the declining population, national patriotism, and paternalism toward workers.[30] Nonetheless, employers' objective of holding down wages was clear in those days. Union criticism, however, has been paradoxical in its logic. When dealing with outside forces, unions strove toward the socialistic principle of "to each according to his needs," and the concept of a living wage was their hue and cry. But within the union, members wanted to keep the well-established capitalist rule of "equal pay for equal work."[31] In short, unions appeared enthusiastic for vertical redistribution of income but not for horizontal redistribution.

Unions' apprehension about children's allowances seems to have dissipated as time went on. Again in France, after World War II, as children's allowances came to be provided under governmental auspices and paid independently of the breadwinner's wage levels, the idea of children's right to economic security emerged, along with the concept of equalizing the burden of child rearing. One theme has persisted: Children's allowances make up for a discrepancy between, on the one hand, wages and their derivatives (for example, social insurance benefits) that are not based on family size and, on the other hand, family needs that depend on family size.

As children's allowances have become an institution in many countries, criticism of the program as a depressant of wages appears to have subsided. Indeed, because unions in all industrialized countries are much stronger than when children's allowances came into being, the provision of children's allowances by the government seems to have had little influence on union bargaining with management. The concern of unions about children's allowances as a possible depressant of wages can therefore be minimized if children's allowances are programmed by the government rather than by industrial organizations and are financed by some form of general revenue rather than by employer or employee contributions or both, so that they are independent of the wage system and collective bargaining.

POLICY ISSUES IN PROGRAM DEVELOPMENT

Once the United States decided to adopt a program of children's allowances, policymakers would need to decide what type of program is most appropriate. The major policy issues related to the development of a program of children's allowances—the issues that all countries with such a program must face—are the following:

- Whether to adopt a universal or employment-related program
- Whether the allowance should commence with the first child or after the family reaches a certain size
- The level of the allowance
- Whether the allowance is to be the same for all eligible children, or to vary with the age or order of the child
- Whether the allowance should be wage-related or uniform
- Whether to condition eligibility on some kind of income test
- What adjustments, if any, to make in the tax treatment of families with children
- Whether the allowance is to be a substitute for, or an addition to, benefits from other income maintenance programs
- The method of financing the program[32]

These issues are not necessarily mutually exclusive. They will be discussed seriatim, with references made to experiences in other countries whenever possible.

Universal Versus Employment-Related Program

Whether a nation opts for a universal or an employment-related program of children's allowances has important ramifications on the distribution of benefits and also on the extent to which other income maintenance programs have to supplement children's allowances. Currently four out of every five programs of children's allowances in the world are employment-related and the rest are universal. Universal programs, although fewer in number, have been adopted by relatively more industrially advanced countries such as Australia, Canada, France, and Sweden, which have had a long tradition of providing children's allowances. In contrast, employment-related programs are widely used in developing nations of Africa and South America. Unlike universal programs, which provide allowances to all children regardless of the employment conditions of their parents, employment-related programs provide allowances contingent upon the work records of the children's parents. In some countries, parents not only must be currently working but also must show at least a minimum degree of attachment to the labor force during the month or the year. An employment-related program of Tunisia provides allowances that are in direct proportion to the wages of parents, although such a computational method is rare.

Employment-related programs may have the legislative intent of adding the work incentive to participants in the labor force and also to some extent the objective of minimizing labor costs. However, such

a program, if adopted, would fail to reach children of parents who do
not work. In 1978, 10 percent of the heads of all families in the United
States who had children under age 18 did not work at all. The incidence
of poverty among such families was 60 percent. The situation was
gloomier among black families. One quarter of the heads of black
families with children under age 18 did not work. The incidence of
poverty among such black families was 75 percent.[33]

If an employment-related program was adopted in the United
States, allowances would go to families who already have some degree
of income security through employment; they would not go to nonworking families who especially need them. The antipoverty effects of such
a program would therefore not be as effective as those of a universal
program. Furthermore, an employment-related program would call
for a larger role being played by income-tested programs to meet
the income needs of nonworking families.

An employment-related program would be difficult to administer,
especially in a country like the United States, where many heads of
families work part time. In 1978, 20 percent of the working heads of
families with children under 18 worked less than a full year. It is
difficult to draw a line between working and nonworking parents in
order to determine which children are eligible for children's allowances.

For these reasons the adoption of an employment-related program is not recommended for the United States. Such a program would
not be effective in solving the problems discussed in earlier chapters.

Coverage of Children

Of the 69 programs in the world, 53 pay children's allowances
beginning with the first child; the rest provide other forms of coverage. Three countries start payment with the second child, Japan and
Mauritius start with the third child, and the Soviet Union starts with
the fourth child. In contrast, 10 countries favor children born earlier
in order, ranging from the first two children in Iran to the first nine
children in Romania. The form of coverage that a country adopts is
related to its population policy. Countries encouraging the increase
of population tend to favor children born later in order. Countries
alarmed by an explosive increase of population favor children born
earlier in order; they thus limit the number of eligible children per
family.

Minimizing public expenditures for a program of children's
allowances may be a factor in a country's choice of the form of coverage. If the United States—instead of providing allowances at a uniform
rate for all children—chose to provide them only to the second and
subsequent children in a family, 50 percent of the benefit cost could
be saved, based on 1978 data. By so doing, however, 41 percent of
the poor children would be bypassed. By not providing allowances to

first and second children, as much as 80 percent of the benefit cost would be saved, but 70 percent of the poor children would by bypassed.[34]

Economy achieved by limiting coverage to later children is one thing. Economic efficiency related to antipoverty effects is another. If the United States had paid children's allowances in 1965 and had used the payment level of $50 a month per child advocated by Mollie Orshansky (the amount equivalent to poverty-line income needed to support a child in that year), the antipoverty effectiveness would have been reduced to less than half by not covering the first and second children.[35] That is, such a program would have pulled 64 percent of poor families out of poverty if it covered all children, but merely 29 percent if it covered only third and subsequent children.

Administrative efficiency should also be considered in deciding the form of coverage. If the United States chose not to provide children's allowances to families with only one child, 39 percent of all families with children, including 29 percent of all poor families with children, would be out of the program, based on 1978 data. If allowances were not provided to families with one or two children, 75 percent of all families with children, including 60 percent of all poor families with children, would be out of the program.[36] This way the scope of administration could be minimized by removing families with one or two children from coverage, but a different kind of administrative complexity is introduced. In addition to showing the order of each child and number of children born to a family, records would have to differentiate between families with three or more children and those with one or two, in order to establish eligibility for children's allowances.

Level of Allowance

The benefit level of children's allowances varies among countries. For example, the Canadian programs offers a modest average amount of $16.50 a month per child up to age 17, which many provinces supplement with additional payments. The Swedish program offers 2,500 kronor per year for each child under age 16—approximately $490 a year at the current exchange rate, but probably equivalent to a higher amount in purchasing power.

Children's allowances can be developed either for partial or full support of a physical minimum for children. In this country, benefit levels ranging from $10 to $50 a month per child were proposed during the late 1960s.[37] the highest amount, $50, was equivalent to the personal exemption allowed in the income tax law in those days and also roughly equivalent to the poverty-line income needed to support a dependent child living in a family.

The antipoverty effect of a program of children's allowances is in direct relationship to the level of the allowances. The greater the provision per child, the greater the proportion of poor families removed from poverty. Orshansky indicated that if in 1965 the United States had provided children's allowances of $50 per month per child, 64 percent of all poor families would have been removed from poverty. With a more modest provision of $25, only 36 percent of poor families would have been removed from poverty. At either rate, a relatively larger percentage of poor families would have been removed from poverty as the number of children in a family increased. Under the program of $50 for every child, 97 percent of poor families with six or more children would have been removed from poverty, whereas only 30 percent of poor families with one child would have been removed.[38] Therefore it is conceivable that, if a program of children's allowances was instituted the government might adopt $100 a month per child (or $1,200 a year) as the level of the allowance. This amount would have been required to support a dependent child living in a family at the 1979 poverty-line level.[39] (In interpreting the findings by Orshansky, great caution is required because she assumed the continuation of all existing programs that benefit children.)

Uniform Versus Differential Provision

The program of children's allowances in Uruguay provides differential allowances based on the age of the child. Children of elementary school age are provided 11 pesos a month, and those of secondary school age 22 pesos a month. The Australian program is based on the order of child. In 1979, the first child received A$15.20 a month, the second child A$21.70, the third or fourth child A$26.00, and the fifth or subsequent children A$30.35. The Canadian scheme also follows the order of child in differentiating children's allowances. Most nations using the order of child as a basis for rates of children's allowances are adopting a progressive scale as in Australia. A few countries such as Bulgaria and France provide a higher allowance for children in the middle, with earlier and later children receiving a lower amount.

The factors involved in deciding the kind of scale to adopt are mainly demographic and administrative. Countries wishing to increase their population tend to use a progressive scale. However, programs of children's allowances become administratively complicated when order of child or age differential is introduced. That is why Beveridge, in his 1942 report, recommended a uniform rate of 8s. per week to the second and each subsequent child.[40] (Beveridge assumed that the cost of raising the first child could be met by the parents' earnings.)

Douglas also recommended a uniform rate for the United States for administrative reasons.[41]

A case can be made for a decreasing rate with an increasing number of children. This argument is based on the fact that family living expenses do not increase proportionately as the number of children increases. On the other hand, a larger number of children is more likely to require the mother to stay at home, thus depriving the family of a second income. A case can be made for paying higher rates of allowances for children because of increasing costs of raising older children. On the other hand, as children become older, there is more opportunity for the mother to go out and work.

At any rate, in a country such as the United States, where three levels of government woud be involved in tracing the age or order of children, the administrative complexity of providing variable rates based on age or order of child might override the favorable considerations for such rates. Therefore it might be a sensible policy choice to use a uniform rate of allowances with universal coverage.

Flat Rate Versus Wage-Related Allowances

Most programs of children's allowances provide a flat rate of payments according to age or order of child or a universal rate that is the same for all children. However, some countries, such as Tunisia, offer wage-related allowances. These are calculated in a manner similar to the way social security benefits are calculated. Thus the Tunisian program provides graduated allowances as earnings of employees increase. On the other hand, the Australian program until 1941 used a tapering scale favoring low-wage earners. It divided wage earners into 12 brackets. As a worker went up each step from the bottom earnings bracket, the children's allowance payment was decreased by one-twelfth until it finally became zero.[42]

It is of interest to note that social reformers in Britain were advocates of children's allowances for the well-to-do. The London School of Economics had adopted a program of children's allowances at the recommendation of Beatrice and Sidney Webb long before the government enacted a public program of children's allowances in 1945.[43] In 1921, William MacDougall, a British economist, recommended a public program of children's allowances that would pay 10 percent of parents' earnings to each child.[44] Beveridge also recommended supplemental children's allowances by employers to high-wage workers.[45] The motive of their suggesting such schemes was their concern about the declining birthrate among middle-class and upper-class families. The social progress of Britain, they thought, required a greater number of children born to professors, lawyers, scientists, and so on.

If a program of children's allowances was developed in the United States as an antipoverty instrument, it is clear that neither regressive nor proportional scales related to wage levels would accomplish the desired objective. The progressive scale used by Australia until 1941 makes more sense. However, once rates of children's allowances are related to wages, they create two problems: administrative complexity and the introduction of a form of income test—and income tests, as this author argued earlier, should be minimized in the American system of income maintenance. If the concentration of payments on low-income families is desired, there are alternatives to bring this about. These include the abolition of personal exemptions in the federal income tax law and the inclusion of children's allowances in taxable income. Financing the program by a progressive tax is another approach to bringing about a similar end. More on this later.

Flat-Rate Versus Income-Tested Allowances

Countries that incorporate an income test in programs of children's allowances tend to take a two-tier approach to providing children's allowances: the first tier providing flat-rate payments and the second tier providing allowances based on need. Second-tier payments are similar to AFDC payments in the United States. New Zealand, the Soviet Union, and Belgium take this approach. Romania and Yugoslavia provide all children's allowances on the basis of need. At any rate, income testing is relatively rare in programs of children's allowances now in operation.

If the United States developed a program of children's allowances based on need, it could incorporate income testing that takes one of the following policy options: (1) uniform payments to a certain limited number of children in all families and equal payments to other children of poor families only; (2) full payments to each child in families below a certain income level and a fraction of the full payments to each child in families above that income level; (3) uniform payments to all children supplemented by special allowances to children in poor families; or (4) uniform payments confined to all children in poor families. All four policy options would require refinement in administrative rules so that such a notch problem as that widely noticed in the current Medicaid program could be avoided. In other words, these policy options would end with income testing similar to procedures now used in AFDC, SSI, and food stamps, if such a notch problem is to be avoided.

Policy options 1 and 4 arouse concern related to the policy regarding population. Under policy option 1, all children of families below a certain income would receive children's allowances, but only a limited number of children of families above that level would receive allowances. Under policy option 4, only children of poor families would receive children's allowances. The United States is not yet alarmed about a declining birthrate, and even if it should face a population crisis such as experienced in European countries, the public might still dislike a public policy that appears to encourage poor families to have more children but not encourage nonpoor families to do so. At such a time, policymakers, whether liberal or conservative, might decide that they prefer to aid middle-income and upper-income families to have more children, as did social reformers in Great Britain.

Provision of children's allowances subject to need is analogous to the Family Assistance Plan (a derivative of a negative income tax) advocated by Richard Nixon. The difference is that the former provides only for children in poor families and the latter for all poor families with children. Once an income test is introduced into a program of children's allowances, practically the same problems are encountered as in current income-tested programs: the administrative problems of defining who the poor are, defining income, defining children dependent on that income, and the weakening of the work incentive. Many advocates of children's allowances, including this author, wish to avoid an income test.

In addition to these problems, an income test implies that people must apply for children's allowances and prove their status of poverty. Not only would such income-tested provisions maintain the stigma associated with current welfare programs, but more important, they would prevent children's allowances from reaching poor families who would otherwise be eligible. Some families would not apply for allowances for many reasons, including ignorance, self-pride, and their individual interpretation of what parental responsibilities should be. As Richard Titmuss asserted, an income or means test, however good its intentions, tends to push people away from the program.[46]

Adjustments in Tax Treatment

Should personal exemptions for dependent children, as allowed in the present federal income tax law, be continued when and if a program of children's allowances is introduced in the United States? Should children's allowances be subject to income tax? Each country with a program of children's allowances deals with these questions differently. Great Britain offers a pertinent example.

In Britain, children's allowances are given to all children. The annual allowance payment in 1979 was £208 (the weekly payment of £4 multiplied by 52 weeks). Taxpayers can claim personal exemptions for all children. They were £300 for a child under 11, £335 for a child between 11 and 16, and £365 for a child over 16 and undergoing full-time education. The marginal tax rate of 35 percent applies to taxable income up to £5,000, and the majority of families have less than that.[47] Therefore for most families the net value of the exemption per child was £105, £117, or £128, depending on the age of the child. The net value of exemptions was correspondingly higher for families with taxable income greater than £5,000 because their marginal tax rate was higher than 35 percent.

British children's allowances and personal exemptions combined definitely favor middle-class and upper-class families with children. Families too poor to pay income taxes simply receive children's allowances for which they pay no taxes. As family income increases, families have to pay taxes on children's allowances, but at the same time they can save taxes by claiming exemptions for children. And at the tax rate of 35 percent, which applies to most taxpaying families in Britain, the taxes saved by claiming exemptions are greater than the taxes they have to pay on children's allowances. Take, for example, a family with a taxable income of £4,000 with one child under 11. This family would pay taxes of £73 on children's allowances of £208. But by claiming a £300 exemption for this child, the family would save £105 in income taxes. As a result, this child brings a combined net benefit of £240. This compares favorably with £208 that a nontaxpaying family receives in the form of children's allowances for a child the same age. The relative advantage of the taxpaying family in this example is even greater if the child falls in an older age bracket, because taxes saved on an exemption are larger for an older child, whereas the taxes the family pays on children's allowances stay the same regardless of the age of the child. Also, the disparity between the combined net benefits accrued to a child of a nontaxpaying family and those accrued to a child of taxpaying family widens as the taxable income increases because of the progressive income tax schedule adopted by the British government.

From the British example, it is clear that under a progressive income tax law the retention of personal exemptions for children definitely favors high-income families with children. On the other hand, inclusion of children's allowances in taxable income disfavors high-income families. If children's allowances are to be provided in the United States with an emphasis of helping poor families, it is clear that exemptions for children should be abolished and that children's allowances be subject to a personal income tax.

The following examples show how the inclusion of children's allowances in taxable income and the abolition of exemptions for children would affect taxpaying families in the United States. Suppose the United States adopted a program of children's allowances that paid

$100 per month per child—the amount required in 1979 to support a child living in a family with poverty-line income. What would be the net gain for a family whose income would be taxed at a marginal rate of 20 percent? In other words, what would be the net gain for this family if such a program of children's allowances was instituted and personal exemptions for children were abolished? The family would lose the value of the exemption for a child (worth $200) but would gain a net value of children's allowances amounting to $960—$1,200 - ($1,200 × .20). The net gain therefore would be $720.

Now suppose the program provided $50 per month per child. The family would lose the same value of the exemption per child (worth $200) but would gain a net value of children's allowances amounting to $480—$600 - ($600 × .20). The net gain therefore would be $240. Finally, suppose the program provided $25 a month per child. The family would again lose the value of the exemption worth $200 and would gain a net value of children's allowances of $240. On balance, this family would have a net gain of only $40.

The following equation calculates the marginal income tax rate at which point children's allowance payments would be completely neutralized, that is, the point when a family would neither gain nor lose by instituting a taxable program of children's allowances and by eliminating personal exemptions for children.

$$(E)(R) = C - (C)(R)$$

in which C is the children's allowance payment per child per year; E is the personal exemption per child; and R is the marginal tax rate. With children's allowance payments of $100 a month (or $1,200 a year), the equation becomes:

$$(1,000)(R) = 1,200 - (1,200)(R)$$

$$R = .55$$

All families paying an income tax at a marginal rate higher than 55 percent would lose on balance with allowance payments of this size; those paying at a lower rate would gain.

Similar calculations show that allowances of $50 a month would be neutralized at a 38 percent tax rate, and $25 a month at a 23 percent rate. As of 1979, the marginal tax rate of 55 percent applies to taxable income in excess of approximately $60,000; a 38 percent tax rate, to income over approximately $29,900; a 23 percent tax rate, to income over approximately $16,000—all for a married couple filing a joint return.[48]

The dilemma involved in the policy choice is clear. The larger the allowance, the larger the number of taxpaying families who would gain by instituting a taxable program of children's allowances and eliminating personal exemptions for children. On the contrary, the smaller the allowance, the fewer the number of taxpaying families who would gain. A modest program of $25 per month per child, for example, could ensure that no family with a taxable income of $16,000 or more would gain by the institution of such a taxable program of children's allowances and the elimination of personal exemptions for children. However, the lower the allowance, the lower the percentage of poor families who would be removed from poverty.

One way to solve the dilemma regarding benefits to poor as well as nonpoor families is to introduce "vanishing allowances" or a tapering scale favoring the poor, similar to that used in Australia until 1941. Under this scheme, as family income rises, children's allowances are proportionately reduced. Vanishing allowances, together with the elimination of personal exemptions for children and the inclusion of such allowances in taxable income, could recoup the original payment from nonpoor families to any extent desired—up to 100 percent. In 1967 Harvey Brazer recommended a plan of vanishing allowances in which the allowances were gradually diminished, with 90 percent vanishing at the $20,000 income level in that year.[49]

As mentioned earlier, providing allowances to each family with children through an income test, using either a progressive or regressive scale, invites administrative complexity. The income test is the price that must be paid for fitting children's allowances more closely to family needs and thus minimizing the net cost. Is it worth paying that price? The question is whether it is desirable to develop a program that would partially benefit near poor and middle-class families. As already mentioned, families sufficiently well-off to pay taxes would retain only a part of the original allowances. The fraction becomes even smaller as the income level rises. Furthermore, they would lose tax savings stemming from the elimination of personal exemptions for children.

In comparison with the British situation, taxable children's allowances with no personal exemptions for children permitted are far more progressive in the provision of benefits and they definitely favor low-income families. Considering all the advantages that come from a uniform provision of $100 a month per child (administrative simplicity, the expectation of taking the majority of poor children and poor families out of poverty, and the absence of an income test), it might be a recommendable plan for the United States, although the program would cost more than others that incorporate income testing. Furthermore, the net benefit that would accrue to near poor and middle-class families might be a fair price to pay in order to gain the wide political support for a program of children's allowances.

Adjustments of Other Benefits for Children

If a program of children's allowances was instituted in the United States, what adjustment, if any, should be made in other income maintenance programs, especially in social security programs, unemployment insurance, and worker's compensation? Should children's allowances be substitution for or an addition to benefits for children under present public assistance programs—AFDC, SSI, and general assistance?

If children's allowances of $100 a month per child were provided, it would appear that dependent benefits for children could and should be eliminated from other income maintenance programs. Reasons are multiple. First, there is inequity in treating families under the existing income maintenance programs. Income-tested programs generally incorporate family size in calculating assistance payments, but social insurance programs fail to do so adequately. Second, as discussed earlier, it is difficult for social insurance programs to relate benefits to family size. Third, savings stemming from the elimination of dependent benefits for children from social insurance programs could be used to increase benefit levels for insured workers, especially the level of the minimum benefit.

From the standpoint of equity among various income maintenance programs, it is desirable that all programs provide comparable dependent benefits for children or that all programs disallow them. Currently, children in only a few states receive dependent benefits either under unemployment insurance or under worker's compensation, although under worker's compensation they receive survivors benefits if the insured worker dies as a result of industrial injury or disease. Social security does provide dependent benefits for children, but only partially. Maximum family benefits are large enough to cover only the insured and one dependent without having benefits for dependents reduced proportionately. For these reasons, once adequate children's allowances are provided to all children, dependent benefits for children should be eliminated from other income maintenance programs. Unless this is done, another type of inequity would arise: Children ineligible for the benefits of such programs would receive only children's allowances but children eligible for benefits from one of these programs would be doubly paid. Such a dual entitlement might aggravate the situation in regard to maintaining the work incentives of their parents.

Provision of children's allowances would also help policymakers rethink the concept of the minimum wage. The concept of a living wage has generally been used in establishing a legal minimum wage. A living wage means a wage that covers the living costs of the worker and his family. [50] However, because of the presence of children at home, a minimum wage so developed has been only an abstract notion for most families. If, for example, a minimum wage was established on the basis of average family size, families below that size would be overpaid and families above that size underpaid. In line with the principle of horizontal equity, therefore, it would seem best to establish a minimum wage based on a living wage for a definite number of family members. If a program of children's allowances was instituted, such a minimum wage would become a reality. In that case, a legal minimum wage could be developed on the basis of a living wage for the worker or for the worker and a spouse.

In a similar fashion, having a program of children's allowances could streamline benefit formulas for social insurance programs. With children's allowances instituted, social insurance programs could focus on distributing benefits to insured workers. As a result, social insurance benefits could be more directly tied to past contributions or previous earnings. Because dependent benefits would be eliminated from social insurance programs, the funds saved could be used to provide more adequately for the insured worker.

What would be the effects of a program of children's allowances on the current public assistance programs? In 1978, there were 1.2 million poor families without children, of which 574,000 were headed by an elderly person. There were 5.4 million unrelated individual poor persons living alone, of whom 2.1 million were elderly.[51] These poor families and unrelated individuals would not benefit from children's allowances directly or indirectly. However, children's allowances, if provided, would make AFDC and AFDC-UP almost redundant. The social security reform recommended in Chapter 6 would also make SSI unnecessary. Therefore, with a children's allowance program adopted and social security reformed, only a small-scale, income-tested cash transfer program would be necessary to deal with income needs of nonaged, nondisabled adult individuals.

Method of Financing

The nations providing children's allowances use various methods of financing. When a universal program exists, benefits are usually financed by general revenue, as in Canada and Britain. In nations with employment-related programs, employers bear the major burden of financing, ranging from 1 percent of the payroll in Greece to as much as 16.7 percent of the payroll in Zaire. Governmental involvement in financing employment-related children's allowance programs is relatively rare. In the majority of countries with such programs, the governments contribute nothing toward financing the programs. In the rest of the countries with such programs, the governments limit their involvement to paying allowances for special categories of children or paying deficits when they occur. No employment-related programs, with the exception of those in Greece and Yugoslavia, require employees to contribute to the system. A few countries—Bulgaria, Cape Verde, Czechoslovakia, Malta, and Tunisia—finance children's allowances through social security funds to which employers and in most cases employees contribute. In some cases, governments, too, contribute to social security funds through general revenue.

Major policy issues involved in financing a program of children's allowances are equity, economic efficiency in collecting adequate revenue without imposing high tax rates, and target efficiency in redistributing income.

The principle of equity requires that all taxpayers pay a fair share of the burden of financing a program of children's allowances. Suppose children's allowances were financed by payroll taxes on employers. Would this method of financing be equitable? Not likely. Inequity arises because firms devoting a large percentage of their production cost to labor would have to pay a relatively large amount of taxes. On the contrary, firms devoting a large percentage of their production cost to capital equipment and only a small percentage to labor would pay a comparatively small amount of payroll taxes. Certainly a firm's payroll is not a good measurement of its financial capability. Thus payroll taxes imposed on employers do not offer an equitable means of financing a program of children's allowances. Inequity also arises when employees are asked to finance children's allowances through payroll taxes. This would be unfair because low-wage earners tend to receive their total income through earnings but high-wage earners tend to obtain income from other sources as well, such as rent, interest, and dividends. A payroll tax cannot tap these sources of income. Therefore, a payroll tax, even without a ceiling in its tax base, is generally known as a regressive tax. For these reasons, payroll taxes, whether levied on employers, employees, or both, violate the principle of equity in financing a program of children's allowances.

Economic efficiency in collecting revenue dictates that the taxable base should be as large as possible. Taxing only certain types of income, certain types of property, or certain types of business transactions limits the taxable base. When the taxable base is small, the tax rate must be correspondingly higher to collect a given amount of revenue. On the other hand, financing the program through general revenue ensures that the funds come from all taxpayers through diverse types of taxes, thus ensuring the largest possible tax base. As a result, the increase in tax rate in any specific tax can be minimized.

An economically efficient way to collect funds to finance children's allowances, however, does not necessarily ensure an efficient way to redistribute income vertically from the well-off to the less well-off. General revenue includes revenue raised through regressive taxes such as property and sales taxes. There seems to be no point in attempting to finance a program of children's allowances in part through a poor man's tax.

So what would be the relationship between the extent of income redistribution and the method of financing? If high-income families pay proportionately more than low-income families, there would be more vertical redistribution of income from the well-off to the less well-off. A program financed by a progressive income tax would ensure a greater degree of redistribution of income than one financed by a proportional or regressive tax. Effective redistribution of income through an income maintenance program can be accomplished by the way benefits are financed, or by the way benefits are distributed, or by a combination of both. Because flat-amount children's allowances, subject to income tax, have been argued for in this chapter, financing the program through a progressive tax would have an added effect on redistribution.

In the final analysis, there is a trade-off between policy concerns in regard to equity, economic efficiency in collecting revenue, and target efficiency in redistributing income. On balance, it appears that a progressive income tax is the best choice as a vehicle to finance a program of children's allowances. A progressive income tax enjoys a sizable tax base, touches everyone who has some sort of income, and offers an efficient means to redistribute income vertically from well-off to less well-off families with children.

RECOMMENDATIONS ON A PLAN OF CHILDREN'S ALLOWANCES FOR THE UNITED STATES

If the United States chooses to adopt a program of children's allowances as an antipoverty instrument, the following plan is recommended by the author as most desirable. The program would provide universal coverage at a uniform amount that is equivalent to income needed to support a dependent living in a family at the poverty line. If the program had been in effect in 1979, all children under 18 would have received $100 per month. The allowance will be taxable. The present personal exemptions for children would be abolished, as well as dependent benefits for children under social insurance and public assistance programs. The financing of the cost would be met by a progressive federal income tax.

The author recommends an allowance per child that is set at the poverty-line income for a dependent living in a family—about $100 in 1979—as it provides for a minimum yet adequate floor of income security for children. This amount compares with the weighted average dependent benefit of $100.90 for children under OAI and DI as of October 1979.[52] Adequate children's allowances would minimize the amount spent on public assistance and other welfare programs, which would nevertheless be retained to meet the needs of the rest of the poor. Adequate children's allowances would also make it possible to establish equitable levels of minimum benefits in all social insurance programs and this, in turn, would lessen the number of families who have to supplement social insurance benefits with benefits from income-tested programs.

The inclusion of children's allowances in taxable income for federal income tax purposes is recommended to recoup a part of the original allowances from well-off families, thus reducing the net cost of the program to a great extent. Applying a finding by Orshansky in regard to a hypothetical program of $50 a month per child in 1965, it would be possible to recoup about 30 percent of the initial benefits by making children's allowances taxable. If this is a plausible projection, the federal government would expect to recoup $22.3 billion out of the gross cost of $74.4 billion for the program recommended here by making allowances taxable.[53] Consequently, a guesstimate of the net cost is about $52.1 billion, based on the number of children in 1978 and the benefit level for 1979 ($100 per month).

Financing children's allowances by progressive federal income taxes is recommended for reasons of equity and effectiveness in achieving vertical redistribution of income from well-off to less well-off families. With such financing arrangements, the federal government would be the most appropriate administrator of the program, ensuring universal coverage and uniform allowances to all children. Also, such financing arrangements and the administration of the program by the federal government would minimize possible union resistance to the program on the grounds that allowances act as a depressant of wages.

A program of children's allowances, despite its desirable characteristics, is not a panacea for resolving the income needs of everyone. It would merely deal with the income insecurity of children and would benefit only indirectly the adults who live with children. In a complex industrial society with diverse causes of income insecurity, no one income maintenance program can be expected to deal with everyone's income insecurity. Nor should it. If one program attempted to solve the problem of income insecurity for all, other problems such as those discussed earlier—inequity, inadequacy, and work disincentives—would arise.

The essential question to ask, therefore, is not which program but what mix of programs should deal with the income insecurity of Americans, and in what manner. In short, this nation needs to move toward establishing a comprehensive system of income maintenance, a system that can provide adequate income to those who need it and yet can preserve the work incentive of those who can work. A program of children's allowances appears to be a vital part of such a system.

NOTES

1. U.S. Department of Health, Education, and Welfare, Social Security Administration, Social Security Programs in the United States, 1973 (Washington, D.C.: U.S. Government Printing Office, 1973), pp. 61, 76-80.

2. James C. Vadakin, Family Allowances (Oxford, Ohio: University of Miami Press, 1958), p. 21.

3. U.S. Department of Health and Human Services, Social Security Administration, Social Security Programs Throughout the World, 1979, Research Report no. 54 (Washington, D.C.: Social Security Administration, 1980).

4. U.S. Bureau of the Census, Current Population Reports, Series P-60, no. 124, Characteristics of the Population Below the Poverty Level: 1978 (Washington, D.C.: U.S. Government Printing Office, 1980), Table 27, pp. 119-27.

5. Alvin L. Schorr, Poor Kids (New York: Basic Books, 1966).

6. San Francisco Chronicle, October 13, 1968.

7. Robert E. Lane, Political Ideology: Why the American Common Man Believes What He Does (New York: Free Press, 1962), pp. 71-72.

8. Scott Briar, "Why Children's Allowances?" Social Work 14 (January 1969): 9.

9. Marc Bendick, Jr., "Targeting Benefit Payments in the British Welfare State," Working Paper 1525-01 (Washington, D.C.: Urban Institute, September 1980).

10. James L. McCamy, "Responsiveness Versus Efficiency in Public Services," Annals of the American Academy of Political and Social Science 292 (March 1954): 34.

11. Joseph W. Willard, "Family Allowances in Canada," International Labor Review 75 (March 1957): 208-09.

12. Sir William H. Beveridge, Social Insurance and Allied Services (New York: Macmillan, 1942), p. 7.

13. U.S. Bureau of the Census, op. cit., Tables B, G, 18, and 34, pp. 4, 11-12, 82, 146.

14. Inga Thorsson, "Children's Allowances in Sweden," in Children's Allowances and the Economic Welfare of Children, ed. Eveline M. Burns (New York: Citizens' Committee for Children of New York City, 1968), p. 117.

15. For detailed discussion see Vadakin, op. cit., Chap. 6.

16. Susan Lee, "Reagan's Economics by a Supply-Side Insider," Wall Street Journal, June 5, 1981.

17. For detailed discussion on political issues, see Paul H. Douglas, Wages and the Family (Chicago: University of Chicago Press, 1927), Chap. 16.

18. Thorsson, op. cit., p. 116.

19. Vadakin, op. cit., p. 115.

20. Douglas, op. cit., p. 93.

21. Schorr, op. cit., p. 69.

22. L. Rasle, "Family Allowances and Decline of Birth-Rates," Population 32 (July-October 1977): 1011-15.

23. Lynn M. Ellingson, "Recent Change in French Family Allowance Policy," Social Security Bulletin 42 (December 1979): 14-19.

24. Phillips Cutright, "Illegitimacy and Income Supplements," in The Family, Poverty, and Welfare Programs: Factors Influencing Family Instability, Studies in Public Welfare, Paper no. 12 (Part I), U.S. Congress, Joint Economic Committee, Subcommittee on Fiscal Policy, 93rd Congr., 1st sess. (Washington, D.C.: U.S. Government Printing Office, 1973), pp. 90-138.

25. Ibid.

26. Phillips Cutright and John Scanzoni, "Income Supplements and the American Family," in The Family, Poverty, and Welfare Programs: Factors Influencing Family Instability.

27. F. Y. Edgeworth, "Equal Pay to Men and Women for Equal Work," Economic Journal 32 (December 1922): 453.

28. Eleanor F. Rathbone, Family Allowances (London: Allen & Unwin, 1949), p. 198.

29. Ibid., pp. 132-33.

30. Ibid., p. 158.

31. Douglas, op. cit., p. 105.

32. Eveline M. Burns, "Childhood Poverty and the Children's Allowances," in Children's Allowances and the Economic Welfare of Children, ed. Eveline M. Burns (New York: Citizens' Committee for Children of New York City, 1968), p. 16.

33. U.S. Bureau of the Census, op. cit., Table 27, p. 119.

34. Ibid., Table B, p. 4.

35. Mollie Orshansky, "Who Was Poor in 1966?" in Children's Allowances and the Economic Welfare of Children, ed. Eveline M. Burns (New York: Citizens' Committee for Children of New York City, 1968), p. 57.

36. U.S. Bureau of the Census, op. cit., Table B, p. 4.

37. Orshansky, op. cit.; and Schorr, op. cit.

38. Orshansky, op. cit., p. 57.

39. As of 1979, $100 per person was the average increment in

poverty-line income as family size increased from 2 through 6. See Social Security Bulletin: Annual Statistical Supplement, 1977-79 (Washington, D.C.: Social Security Administration, 1980), Table 9, p. 59.

40. Beveridge, op. cit., p. 156.

41. Douglas, op. cit., p. 212.

42. Ibid., p. 158; and Vadakin, op. cit., p. 33.

43. Bentley B. Gilbert, The Evolution of National Insurance and Great Britain (London: Michael Joseph, 1966), p. 91.

44. William MacDougall, National Welfare and National Decay (London: Methuen, 1921), p. 197.

45. Sir William H. Beveridge, The Pillars of Security (London: Allen & Unwin, 1942), p. 159.

46. Richard M. Titmuss, Commitment to Welfare (London: Allen & Unwin, 1968), p. 68.

47. U.S. Department of Health and Human Services, Social Security Administration, Social Security Programs Throughout the World, 1979, op. cit., p. 251; and Hilary Land and Roy Parker, "United Kingdom," in Family Poverty: Government and Families in Fourteen Countries, ed. Sheila B. Kamerman and Alfred J. Kahn (New York: Columbia University Press, 1978), p. 345.

48. U.S. Department of the Treasury, Internal Revenue Service, 1979 Instructions for Preparing Form 1040 (Washington, D.C.).

49. Harvey E. Brazer, "Tax Policy and Children's Allowances," in Children's Allowances and the Economic Welfare of Children, ed. Eveline M. Burns (New York: Citizens' Committee for the Children of New York City, 1968), pp. 140-49.

50. For detailed discussion on living wages, see Eveline M. Burns, Wages and the State (London: R. S. King and Son, 1926).

51. U.S. Bureau of the Census, op. cit., Tables 1, 7, and 19, pp. 16-18, 36-37, 83-86.

52. U.S. Department of Health and Human Services, Social Security Administration, Monthly Benefit Statistics, Note no. 11, October 15, 1979, Table 1.

53. Orshansky, op. cit.; and U.S. Bureau of the Census, op. cit., Table 9, p. 42.

8

TOWARD ESTABLISHING
A SYSTEM OF
INCOME MAINTENANCE

After 40 years of growth in social welfare programs since the New
Deal, with philosophical inertia along the way, this nation is ready to
awaken. With a president in the White House who has a view about the
economy and about the role of government that is distinctly different
from his predecessors', the nation seems ready to go through a kind
of rebirth. Whether the majority of the public supports Ronald Reagan's
view remains to be seen. However, it seems clear that the public is
demanding that Congress find a new approach to solving many of the
nation's social welfare problems, including income maintenance. It
may be the greatest opportunity for this nation since the New Deal to
clarify its philosophical stance on income maintenance and to develop
a coherent system of income maintenance programs, so that what the
government does in this area will make sense to awakened Americans.

As mentioned time and time again in this book, the public senses
that income maintenance programs are getting out of control. The public is concerned not only about the growing public expenditures for
these programs but also about the lack of rationale behind the whole
system. Somehow the public believes that the system has its own
dynamics of growth beyond anybody's control. As a result, a sense of
helplessness and hostility against the system grows.

All this does not mean that the American public lacks a desire
"to do good" in helping those in need. It's just that, because the system
works as it does, the public is concerned that it cannot be truly generous to certain segments of society without destroying the work incentive of other segments. The public is simply caught in the bind because
of the way the system works. If the system is disentangled and rebuilt
so that the public is given a chance to be generous to certain segments
of the population and, at the same time but quite separately, satisfy

its concern about maintaining the work incentive of others, this could constitute an improvement in income maintenance policy.

A sensible system of income maintenance programs can give citizens an opportunity to practice fraternity and build a nation of people who can feel a sense of unity, interdependence, and mutual cooperation. However, the planners of an income maintenance system must accept the conditions of an essentially nontotalitarian society that bases its economic activities on free enterprise. Such a system, although giving the public a chance to be generous to those in need of public income support, must be so built that work is always preferred over nonwork. This point cannot be overemphasized. A nontotalitarian society that thrives on free enterprise must depend on the voluntary choice of the population to work rather than not to work. It cannot force people one way or the other. But if such a society is to be preserved and to prosper, incentives must be built into the system so that work is preferred. The price for not building such incentives is the acceptance of governmental coercion to make certain people work against their will. When this occurs, the texture of the society changes. Nobody wants this to happen, of course.

Such a system can be built only when the planner has sorted out the divergent causes of income insecurity in a modern capitalistic society and has come up with a composite of programs. Each part in such a system should address itself to a specific cause of income insecurity. Most European countries have evidently proceeded with building such a system during this century. They have recognized, for example, family size and old age as distinct causes of income insecurity, thus introducing "demogrants" into their systems of income maintenance. Demogrants typically are payments made to all persons in a certain demographic category, such as children and the aged. The idea of demogrants is as yet foreign to the United States, although the "$1,000 for everyone" promised by then Senator McGovern (South Dakota) in his 1972 presidential campaign constituted one type of demogrant. A number of countries have implemented the idea of demogrants by providing children's allowances and noncontributory old-age pensions. Because the public does not raise the question of the work incentive in regard to children and the elderly, society is given a chance to care for these categories of individuals without much concern about this question. Through the use of demogrants, society is given an opportunity to project its generosity and its care without experiencing conflict with other concerns.

In addition to the adoption of the demogrant approach to providing income support for children and the aged, European countries have come a long way toward perfecting social insurance programs to deal with income insecurity caused by industrial risks—retirement, unemployment, short-term and long-term disability, and the death of the

breadwinner.[1] Their commitment to social insurance programs is
generally much stronger than the commitment made in this country.[2]
Because social insurance programs justify their existence on the basis
of the contributory principle, the notion of entitlement is instilled in
the public's mind. As a result, again the question of the work incentive is not often raised in social insurance. The public knows and
understands why social insurance beneficiaries are receiving benefits
and feel that they are justified.

Because European countries have been capitalizing on the new
approach of demogrants and on strengthened social insurance programs, they have been able to contain income-tested welfare programs
within manageable and tolerable limits. In contrast, the United States
has, during the past 15 to 20 years, opted for the expanded use of the
welfare approach. The idea of negative income tax, which sounded
novel when it was popularized in the early 1960s by Milton Friedman,
is not, in fact, so revolutionary.[3] Negative income tax, too, falls
into the category of income-tested transfer programs. It simply is an
impersonal, bureaucratized version of old, individually income-tested
public assistance.[4] It simply is another welfare program, although
probably with fewer strings attached to it. In essence, then, the United
States has been attempting to solve the problem of poverty—the causes
of which are increasingly diverse and complex—through the single approach of income-tested welfare programs, as compared with the
multiple approaches taken by European countries.

European countries have evolved in their approaches to solving
income insecurity, but the United States has stagnated. European countries have evolved from relying solely on the welfare approach to
adopting social insurance and then to introducing demogrants. The
United States, in contrast, has advanced as far as adopting social
insurance but has never advanced to the stage of adopting the demogrant approach. Instead, during the past two decades, the United States
has regressed toward heavy reliance on income-tested welfare programs as a way to solve diverse problems of income insecurity for
low-income families.[5]

The price that the United States is paying for not having advanced
in the evolutionary path to establishing a system of income maintenance
programs is the welfare mess, and no one has a clear answer as to
what to do with it. Confusion and anxiety among the politicians and the
public are understandable. Because income-tested transfer programs
are heavily relied upon, diverse types of families and individuals are
covered and provided for by particular programs, no matter what the
nature of the income insecurity. The food stamp program is a good
example. It provides for widely different families and individuals whose
reasons for lack of income range from large family size, disability,
and old age to being a student, being on strike, or simply being unwilling

to work. From the point of view of simple economic equity, they are all entitled to food stamps as long as their income level is below a cutoff point. However, the public may feel that some of these people should not receive food stamps. The public's misgivings arise precisely because the U.S. government is not differentiating its approaches to income maintenance on the basis of different causes of income insecurity. It can be expected, therefore, that as long as the government continues to rely heavily on the welfare approach, as long as it fails to sort out the causes of income insecurity, and as long as it fails to take multiple approaches to income maintenance, such public misgivings will continue.

For the public to be able to make sense out of the system, it needs to know why people are receiving income support from the government. The public seems to consider that just being in need of money is an insufficient reason for justifying income support. In contrast, if the system is developed so as to enable the public to understand the rationale behind each income maintenance program and behind the system as a whole, the public may in fact support even greater expenditures for certain programs, and it may favor tighter control of expenditures for other programs. At any rate, such a system would enable the public to feel in control of public expenditures for income maintenance programs. Only when this occurs can the public feel free to extend its support. For these reasons, public provision of income support should be linked to specific types of income insecurity.

So what principles should guide policymakers in envisioning the future system of income maintenance for the United States? It should be a system that, on one hand, offers the public a chance to be mutually supportive for income transfers for certain segments of society and, on the other hand, makes the public feel in control of maintaining the work incentive of other segments of society. It seems that the following four principles should guide the development of such a system: separate treatment of children, the use of individuals as a unit for allocating income for adults, hierarchical order of income provision for adults, and less eligibility.

Separate Treatment of Children

As mentioned earlier, the United States had landed in the current welfare mess in part because the government has attempted to provide income security for children contingent upon their parents' employment status and level of earnings. Because children are provided for only when their parents cannot earn enough, and because the level of transfer payments depends on the number of children in the family, there is a gap between the level of income that the government provides and the level of income that the head of household can potentially earn. Even if families are headed by single females or the disabled, the public concern still remains.[6] As long as the possibility exists that transfer payments for families are higher than their potential earnings, the political passion of the public can be aroused. Such public outrage stems not so much from hostility toward recipient families as concern for the maintenance of the work incentive in free enterprise America. If, under any circumstances, some families are better off by not working, how can the fundamental structure of a society based on a work-related reward system be preserved?

One way out of this dilemma is to deal with income security of children separately and independently of their parents' economic pursuits and work efforts. This was the essential ground on which this author based the recommendation in Chapter 7 that children's allowances be introduced into the American system of income maintenance.

The British economist Juliet Rhys-Williams long ago advocated that adequate provision to meet family need be made quite separately from the wage structure. She advocated the provision of "social dividends" for every British citizen. The ground for her advocacy was quite similar to the concern discussed here. She was concerned about work disincentives associated with adequate provision of unemployment insurance benefits, which included benefits for dependents. She argued that providing amply for dependents only when unemployment occurs destroys the incentive for the head of the family to return to work. Her answer was to provide a minimum guaranteed income—a social dividend—to each citizen in return for a pledge from the adults to accept available jobs at prevailing wages.[7]

In developing a system of income maintenance, therefore, the adoption of an independent program to provide for children is the first step. The second step is to program the rest of the system to deal with income security for the adult population. In that part of the system, the preservation of the work incentive should be the paramount concern.

Individuals as a Unit of Allocation

Having dealt with the problem of income security for children under a completely separate program that has no relation with their parents' employment or level of earnings, one can now proceed with developing a parallel system of income provision for adults. In this system the concept of minimum wages is operationalized as living wages to support individual workers, per se, not households or families. Similarly, social insurance and an income-tested cash transfer program (or noncategorical public assistance) deal with income maintenance for individuals, not households or families. When all layers of income provisions—from minimum wages on down to an income-tested cash transfer program—address themselves to individuals as the unit for allocating income, the planner of a system of income maintenance can establish a hierarchical order of income provision for adults.

Hierarchical Order of Income Provision

In this hierarchical order of income provision for adults, minimum wages constitute the first layer of the protection society provides to make sure that individuals have a decent minimum of income in the United States. Social insurance benefits constitute the second layer of income provision. Benefits from an income-tested cash transfer program (noncategorical public assistance) constitute the third layer. In operationalizing the national minimum for each layer of income provision for adults, the policymaker needs to make sure that the national minimum of wages is always higher than the national minimum of social insurance benefits, which in turn must be higher than the national minimum of income provided under an income-tested cash transfer program.

Implementation of the Principle of Less Eligibility

The development of a hierarchical order of income provision in effect means that the government upholds and practices the principle of less eligibility, but with a quite different philosophical stance than in the past. Less eligibility was a principle guiding the administration of the poor laws in England after the adoption of the 1834 Report by the Poor Law Commission and into the twentieth century. The doctrine was also adopted and widely put into practice in the United States. Under this principle, the assistance provided to a person in need must be such as to make his condition less desirable—that is, in old English less eligible—than the condition of the lowest-paid laborer who does not receive welfare.[8] Administrators of the poor laws in England and in the United States believed that only by setting levels of income transfers lower than the lowest wages in town and/or providing living conditions more miserable than what the lowest wage earner could afford could they deter poor people from seeking welfare. The principle of less eligibility was practiced with nuances and attitudes that were associated with the treatment of criminals.[9] Because of the harshness surrounding the implementation of this principle, students of social welfare, except for a few in the nineteenth century, have never positively identified with the principle of less eligibility. Added to the moral indignation that they felt against this principle was their conviction that the level of welfare payments based on such a principle was too inadequate to support families who often had many children to care for. Implementing the principle of less eligibility always penalized children.

But this book proposes a totally different way of implementing the principle of less eligibility in the system of income maintenance. Because income insecurity of children is dealt with in a separate program of children's allowances, the question does not arise regarding an inadequate level of transfer payments to families in relation to their size. Family size is built into the system as a whole, although no single program other than children's allowances addresses the question of family size. Therefore, the implementation of the principle of less eligibility in the proposed system does not penalize children as it has done in the past. Furthermore, the application of this principle does not mean that contemporary America, in administering the income maintenance programs, would adopt the practices used in administering poor laws, such as detaining the poor in poorhouses and workhouses. The principle of less eligibility is adopted simply to define the differential national minima for various layers of income provision for adults. As a matter of fact, the adoption of this principle in defining the national minima is the key to preserving the work incentive.

RECOMMENDATIONS ON A SYSTEM
OF INCOME MAINTENANCE

With the concerns discussed in regard to the development of a system of income maintenance in mind, Table 8.1 presents the national minima under different components and layers of income provision. A program of children's allowances provides monthly payments to all children under age 18. The level of allowances is equivalent to the income necessary to support a child living in a family at the poverty level. The provision of children's allowances is not contingent upon the provision of income to the adult population. Thus children's allowances are placed alongside income provision for adults. For reasons of economy and effectiveness of redistribution, however, children's allowances would be subject to income taxes. For the same reasons, current personal exemptions for children would be abolished.

As the first layer of income provision for adults, it is recommended that the national minimum wage be set at 200 percent of the poverty-line income for a one-person family. Currently, minimum wage earners working full time year-round are ensured of an income approximately equivalent to 200 percent of the poverty-line income for

TABLE 8.1

A System of National Minima of Income Security, Expressed as
Percentage of Poverty-Line Income

Income Provision for Children	Income Provision for Adults		
Children's allowances: 100% of poverty-line income for a dependent ($1,200* per child per year)	Minimum Wages		
	200% of poverty-line income for a one-person family.		

Note: All children under
        age 18 to be eligible;
        children's allowances
        to be subject to income
        tax; personal exemp-
        tions for children to be
        abolished.
	Social Insurance		

	OASDI	UI	WC
	100%	100%	100%

	Note: Benefits under UI and WC to
	        be subject to the maximum
	        duration as provided under
	        state statutes; OASDI benefits
	        subject to income tax.		

	Noncategorical Public Assistance		
	50%		

	Note: A 50 percent implicit tax rate
	        on earnings; a 100 percent im-
	        plicit tax rate on unearned in-
	        come; beneficiaries of social
	        insurance programs not
	        eligible.		

*Effective as of 1979.

a one-person family. (Earnings from a minimum-wage job would also
ensure 150 percent of the poverty-line income for a two-person family.)

As the second layer of income provision for adults, it is recommended that social insurance programs—that is, old-age, survivors,
and disability insurance (OASDI), unemployment insurance (UI), and
worker's compensation (WC)—guarantee income at 100 percent of the
poverty-line income for a one-person family. In 1979, the poverty-
line income for a one-person family was $3,690 (or $307 a month).[10]
This compared with the weighted monthly average benefit of $297 for

retired and disabled workers under social security that year.[11] Because the minimum proposed here is as high as the average benefit, it is expected that greater expenditures would be incurred for financing benefits to retired and disabled workers. On the other hand, as discussed earlier, this author's proposal on social security would eliminate all benefits for dependents. Savings derived from such elimination would help offset the additional expenditures necessary to implement the national minimum recommended here.

In most states, unemployment insurance provides 50 percent of weekly wages, and worker's compensation 67 percent of weekly wages, both subject to a maximum. Guaranteeing the national minimum benefit under UI and WC at 100 percent of poverty-line income for a one-person family, or 50 percent of the minimum wages, seems quite reasonable. The proposed national minimum benefit would be about two thirds of the take-home pay of minimum wage earners.

The minimum benefit under social security (OASDI) would be tied to the first-tier flat-amount benefits for the aged, the disabled, and nonaged surviving spouses with children. Beyond this national minimum (the first-tier benefits) retired workers would receive an annuity based on past contributions and interest, and the disabled and nonaged surviving spouses with children would receive a percentage replacement of the worker's average indexed monthly earnings. The level of the first-tier benefits pegged to 100 percent of poverty-line income for a one-person family seems reasonable in the light of the recommendation by the National Commission on Social Security, which stated that SSI benefits should approach the poverty line.[12]

There would be no earnings test for retired workers, although all social security benefits—both in tier one and tier two—may be subject to income tax, depending on the legislative intent in regard to economizing on the program. Benefits for the disabled would stop after recovery and a trial period of gainful work and could be subject to income tax. As discussed in Chapter 6, this author recommends that benefits for nonaged surviving spouses with children should not be subject to an earnings test either but instead subject to income tax. The reason is that the repeal of the earnings test from survivors insurance (SI) would underscore the insurance character of the program. Not only would such a policy enhance the work incentive of survivors but it would also give them freedom to plan ahead. Some might use three-year benefits to obtain education and vocational training; others might accumulate savings toward educational costs for their children. The bottom line is that they would know they could count of benefits flowing in for three years and they would also know that benefits would stop in three years. The earnings test, on the contrary, might stifle the survivors' options to plan and proceed creatively with their lives after the death of the breadwinner, let alone stifle the incentive to go out and work.

Because the first-tier benefits under social security would be provided to all elderly and disabled persons regardless of their employment records and level of earnings, SSI would become redundant and therefore should be abolished. Those on SSI, with the exception of disabled children, would simply receive the first-tier flat-amount benefits. There would be no income test for the aged or the disabled. However, benefits for the disabled would stop after recovery and a trial period of gainful work. Income security of disabled children is dealt with through children's allowances.

As the third layer of income provision for adults, an income-tested cash assistance program is recommended. This program deals with individuals who do not come under any of the upper layers of income provision, that is, under minimum wages or social insurance. Recipients of this cash assistance program would be nonaged, nondisabled individuals who cannot earn enough to support themselves. By and large, they would be single female parents who have children under their care and individuals who have exhausted the benefits from UI.

The recommended level of assistance is half of the poverty-line income for a one-person family with no income from other sources. The work incentive measure would be so provided as to reduce payments at the rate of 50 percent of earnings. Unearned income such as rent, interest, and dividends would be offset against assistance payments at a 100 percent rate. Some sort of assets test might also be instituted.

At a glance, the level of the basic guarantee (or the maximum payment) at 50 percent of the poverty line appears inadequate. However, recipients of this assistance would also benefit indirectly from children's allowances if they have children under their care. Because the allowance for each child is equivalent to 100 percent of the poverty-line income necessary to support a dependent living in a family, children's allowances and assistance payments put together would approach closer to the poverty-line income for the respective family size.

EFFECTS OF THE RECOMMENDED SYSTEM
OF INCOME MAINTENANCE

Perhaps the most striking feature of the recommended system is that each component deals with individuals as the unit for allocating benefits, but the system as a whole can meet family need. Family need is met because income that flows to a family comes from one of the layers of income provision for adults and also from children's allowances. For example, for working families with children, income is a composite of earnings and children's allowances. For those families on a

social insurance program, income transfers come from one of the
social insurance programs and the program of children's allowances.
Similarly, for those on the noncategorical public assistance program,
income transfers are the sum of assistance payments and children's
allowances. Therefore, although all programs for adults are based
on individuals as beneficiary units, families receive income adjusted
for family size, thanks to children's allowances.

The system accomplishes the objective of meeting family need
without creating work disincentives and without distorting the ranking
of income provisions as related to work effort. The system accomplishes this precisely because each program for adults deals with
individuals, not households or families. Because a minimum wage job
can bring more income than any social insurance program, which in
turn can bring more income than the noncategorical public assistance
program, the system always rewards individuals according to their
degree of attachment to the labor force. Furthermore, as no program
for adults provides for dependents, the ranking of levels of income
provided by the three layers of income provision can be preserved.
A higher layer of income provision always provides a larger income
than does a lower layer of income provision.

This recommended scheme for a system of income maintenance
departs drastically from the traditional approach to meeting family
need. Current income-tested transfer programs attempt to meet family
need by adjusting the level of payments to family size. Even social
insurance programs go half way in meeting family need by providing
benefits for dependents. However, by so doing, the current income
maintenance programs have created the problems of work disincentives
and inequity. Ironically, the recommended system meets family need—
and succeeds in so doing without creating such adverse effects—by
having each program deal with individuals. The reason for this is
straightforward. Wages are paid on the basis of individuals' work.
Both social insurance benefits and public assistance payments also
are provided on the basis of individuals as a beneficiary unit. Then
the three layers of income provision for adults are rank-ordered according to the principle of less eligibility.

And yet the system meets the income need of vulnerable groups
of individuals to whom the concept of presumptive need can justifiably
be applied. They are the children, the aged, and the disabled. The
system meets their income needs by providing, in essence, demogrants.
Children's allowances are one type of demogrant. The first-tier flat-
amount benefits under social security for the elderly and the disabled
(and the survivors) are another type of demogrant.

The system, although guaranteeing income for all these groups
of individuals, still clearly differentiates between those who worked
and contributed to the system and those who never worked. The system

differentiates its treatment of beneficiaries who were workers by providing them second-tier benefits based on their past contributions to the system in addition to first-tier flat-amount benefits.

Differentiating between the different layers of income provision for adults and putting the national minima in hierarchical order ensure that overlaps between programs are eliminated. An adult who works at a minimum wage job the year around is considerably above the poverty line. If for some reason the worker becomes a beneficiary of one of the social insurance programs, he is guaranteed at least poverty-line income. An individual who neither works nor receives social insurance benefits receives a basic guarantee of half of poverty-line income under the noncategorical public assistance program. As this person starts earning, the assistance payment is reduced by 50¢ for each $1 earned. When earnings reach the level of poverty-line income for a one-person family, the person no longer receives assistance payments. Thus no one individual comes under two layers of income provision at the same time. Eliminating overlaps between programs and thus avoiding multiple recipiency of benefits is the key to minimizing the adverse effect of the implicit cumulative tax rates that are detrimental to preserving the work incentive. This was discussed at length in Chapter 5.

Of course, if an adult individual lives with his or her children, this family may receive income from two income transfer programs. However, because the children's allowances recommended in this book are taxable demogrants (and most poor families do not pay income taxes), such allowances are not withdrawn as quickly as current welfare payments are, as the earnings of the head of the household increase. Therefore, the disincentive effect created by the dual recipiency of children's allowances and benefits from one of the income maintenance programs for adults is not expected to be of great concern.

Because the system has been developed to eliminate overlaps between programs, and because the national minima are differentiated in hierarchical order on the basis of the principle of less eligibility, the number of recipients of noncategorical public assistance is expected to be small. There will no longer be families receiving payments from public assistance to supplement earnings from work. There will no longer be individuals on social security who must supplement those benefits with public assistance payments. The income security of individuals is dealt with by one program, and no more, according to the nature of income insecurity. Thus it is expected that the "welfare caseloads" that the public talks about with distaste will be minimized. Work and welfare are not mixed much under the recommended system, nor do social insurance and public assistance go together. Furthermore, the scope of public assistance will be so small a part of the recommended system of income maintenance that negative political passion against public expenditures for income support in general will be minimized.

A question may arise, however, as to the handling of a nonaged, nondisabled couple when one spouse works and the other does not. How does the concept of the individual as a unit for allocating income work in this case? Does the nonworking spouse receive public assistance? The answer depends on the earnings of the working spouse. That is, as in the case of social security, it is advisable to assume that earnings belong equally to both spouses and therefore assume that half of the earnings of the working spouse is available to support the other spouse. If the earnings when split in half are smaller than the break-even level in the noncategorical public assistance program, both spouses receive public assistance on their own. However, cases like this would be rare. The national minimum wage recommended here is 200 percent of poverty-line income for a one-person family and 150 percent of the poverty-line income for a two-person family. Thus as long as one spouse works and earns at least minimum wages the year around, both spouses would be out of poverty and thus would be ineligible for public assistance.

The last but not least important point that should be made about the recommended system of income maintenance is that the system reflects the reward system in a free enterprise society. Current work would always bring more income than nonwork. Prior participation in the labor force would ensure more income than lack of prior participation. Thus, it is reasonable to expect that able-bodied individuals would prefer work over nonwork if at all possible. Even if able-bodied individuals choose not to work, there would be less public concern over such individuals' behavior than under the current system. Because such individuals would receive the least eligible (least desirable) level of income support in the system, the public would probably feel that such individuals were being treated equitably, and so would the individuals themselves. There would be little public dispute over the system's treatment of such able-bodied individuals or over such individuals' choosing not to work. On the other hand, if they did choose to work it would be much easier to put their families above the poverty line than it is under the current system. All that they would have to do is to work at a minimum-wage job for at least half the year. Currently, the amount of earnings one has to make to pull a family out of poverty is a function of the number of dependents to be supported. Thus it is extremely difficult for a single female parent on AFDC, for example, to earn enough to pull her family out of the program and out of poverty as well.

FURTHER CONSIDERATIONS AND CAVEATS

The system envisioned here is much more simplistic than the current system. For one thing, the recommended system does not deal with various in-kind programs, such as Medicare, Medicaid, food stamps, public housing assistance, and day care services. Therefore, further consideration of such programs is required before the merit of the recommended system can be assessed. For example, if the recommended system is implemented along with all these in-kind transfer programs, many of the problems discussed in Chapter 5 would remain—implicit cumulative tax rates, caused by multiple recipiency, work disincentives, and inequity.

Before discussing the future fate of in-kind transfer programs, one needs to discuss the inherent differences between health care benefits provided under Medicare and Medicaid on one hand and food stamps, public housing assistance, and day care services on the other. What chiefly distinguishes health care benefits from other in-kind benefits is the uncertainty involving costs of health care, in terms of amount and in terms of timing.[13] Illness strikes anyone unexpectedly and regardless of income level; furthermore, the incidence of illness is uneven among people. Because of such uncertainties, it is difficult to cash out health care benefits and include them in cash payments. It is also difficult to limit the provision of health care to the truly needy.

Another distinguishing characteristic of health care is that nobody really wants to consume it. To make matters worse, nobody really contemplates being sick. Thus few individuals willingly set aside a portion of current income for the contingency of future illness. These are some of the reasons why people buy health insurance. By buying health insurance, they transform the uncertain risk of future illness into a calculated risk with the certainty of being able to pay for costs of health care; they succeed in forcing themselves to pay in advance for health care services for future illness.

Another important difference between health care benefits and other in-kind benefits is that the former are perceived more strongly as a "public good" than the latter. The public has a stake in keeping people in the community healthy because of the strong spillover effects involved. If, for example, a person fails to obtain an innoculation for a communicable disease, the entire population in the community may suffer from that disease. Also, without a healthy population, society's essential tasks may not be accomplished. Therefore the public has a stake in providing a minimum level of health care to the entire population and in making sure that the entire population uses certain types of health care services.

In contrast, in-kind benefits—such as day care services and the food and shelter obtained through food stamps and public housing assistance—are items of more normal consumption that people daily buy and willingly pay for. They are items pleasurable to consume. Also, because they are used day after day, people can pretty well allocate current income to buy an assortment of such items according to their need and tastes. Furthermore, because these items of consumption are not so closely associated with crisis situations as health care services are, future expenditures for them can be planned better than for health care services. Although no publicly provided goods and services escape the notion of being a public good, the degree of being a public good seems lower for these in-kind benefits than for health care benefits.

Because of these reasons, it is sensible to deal with health care benefits and other in-kind benefits separately.

First, focusing on in-kind benefits other than health care benefits, it seems advisable for the government to provide these in-kind benefits as alternatives to cash assistance. To make this possible, the levels of benefits should be made equivalent in terms of cost to the government. Under such a scheme, single female parents, for example, my choose to receive day care services over cash assistance for themselves. Some individuals may prefer public housing assistance instead.

Next, because of the unique nature of health care benefits, it seems desirable for the U.S. government to ensure a minimum level of health care for the entire population through some form of national health insurance. For example, the government can require all employers to insure their employees. For those persons not employed, the government may buy insurance coverage on their behalf. As far as consumers are concerned, health care becomes a pure public good just like public education. Aside from health care benefits, children and adults who work or are on social insurance should not receive other income-tested, in-kind benefits.

Some may maintain that the level of in-kind benefits other than health care benefits is inadequate. However, if adult recipients of income-tested programs are ensured of a minimum level of health care and either cash assistance payments or one type of in-kind transfer benefits, the level of financial anxiety is expected to be relatively low. There is some indication that many on AFDC stay on assistance rolls in order to maintain eligibility for Medicaid.[14] Furthermore, under the recommended system, adult individuals benefit indirectly from children's allowances if they have children under their care.

Another issue that may be raised on the recommended scheme of income-tested benefits—that is, letting recipients choose one type among several types—is the question of the public's desire to control the consumption of recipients of public aid programs. The public wants to make sure that low-income families use public aid to acquire certain items of consumption and not others. This was a major force supporting public expenditures for food stamps, public housing, day care, and so on. However, the proliferation of various income-tested, in-kind programs along with cash transfer programs has created many of the adverse effects discussed in Chapter 5.

The issue of whether poor people should be permitted to choose among various types of transfer payments hinges also on whose value is at stake in evaluating in-kind transfers. In-kind transfers can be assessed in many ways. One way is to measure how much the government spends for a particular program and how much each individual recipient receives in terms of the cost to the government. Another way to measure the value of in-kind benefits is to calculate "cash equivalence to recipients."[15] Under this approach, one measures how many dollars the recipient is willing to give up to obtain particular in-kind transfer benefits. At any rate, when the focal point is shifted from the supplier (the government) to the consumer (recipient), it is generally believed that the value of in-kind benefits as perceived by the recipient is smaller than the value that the recipient attaches to cash payments of equal amount. The reason behind such a conclusion is that, when the recipient is given freedom in buying goods and services, the level of utility that the recipient feels in such goods and services is higher than when the recipient is forced to consume certain commodities. Giving low-income families an opportunity to choose between cash assistance payments and in-kind benefits enhances the value of tax dollars as perceived by the recipient. On the other hand, the public loses its opportunity to force poor people, through legislation, to consume in a certain prescribed manner.

But one cannot ignore the advantage that the recommended scheme has in providing options to recipients of income-tested programs. It eliminates multiple recipiency of benefits, which in turn improves the current situation in regard to work disincentives. Furthermore, greater equity between recipients of income-tested benefits is achieved. Because all recipients receive equivalent levels of benefits from one of the alternative programs, the situation does not arise in which some benefit more than others, although they benefit from different programs. In addition, because they enroll in a program of their choice, the level of utility perceived by the recipient is expected to be higher than when they receive any other kind of benefit. Thus the equivalence of perceived value between recipients may also be attained.

Another policy option open to the decision maker is to phase out all income-tested, in-kind transfer programs with the exception of national health insurance. If this is done, the future system of income maintenance would be composed of programs presented in Table 8.1 plus national health insurance. Recipients of noncategorical public assistance, in that case, would simply use their cash assistance

payments and children's allowances (if they have children) to buy in
the marketplace needed services such as day care and baby sitting.
By letting private providers in the marketplace supply such services,
the government would be freed from the bureaucratic burden of administering income-tested, in-kind transfer programs.

There is one important caveat in regard to the feasibility of the
recommended system of income maintenance: Job opportunities must
be plentiful. If the private sector cannot provide enough jobs, the
government has to make sure that jobs are available to all adults able
and willing to work. This caveat is extremely important because,
without available jobs, many adult individuals may be forced to take
options downward, that is, apply for social insurance benefits or for
noncategorical public assistance. Many with marginal employability
may be forced to claim disability benefits. Others may be forced to
claim unemployment insurance benefits. Those without the protection
of social insurance may be forced to apply for public assistance as a
last resort. If this happens, public expenditures for income maintenance programs in the recommended system quickly swell. When jobs
are not available, the incentives incorporated in the system are mean-
ingless and unworkable. This is true because, if the incentive mechanism is to function effectively, there must be options for adult individuals to go upward in the system.

For the recommended system to function, therefore, the creation
of public jobs at minimum wages may be called for. In order to preserve the work habit of the adult population, such public investment
may be worthwhile. Only 20 years ago, the government of Japan was
obligated to provide jobs at 240 yen a day (at that time) to anyone who
showed up at a local employment office. In those days, government-
provided jobs certainly were "made-work." For example, hundreds
of workers were hired to pave one and one-half miles of road leading
to the Haneda Airport in Tokyo. It took two and one-half years to com-
plete the project. By the time the project was completed, the other
end of the road was ready for repair! Many workers were kept working
on the same road for several years.

In Japan, belonging to the mainstream of society is of the utmost
importance for individuals to develop identity as productive members
of society. For example, a father without a job ceases to be a father
in Japan. Thus working even at a menial job is important for adults as
a support to their claim to parenthood. Therefore, having a job is
more than an economic proposition. It is the key to being accepted and
acquiring a sense of belonging to the family, the town, and the nation.

The situation does not seem so different in the United States. In
this country work seems to be the most important link between individuals and society. Through work, families extract resources from
the community to sustain their livelihood. Through work, persons can

test their marketable capabilities, and that can give a sense of mastery over certain skills. Work, through its earnings, gives a feeling of continuity in life: The future becomes more secure. Work provides social relationships in the work place, as a person's functions are inevitably coordinated with those of others in the common pursuit of producing goods and services.[16] In short, work is a cornerstone of life, which helps individuals and families live both as private and social beings. In America work unites people of diverse cultural backgrounds. Nothing else is so powerful for binding the nation together as the concept of work.

When work is understood as a powerful vehicle for accomplishing not only economic objectives but also cultural and political objectives, it is difficult to compare public works and income maintenance using the common dollars-and-cents measurement. Probably the provision of public works at the minimum wage is more costly to the government than the provision of income transfers. But the effects of these two approaches seem diametrically opposed. Providing jobs helps to put individuals into the mainstream of society; providing income transfers may isolate recipients and may lead nonrecipients to castigate them. Furthermore, with income transfers, the government has to care for a relatively large segment of society as a dependent population for a long time. The social and psychological impact of such dependence is hard to measure in dollars and cents.

LEAPING INTO A FUTURE BASED ON TRADITION

Public support, or nonsupport, for particular income maintenance programs has roots in the American tradition of two opposing ideologies. These are the old liberalism and the new liberalism discussed in Chapter 1. Even today, passions are evoked in regard to the governmental role in providing income security, according to which ideology people believe in. Some people side with old liberalism; others feel comfortable with new liberalism. But both ideologies are still alive and strong in the minds of people in America today.

The planner of a system of income maintenance, therefore, cannot recommend a system with a philosophical rationale aligned exclusively to one ideology and ignore the other. This point cannot be overemphasized, because each ideology is a guiding force for preserving the basic principles of this society. For example, the notions of collectivism, interdependence, altruism, and the pooling of resources to meet life contingencies, which new liberalism espouses, give impulse to people in the society to give up a portion of their own resources to ensure a basic minimum of living for certain segments of society. On the other hand, the notions of individualism, independence, free enterprise, and a reward system linked to individual productivity, which old liberalism espouses, give impulse to people in the society to channel their energy and engage in activities so that individual well-being can be achieved. In the context of capitalism as American people know it, the basic rules of the game according to old liberalism are essentially played in individual pursuit of well-being. In the context of a capitalistic political system, therefore, old liberalism too is a guiding force for preserving the basic principles of this society.

The challenge to the policymaker, then, is to adopt a system of income maintenance in which the ideological forces coming from old and new liberalism interact in a complementary manner. The current system is not achieving this objective. AFDC is a good example of a program in which forces from these two ideologies are allowed to fight each other. On the one hand, policymakers provide and the public seems to support the provision of a minimum level of living for children. Such support rests with the public's vested interest in preserving the human capital of the society, and the impulse indeed comes from new liberal thinking. On the other hand, again in the AFDC program, one focus of policymakers is maintaining the work incentive of AFDC mothers, an idea that stems from old liberalism. Thus one of the policy goals of AFDC is to help AFDC mothers become self-sufficient. The public seems to support this policy too, although it may not always be in the interest of the children's well-being. Nor is it being achieved with any marked degree of success. Having these two ideologies in conflict in the same program inevitably leads to confusion, inefficiency in attaining policy goals, and perhaps even to public despair.

Another area in which these forces are allowed to clash with each other is social security. Under the present system of social security, the objectives of individual equity and social adequacy fight each other. Individual equity is aligned to a great extent to an old liberal impulse, whereas social adequacy reflects the spirit of new liberalism. These ideological forces are not allowed to react in an orderly and complementary manner because, under the current scheme of benefits, it is hard to divide the benefits so that each part clearly relates to one of these ideological forces.

In this book, this author has attempted to explore a system of income maintenance in which these ideological forces are allowed to interact in a complementary manner. The provision of children's allowances and the provision of a guaranteed income for the aged and the disabled through the first-tier flat-amount benefits under social security reflect the philosophical stance of new liberalism. The second-tier benefits in social security reflect individual equity, a concept that is heavily dependent on old liberalism. The layers of income provision for adults in hierarchical order based on the principle of less eligibility clearly reflect the spirit of old liberalism. And yet there does not seem to be ideological conflict between the components in any particular program or between the various income maintenance programs proposed.

Furthermore, two important policy objectives of the recommended plan—to provide adequate income to vulnerable segments of the society and at the same time to maintain the work incentive among able-bodied adults in the rest of the society—have the common aim of preserving and enhancing society as a macrosystem. Attaining both these objectives seems essential to the survival and prosperity of this macrosystem in contemporary America. And the recommended plan as a whole seems able to attain them. The adoption of this plan might even bring a bonus. If the society thrives economically under this plan, it is quite possible that the lowest fifth of the nation may increase its share of income as well. It would be a significant step in the long, long struggle against poverty.

NOTES

1. See James H. Schulz, Providing Adequate Retirement Income: Pension Reform in the United States and Abroad (Hanover, N.H.: University Press of New England, 1974); Sheila B. Kamerman and Alfred J. Kahn, eds., Family Policy: Government and Families in Fourteen Countries (New York: Columbia University Press, 1978); and U.S. Department of Health and Human Services, Social Security Administration, Social Security Programs Throughout the World, 1979, Research Report no. 54 (Washington, D.C.: Social Security Administration, 1980).

2. Max Horlick, "National Expenditures on Social Security in Selected Countries," Research and Statistics Note, no. 29-1974, U.S. Department of Health, Education, and Welfare, Social Security Administration, Office of Research and Statistics, October 18, 1974.

3. Milton Friedman, Capitalism and Freedom (Chicago: University of Chicago Press, 1962), p. 192.

4. Eveline M. Burns, "Social Security in Evolution: Toward What?" Social Service Review 39 (June 1965): 120-40.

5. Ibid.

6. Timothy M. Smeeding, "The Anti-Poverty Effect of In-Kind Transfers: A 'Good Idea' Gone Too Far?" Policy Studies Journals (forthcoming).

7. Juliet Rhys-Williams, Something to Look Forward To (London: MacDonald, 1943), pp. 138-59.

8. Karl de Schweinitz, England's Road to Social Security (New York: A. S. Barnes, 1943), p. 123.

9. Benjamin Disraeli, a prominent English politician about the time the 1834 Report by the Poor Law Commission was adopted, commented on the report as follows: "It announced to the world that in England poverty is a crime." See William Flavelle Moneypenny, The Life of Benjamin Disraeli, Earl of Beaconsfield (New York: Macmillan 1910), vol. 1, p. 374.

10. U.S. Department of Health and Human Services, Social Security Administration, Social Security Bulletin: Annual Statistical Supplement, 1977-1979 (Washington, D.C.: Social Security Administration, 1980), Table 9, p. 59.

11. Monthly Benefit Statistics, no. 11, U.S. Department of Health, Education, and Welfare, Social Security Administration, Office of Research and Statistics, October 15, 1979.

12. U.S. Congress, National Commission on Social Security, Social Security in America's Future (Washington, D.C.: U.S. Government Printing Office, 1981).

13. Herbert E. Klarman, Economics of Health (New York: Columbia University Press, 1970), pp. 10-19; and Kenneth J. Arrow, "Uncertainty and the Welfare Economics of Medical Care," American Economic Review 53 (December 1963): 941-73.

14. Jacque E. Gibbons, "Incentives for Dependency: Non-Cash Transfers in the Aid to Families with Dependent Children Program," Ph.D. dissertation, Washington University, 1981.

15. Eugene Smolensky, Lenna Stiefel, Maria Schmundt, and Robert Plotnick, "In-Kind Transfers and the Size Distribution of Income," in Improving Measures of Economic Well-Being, ed. Marilyn Moon and Eugene Smolensky (New York: Academic Press, 1977).

16. Martha N. Ozawa, "Work and Social Policy," in Work, Workers and Work Institutions: A View from Social Work, ed. Sheila H. Akabas and Paul A. Kurzman (Englewood Cliffs, N.J.: Prentice-Hall, 1982), p. 41; and Lee Rainwater, "Work, Well-Being, and Family Life," in Work and the Quality of Life: Resource Papers for Work in America, ed. James O'Toole (Cambridge, Mass.: MIT Press, 1974), pp. 366-67.

BIBLIOGRAPHY

Aaron, Henry J. "Social Security: International Comparisons." In Studies in the Economics of Income Maintenance, edited by Otto Eckstein, pp. 13-48. Washington, D.C.: Brookings Institution, 1967.

____. "Demographic Effects of the Equity of Social Security Benefits." In Economics of Public Services, edited by Martin S. Feldstein and Robert I. Inman, pp. 151-73. New York: Macmillan, 1977.

____. Politics and the Professors. Washington, D.C.: Brookings Institution, 1978.

Anderson, Martin. Welfare. Stanford, Calif.: Stanford University, Hoover Institution Press, 1978.

Arrow, Kenneth J. "Uncertainty and the Welfare Economics of Medical Care." American Economic Review 53 (December 1963): 941-73.

Barr, Nicholas, and Robert Hall. "The Probability of Dependence on Public Assistance." Economica 48 (May 1981): 109-23.

Bawden, D. Lee, Glen G. Cain, and Leonard J. Hausman. "The Family Assistance Plan: Analysis and Evaluation." Public Policy 19 (Spring 1971): 323-53.

Bendick, Marc, Jr. "Targeting Benefit Payments in the British Welfare State." Working Paper 1525-01. Washington, D.C.: Urban Institute, September 1980.

Beveridge, Sir William H. The Pillars of Security. London: Allen & Unwin, 1942.

____. Social Insurance and Allied Services. New York: Macmillan, 1942.

____. Full Employment in a Free Society. London: Allen & Unwin, 1944.

251

Boland, Barbara. "Participation in the Aid to Families with Dependent Children Program (AFDC)." Working Paper 971-02. Washington, D.C.: Urban Institute, 1973. Mimeographed.

Booth, Charles. Life and Labour of the People of London. London: Williams and Norgate, 1891.

Boskin, Michael J. "Social Security and Retirement Decisions." Economic Inquiry 15 (January 1977): 1-25.

Boulding, Kenneth E. "The Boundaries of Social Policy." Social Work 21 (January 1967): 3-11.

Bowen, William G., and T. Aldrich Finegan. The Economics of Labor Force Participation. Princeton, N.J.: Princeton University Press, 1969.

Brazer, Harvey E. "Tax Policy and Children's Allowances." In Children's Allowances and the Economic Welfare of Children, edited by Eveline M. Burns, pp. 140-49. New York: Citizens' Committee for Children of New York, 1968.

Break, George F. "Social Security as a Tax." In The Crisis in Social Security, edited by Michael J. Boskin, pp. 107-23. San Francisco: Institute for Contemporary Studies, 1977.

Briar, Scott. "Welfare from Below: Recipients' View of the Public Welfare System." California Law Review 54 (May 1966): 370-85.

Burke, Vee, and Alair A. Townsend. "Public Welfare and Work Incentives: Theory and Practice." Studies in Public Welfare, Paper no. 14. U.S. Congress, Joint Economic Committee, Subcommittee on Fiscal Policy, 93rd Congr., 2nd Sess. Washington, D.C.: U.S. Government Printing Office, 1974.

Burke, Vincent J., and Vee Burke. Nixon's Good Deed: Welfare Reform. New York: Columbia University Press, 1974.

Burkhauser, Richard V. "Are Women Treated Fairly in Today's Social Security System?" Discussion Paper no. 53-78. Madison: Institute for Research on Poverty, University of Wisconsin, 1978. Mimeographed.

_____. "Earnings Sharing: Incremental and Fundamental Reform."

Paper presented to the Conference on Social Security and the Changing Roles of Women. Cosponsored by the Institute for Research on Poverty and the Women's Studies Research Center, University of Wisconsin, April 11-12, 1980, Madison.

____. "The Early Acceptance of Social Security: An Asset Maximization Approach." Industrial Labor Relation Review 33 (July 1980): 484-92.

Burns, Eveline M. Wages and the State. London: R.S. King and Son, 1926.

____. The American Social Security System. New York: Houghton Mifflin Co., 1949.

____. "Social Security in Evolution: Toward What?" Social Service Review 39 (June 1965): 129-40.

____. "Childhood Poverty and the Children's Allowances." In Children's Allowances and the Economic Welfare of Children, edited by Eveline M. Burns, pp. 3-18. New York: Citizens' Committee for Children of New York City, 1968.

Campbell, Rita Ricardo. "The Problems of Fairness." In The Crisis in Social Security, edited by Michael J. Boskin, pp. 125-45. San Francisco: Institute for Contemporary Studies, 1977.

____. Social Security: Promise and Reality. Stanford, Calif.: Stanford University, Hoover Institution, 1977.

Coe, Richard D. "Sensitivity of the Incidence of Poverty to Different Measures of Income: School-Aged Children and Families." In Five Thousand American Families: Patterns of Economic Progress, vol. IV, edited by Greg J. Duncan and James N. Morgan, pp. 357-409. Ann Arbor: University of Michigan, Institute of Social Research, 1976.

____. "Participation in the Food Stamp Program Among the Poverty Population." In Five Thousand American Families, Patterns of Economic Progress, vol. VII, edited by Greg J. Duncan and James N. Morgan, pp. 249-71. Ann Arbor: University of Michigan, Institute of Social Research, 1977.

Commons, John R., and John Andrews. Principles of Labor Legislation. 3rd ed. New York: Harper & Bros., 1920.

Curti, Merle. The Growth of American Thought. New York: Harper & Bros., 1943.

Cutright, Phillips. "Illegitimacy and Income Supplements." In The Family, Poverty, and Welfare Programs: Factors Influencing Family Instability. Studies in Public Welfare, Paper no. 12 (Part I). U.S. Congress, Joint Economic Committee, Subcommittee on Fiscal Policy, 93rd Congr., 1st Sess. pp. 90-138. Washington, D.C.: U.S. Government Printing Office, 1973.

Danziger, Sheldon. "The Measurement and Trend of Inequality: Comment." American Economic Review 67 (June 1977): 505-12.

Danziger, Sheldon, Robert Haveman, and Eugene Smolensky. "The Program for Better Jobs and Income—A Guide and a Critique." Study prepared for the use of the U.S. Congress, Joint Economic Committee, 95th Congr., 1st Sess. Washington, D.C.: U.S. Government Printing Office, 1977.

Danziger, Sheldon, Robert Haveman, and Robert Plotnick. "How Income Transfers Affect Work, Savings, and the Income Distribution: A Critical Review." Journal of Economic Literature 19 (September 1981): 975-1028.

Danziger, Sheldon, and Robert Plotnick. "Demographic Change, Government Transfers, and Income Distribution." Monthly Labor Review 100 (April 1977): 7-11.

_____. Has the War On Poverty Been Won? (in press).

Derthic, Martha. Policymaking for Social Security. Washington, D.C.: Brookings Institution, 1979.

Economic Report of the President, 1964. Washington, D.C.: U.S. Government Printing Office, 1964.

Edgeworth, F. Y. "Equal Pay to Men and Women for Equal Work." Economic Journal 32 (December 1922): 431-57.

Edstrom, Eve. "Newburgh Is a Mirror Reflection on Us All." Washinton Post, August 6, 1961.

Ellingson, Lynn M. "Recent Change in French Family Allowance Policy." Social Security Bulletin 42 (December 1979): 14-19.

Feagin, Joe R. "America's Welfare Stereotypes." Social Science Quarterly 52 (March 1974): 921-33.

Feldstein, Martin S. "Unemployment Insurance: Time for Reform." Harvard Business Review 53 (March-April 1975): 51-61.

Fox, Alan. "Income of New Beneficiaries by Age at Entitlement to Benefits." In Reaching Retirement Age: Findings from a Survey of Newly Entitled Workers, 1968-70. Research Report no. 47. U.S. Department of Health, Education, and Welfare, Social Security Administration, pp. 95-119. Washington, D.C.: U.S. Government Printing Office, 1976.

Friedman, Milton. Capitalism and Freedom. Chicago: University of Chicago Press, 1962.

Galbraith, John Kenneth. American Capitalism. Boston: Houghton Mifflin, 1952.

Garfinkel, Irwin, and Larry L. Orr. "Welfare Policy and the Employment Rate of AFDC Mothers." National Tax Journal 27 (June 1974): 275-84.

Garfinkel, Irwin and Felicity Skidmore. "Income Support Policy: Where We've Come From and Where We Should Be Going." Discussion Paper no. 490-78. Institute for Research on Poverty, University of Wisconsin, April 1978. Mimeographed.

Gibbons, Jacque E. "Incentives for Dependency: Non-Cash Transfers in the Aid to Families with Dependent Children Program." Ph.D. Dissertation, Washington University, 1981.

Gilbert, Bentley B. The Evolution of National Insurance and Great Britain. London: Michael Joseph, 1966.

Gilbert, Neil. "The Transformation of Social Services." Social Service Review 51 (December 1977): 624-41.

Golladay, Fredrick, and Robert Haveman. "Regional and Distributional Effects of a Negative Income Tax." American Economic Review 66 (September 1976): 629-41.

Gordon, Margaret S. "The Case for Earnings-Related Social Security Benefits, Restated." In Old Age Income Assurance, Part II: The

Aged Population and Retirement Income Programs. U.S. Congress, Joint Economic Committee, Subcommittee on Fiscal Policy, 90th Congr., 1st Sess., pp. 312-39. Washington, D.C.: U.S. Government Printing Office, December 1967.

Grad, Susan, and Karen Foster. "Income of the Population 55 and Over." Staff Paper no. 35. U.S. Department of Health, Education, and Welfare, Social Security Administration, Office of Research and Statistics, December 1979.

Greenfield, Meg. "The Welfare Chiseler of Newburgh, N.Y.," The Reporter, August 1, 1961.

Gronbjert, Kirsten, David Street, and Gerald Suttles. Poverty and Social Change. Chicago: University of Chicago Press, 1978.

Groves, Harold M. Financing Government. 6th ed. New York: Holt, Rinehart, and Winston, 1965.

Grundmann, Herman. "Treatment of Short-Service Workers Under OASDI Retirement Provisions." Policy Analysis with Social Security File. Proceedings of a workshop at Williamsburg, Va., March 15-17, 1978, pp. 489-517. Washington, D.C.: U.S. Department of Health, Education, and Welfare, Social Security Administration, Office of Research and Statistics, 1978.

Hacker, Louis M., et al., eds. The Shaping of the American Tradition. New York: Columbia University Press, 1947.

Handler, Joel F. Reforming the Poor: Welfare Policy, Federalism, and Morality. New York: Basic Books, 1972.

Handler, Joel F. and Ellen Jane Hollingsworth. "Stigma, Privacy, and Other Attitudes of Welfare Recipients." Stanford Law Review 22 (November 1969): 1-19.

Hannan, Michael T., Nancy Brandon Tuma, and Lyle P. Groeneveld. "Income Maintenance and Marriage: An Overview of Results from the Seattle-Denver Income Maintenance Experiments." Center for Advanced Study in the Behavioral Sciences, Stanford University, Stanford, Calif., January 25, 1978. Mimeographed.

Harrington, Michael. The Other America: Poverty in the United States. New York: Macmillan, 1962.

Hausman. Leonard J. "Cumulative Tax Rates in Alternative Income Maintenance Systems." In Integrating Income Maintenance Programs, edited by Irene Lurie, pp. 39-77. New York: Academic Press, 1975.

Hendricks, Gary, and James R. Storey. "Disincentives for Continued Work by Older Americans: Final Report." Working Paper 1394-03. Washington, D.C.: Urban Institute, July 1980.

Henle, Peter. "Recent Trends in Retirement Benefits Related to Earnings." Monthly Labor Review 95 (June 1972): 12-20.

____. "Exploring the Distribution of Earned Income." Monthly Labor Review 95 (December 1972): 16-27.

Hirshchleifer, Jack. Price Theory and Applications. Englewood Cliffs, N.J.: Prentice-Hall, 1976.

Hoagland, G. William. "The Effectiveness of Current Transfer Programs in Reducing Poverty." Paper presented at Middlebury College Conference on Economic Issues, April 19, 1980, Middlebury, Vt. Mimeographed.

Horlick, Max. "National Expenditures on Social Security in Selected Countries." Research and Statistics Note no. 29-1974. U.S. Department of Health, Education, and Welfare, Social Security Administration, Office of Research and Statistics. Washington, D.C.: Social Security Administration, Office of Research and Statistics, October 18, 1974.

Hunter, Robert. Poverty. New York: Macmillan, 1909.

Johnson, E. A. J., and Herman E. Krooss. The American Economy: Its Origins, Development, and Transformation. Englewood Cliffs, N.J.: Prentice-Hall, 1960.

Kershaw, Joseph A. Government Against Poverty. Washington, D.C.: Brookings Institution, 1970.

Keynes, John Maynard. General Theory of Employment, Interest and Money. New York: Macmillan, 1973.

Klarman, Herbert E. Economics of Health. New York: Columbia University Press, 1970.

Klodrubetz, Alfred W. "Two Decades of Employee-Benefit Plans, 1950-70: A Review." Social Security Bulletin 35 (April 1972): 10-22.

Lampman, Robert J. The Share of Top Wealth Holders in National Wealth. Princeton, N.J.: Princeton University Press, 1962.

Lampman, Robert J., and Christopher Green. "Schemes for Transferring Income to the Poor." Industrial Relations 6 (February 1967): 122-37.

Lampman, Robert J., and Maurice MacDonald. "Underlying Concepts and Institutions." Paper presented to the Conference on Social Security and the Changing Roles of Women. Cosponsored by the Institute for Research on Poverty and Women's Studies Research Center, University of Wisconsin, April 11-12, 1980.

____. "Transfer and Redistribution as Social Process." In Social Security in International Perspective, edited by Shirley Jenkins, pp. 29-54. New York: Columbia University Press, 1969.

____. Ends and Means of Reducing Income Poverty. Chicago: Markham, 1971.

____. "What Does It Do for the Poor? A New Test for National Policy." The Public Interest 34 (Winter 1974): 66-82.

____. "Employment Versus Income Maintenance." In Jobs for Americans, edited by Eli Ginzberg, pp. 163-83. Englewood Cliffs, N.J.: Prentice-Hall, 1976.

Land, Hilary, and Roy Parker. "United Kingdom." In Family Poverty: Government and Families in Fourteen Countries, edited by Sheila B. Kamerman and Alfred J. Kahn, pp. 331-66. New York: Columbia University Press, 1978.

Lando, Mordechai E. "The Effect of Unemployment on Applications for Disability Insurance." In 1974 Business and Economic Section Proceedings of the American Statistical Association, pp. 438-42. Washington, D.C.: American Statistical Association, 1975.

Lando, Mordechai E., Malcolm B. Coate, and Ruth Kraus. "Disability Benefit Applications and the Economy." Social Security Bulletin 42 (October 1979): 3-17.

Lane, Robert E. Political Ideology: Why the American Common Man Believes What He Does. New York: Free Press, 1962.

Lee, Susan. "Reagan's Economics by a Supply-Side Insider." Wall Street Journal, June 5, 1981.

Lerman, Robert I. "JOIN: A Jobs and Income Program for American Families." In Public Employment and Wage Subsidies. Studies in Public Welfare, Paper no. 19. U.S. Congress, Joint Economic Committee, Subcommittee on Fiscal Policy, 93rd. Congr., 2nd Sess., pp. 3-67. Washington, D.C.: U.S. Government Printing Office, 1974.

Levey, Frank. "The Labor Supply of Female Household Heads, or AFDC Work Incentives Don't Work Too Well." Journal of Human Resources 14 (Winter 1979): 76-97.

Levitan, Sar A. The Great Society's Poor Law. Baltimore: Johns Hopkins University Press, 1969.

Lindsey, Duncan, and Martha N. Ozawa. "Schizophrenia and SSI: Implications and Problems." Social Work 24 (March 1979): 120-26.

MaCamy, James L. "Responsiveness Versus Efficiency in Public Services." Annals of the American Academy of Political and Social Science 292 (March 1954): 30-38.

MacDonald, Maurice. Food Stamps and Income Maintenance. New York: Academic Press, 1977.

____. "Food Stamps: An Analytical History." Social Service Review 51 (December 1977): 642-58.

McMillan, Alma W., and Ann Kallman Bixby. "Social Welfare Expenditures, Fiscal Year 1978." Social Security Bulletin 43 (May 1980): 3-17.

Malthus, Thomas Robert. An Essay on the Principle of Population. London: Ward, Lock, 1890.

Marmor, Theodore R., and Martin Rein. "Reforming 'the Welfare Mess': The Fate of the Family Assistance Plan, 1969-72." In Policy and Politics in America: Six Case Studies, edited by Allen P. Sindler, pp. 3-28. New York: Little, Brown, 1973.

Mencher, Samuel. "Newburgh: The Recurrent Crisis of Public Assistance." Social Work 7 (January 1962): 3-11.

Meriam, Lewis. Relief and Social Security. Washington, D.C.: Brookings Institution, 1946.

Mill, John Stuart. Principles of Political Economy. New York: D. Appleton, 1887.

Millis, Harry A., and Royal E. Montgomery. Labor's Progress and Basic Problems. New York: McGraw-Hill, 1938.

Moneypenny, William Flavelle. The Life of Benjamin Disraeli, Earl of Beaconsfield. Vol. I. New York: Macmillan, 1910.

Moon, Marilyn. The Measurement of Economic Welfare: Its Application to the Aged Poor. New York: Academic Press, 1977.

Mueller, Eva. "Public Attitudes Toward Fiscal Programs." Quarterly Journal of Economics 77 (May 1963): 210-35.

Munnell, Alicia H. The Future of Social Security. Washington, D.C.: Brookings Institution, 1977.

Munts, Raymond, and Irwin Garfinkel. The Work Disincentive Effects of Unemployment Insurance. Kalamazoo, Mich.: W.E. Upjohn Institute for Employment Research, 1974.

Myers, Robert J. Social Security. Homewood, Ill.: Irwin, 1981 (second edition).

Nichols, Orlo R., and Richard G. Shcreitmueller. "Some Comparisons of the Value of a Worker's Social Security Taxes and Benefits." Actuarial Note no. 95. Washington, D.C.: U.S. Department of Health, Education, and Welfare, Social Security Administration, April, 1978.

Okun, Arthur M. Equality and Efficiency: The Big Tradeoff. Washington, D.C.: Brookings Institution, 1975.

Ornati, Oscar. Poverty Amid Affluence. New York: Twentieth Century Fund, 1966.

Orshansky, Mollie. "Counting the Poor: Another Look at the Poverty Profile." Social Security Bulletin 28 (January 1965): 3-29.

_____, et al. "Measuring Poverty: A Debate." Public Welfare 36 (Spring 1978): 46-55.

Ozawa, Martha N. "Four More Years of Welfare Nightmare?" Public Welfare 31 (Spring 1973): 6-11.

_____. "Individual Equity Versus Social Adequacy in Federal Old-Age Insurance." Social Service Review 48 (March 1974): 24-38.

_____. "SSI: Progress or Retreat." Public Welfare 32 (Spring 1974): 33-40.

_____. "Income Redistribution and Social Security." Social Service Review 50 (June 1976): 209-23.

_____. "Social Insurance and Redistribution." In Jubilee for Our Times: A Practical Program for Income Equality, edited by Alvin L. Schorr, PP. 123-77. New York: Columbia University Press, 1977.

_____. "Anatomy of President Carter's Welfare Reform Proposal." Social Casework 58 (December 1977): 615-20.

_____. "An Exploration into States' Commitment to AFDC." Journal of Social Service Research 1 (Spring 1978): 245-59.

_____. "Impact of SSI on the Aged and Disabled Poor." Social Work Research and Abstracts 14 (Fall 1978): 3-10.

_____. "Income Maintenance Programs." In Handbook of the Social Services, edited by Neil Gilbert and Harry Specht, pp. 353-79. Englewood Cliffs, N.J.: Prentice-Hall, 1981.

_____. "Who Seeks SSI? An Empirical Study of the Determinants of Seeking SSI Payments Among the Low-Income Elderly." Final Report to the Administration on Aging. St. Louis, Washington University, 1981. Mimeographed.

_____. "Work and Social Policy." In Work, Workers and Work Organizations: A View from Social Work, edited by Sheila H. Akabas and Paul A. Kurzman, pp. 32-60. Englewood Cliffs, N.J.: Prentice-Hall, 1981.

_____. "SSI Recipients in Mississippi and California: A Comparative Study," Journal of Social Service Research (forthcoming).

____. "Who Receives Subsidies Through Social Security, and How Much?" Social Work (forthcoming).

Ozawa, Martha N., and Duncan Lindsey. "Is SSI Too Supportive of the Mentally Ill?" Public Welfare 35 (Fall 1977): 48-52.

Paglin, Morton. "The Measurement and Trend of Inequality: A Basic Revision." American Economic Review 65 (September 1975): 598-609.

____. Poverty and Transfers In-Kind. Stanford, Calif.: Stanford University, Hoover Institution Press, 1980.

Pareto, Vilfredo. Cours d'economie politique professé a l'Université de Lausanne. Lausanne: I. Rouge, 1896.

Patton, Carl V. "The Politics of Social Security." In The Crisis in Social Security, edited by Michael J. Boskin, pp. 147-71. San Francisco: Institute for Contemporary Studies, 1977.

Pechman, Joseph A., Henry J. Aaron, and Michael K. Taussig. Social Security: Perspectives for Reform. Washington, D.C.: Brookings Institution, 1968.

Pigou, A. C. Wealth and Welfare. London: Macmillan, 1912.

Plotnick, Robert D., and Felicity Skidmore. Progress Against Poverty: A Review of the 1964-1974 Decade. New York: Academic Press, 1975.

Polanyi, Karl. The Great Transformation. New York: Farrar & Rinehart, 1944.

Quinn, Joseph F. "The Early Retirement Decision: Evidence from the 1969 Retirement History." Staff Paper no. 29. Washington, D.C.: Social Security Administration, Office of Research and Statistics, 1978.

Rainwater, Lee. "Poverty, Living Standards, and Family Well-Being." In The Family, Poverty, and Welfare Programs: Household Patterns and Government Policies. Welfare Paper no. 12 (Part II). U.S. Congress, Joint Economic Committee, Subcommittee on Fiscal Policy, 93rd Congr., 1st Sess., pp. 207-54. Washington, D.C.: U.S. Government Printing Office, 1973.

____. "Work, Well-Being, and Family Life." In Work and the Quality of Life: Resource Papers for Work in America, edited by James O'Toole, pp. 361-99. Cambridge, Mass.: MIT Press, 1974.

____. "Stigma in Income-Tested Programs." Paper delivered at the Conference on Universal Versus Income-Tested Program, Institute for Research on Poverty, University of Wisconsin, March 15-16, 1979, Madison.

Rasle, L. "Family Allowances and Decline of Birth-Rate." Population 32 (July-October 1977): 1101-15.

Rathbone, Eleanor. Family Allowances. London: Allen & Unwin, 1949.

Rein, Martin. "Problem in the Definition of Measurement of Poverty." In The Concept of Poverty, edited by Peter Townsend, pp. 46-63. London: Heineman Educational Books, 1970.

Reno, Virginia. "Retirement Patterns of Men." In Reaching Retirement Age: Findings from a Survey of Newly Entitled Workers, 1968-70. Research Report no. 47. U.S. Department of Health, Education, and Welfare, Social Security Administration, pp. 31-40. Washington, D.C.: U.S. Government Printing Office, 1976.

Reno, Virginia, and Carl Zuckert. "Income of New Beneficiaries by Size of Social Security Benefit." In Reaching Retirement Age: Findings from a Survey of Newly Entitled Workers, 1968-70. Research Report no. 47. U.S. Department of Health, Education, and Welfare, Social Security Administration, pp. 121-44. Washington, D.C.: U.S. Government Printing Office, 1976.

Rhys-Williams, Juliet. Something to Look Forward To. London: MacDonald, 1943.

____. A New Look at Britain's Economic Policy. Baltimore: Penguin, 1965.

Rivlin, Alice M. "Income Distribution—Can Economists Help?" American Economic Review 65 (May 1967): 1-15.

Robertson, A. Haeworth. "Financial Status of Social Security Program After the Social Security Amendments of 1977." Social Security Bulletin 41 (March 1978): 3-20.

Rowntree, B. Seeborhm. Poverty: A Study of Town Life. London: Macmillan, 1903.

Sander, Kenneth G. "The Retirement Test: Its Effect on Older Workers' Earnings." Social Security Bulletin 31 (June 1968): 3-6.

Saville, Lloyd. "Flexible Retirement." In Employment, Income, and Retirement Problems of the Aged, edited by Juanita M. Kreps, pp. 140-77. Durham, N.C.: Duke University Press, 1963.

Schiltz, Michael E. Public Attitudes Toward Social Security, 1932-65. Research Report no. 33. Social Security Administration, Office of Research and Statistics. Washington, D.C.: U.S. Government Printing Office, 1969.

Schorr, Alvin L. Poor Kids. New York: Basic Books, 1966.

_____. "Against Negative Income Tax." Public Interest 5 (Fall 1966): 110-19.

Schulz, James H. Providing Adequate Retirement Income: Pension Reform in the United States and Abroad. Hanover, N.H.: University Press of New England, 1974.

Schweinitz, Karl de. England's Road to Social Security. New York: A. S. Barnes, 1943.

Smeeding, Timothy. "The Antipoverty Effectiveness of In-Kind Transfers." Journal of Human Resources 12 (Summer 1977): 360-78.

_____. "On the Distribution of Net Income: Comment." Southern Economic Journal 45 (January 1979): 932-44.

_____. "The Anti-Poverty Effect of In-Kind Transfers: 'A Good Idea' Gone Too Far?" Policy Studies Journal (forthcoming).

Smith, Adam. An Inquiry into the Nature and Causes of the Wealth of Nations. London: W. Strahan and T. Cadell, 1776.

Smolensky, Eugene, et al. "In-Kind Transfers and the Size Distribution of Income." In Improving Measures of Economic Well-Being, edited by Marilyn Moon and Eugene Smolensky, pp. 131-53. New York: Academic Press, 1977.

Spencer, Herbert. Social Statistics: Abridged and Revised Together with the Man Versus the State. New York: D. Appleton, 1892.

Spengler, Joseph J., and Juanita M. Kreps. "Equity and Social Credit for the Retired." In Employment, Income, and Retirement Problems of the Aged, edited by Juanita M. Kreps, pp. 198-229. Durham, N.C.: Duke University Press, 1963.

Tawney, R. H. Equality. London: Allen & Unwin, 1964.

Thorsson, Inga. "Children's Allowances in Sweden." In Children's Allowances and the Economic Welfare of Children, edited by Eveline M. Burns, pp. 115-20. New York: Citizens' Committee for Children of New York City, 1968.

Thurow, Lester. "Toward a Definition of Economic Justice." Public Interest 31 (Spring 1973): 56-80.

_____. "The Political Economy of Income Redistribution Policies." Annals of the American Academy of Political and Social Science 409 (September 1973): 146-55.

Titmuss, Richard M. Commitment to Welfare. London: Allen & Unwin, 1968.

Tobin, James. "The Case for an Income Guarantee." Public Interest 4 (Summer 1966): 31-41.

U.S., Bureau of the Census. Statistical Abstract of the United States: 1979. Washington, D.C.: U.S. Government Printing Office, 1979.

_____. Characteristics of the Population Below the Poverty Level: 1978. Current Population Reports, Series P-60, No. 124. Washington, D.C.: U.S. Government Printing Office, 1980.

U.S., Congress, Advisory Council on Social Security. Reports of the Quadrennial Advisory Council on Social Security. 94th Congr., 1st Sess. Washington, D.C.: U.S. Government Printing Office, 1975.

_____. Social Security Financing and Benefits: Reports of the 1979 Advisory Council on Social Security. Washington, D.C.: U.S. Government Printing Office, 1980.

U.S., Congress, Congressional Budget Office. Poverty Status of

Families Under Alternative Definitions of Income. Washington, D.C.: U.S. Government Printing Office, 1977.

U.S., Congress, Joint Economic Committee, Subcommittee on Fiscal Policy. Handbook of Public Income Transfer Programs. 92nd Congr., 2nd Sess., Studies in Public Welfare, Paper no. 2. Washington, D.C.: U.S. Government Printing Office, 1972.

U.S., Congress, National Commission on Social Security. Social Security in America's Future. Washington, D.C.: U.S. Government Printing Office, 1981.

U.S., Department of Commerce, Bureau of Labor Statistics. Consumer Expenditures and Income. Supplement 3, Part A, to BLS Report no. 237-38. Washington, D.C.: U.S. Government Printing Office, 1964.

U.S., Department of Health, Education, and Welfare. Estimated Employability for Recipients of Public Assistance Money Payments, July 1968. Washington, D.C.: U.S. Government Printing Office, 1969.

_____. Social Security and the Changing Roles of Men and Women. Washington, D.C.: U.S. Department of Health, Education, and Welfare, 1979.

_____. Office of the Assistant Secretary for Planning and Evaluation. "General Approaches to Welfare Reform." Discussion Paper. February 12, 1977. Mimeographed.

_____. Social and Rehabilitation Service, Assistance Payments Administration. Characteristics of State Plans for Aid to Families with Dependent Children. 1974 ed. Washington, D.C.: U.S. Government Printing Office, 1974.

_____. Social Security Administration. Social Security Programs in the United States: 1973. Washington, D.C.: U.S. Government Printing Office, 1973.

_____. Social Security Administration. "Supplemental Security Income: The Aged Eligible." Social Security Bulletin 36 (July 1973): 31-35.

_____. Social Security Administration. Social Security Bulletin:

Annual Statistical Supplement, 1977-1979. Washington, D.C.: Social Security Administration, 1980.

U.S., Department of Health and Human Services, Social Security Administration, Office of Research and Statistics. Monthly Benefit Statistics. No. 10. Washington, D.C.: Social Security Administration, November 6, 1981.

_____. Social Security Administration, Office of Research and Statistics. AFDC Standards for Basic Needs, July 1980. Washington, D.C.: Social Security Administration, Office of Research and Statistics, March 1981.

Vadakin, James C. Family Allowances. Oxford, Ohio: University of Miami Press, 1958.

Warlick, Jennifer N. "The Relationship of the Supplemental Security Income Program and Living Arrangements of the Low-Income Elderly." Paper presented to the National Conference on Social Welfare, May 15, 1979, Philadelphia.

Warlick, Jennifer N., David Berry, and Irwin Garfinkel. "The Double Decker Alternative for Eliminating Dependency Under Social Security." Paper presented to the Conference of Social Security and the Changing Roles of Women. Cosponsored by the Institute for Research on Poverty and the Women's Studies Research Center, University of Wisconsin, April 11-12, 1980, Madison.

Warner, Amos Criswold, Stuart A. Queen, and Earnest Bouldin Harper. American Charities and Social Work. New York: Thomas Y. Crowell, 1930.

Webb, Mrs. Sidney, and B. L. Hutchings. Socialism and National Minimum. London: A. C. Fifield, 1909.

Webb, Sidney, and Beatrice Webb. The Prevention of Destitution. New York: Longmans, Green, 1916.

_____. The History of Trade Unionism. New York: Longmans, Green, 1920.

Weisbrod, Burton A., and W. Lee Hansen. "An Income—Net Worth Approach to Measuring Economic Welfare." In Improving Measures of Economic Well-Being, edited by Marilyn Moon and Eugene Smolensky, pp. 34-50. New York: Academic Press, 1977.

Wholenberg, Ernest H. "A Regional Approach to Public Attitudes and Public Assistance." Social Service Review 50 (September 1967): 491-505.

Wilensky, Harold L. The Welfare State and Equality: Structural and Ideological Roots of Public Expenditures. Berkeley: University of California Press, 1975.

Willard, Joseph W. "Family Allowances in Canada." International Labor Review 75 (March 1957): 207-29.

Zeckhauser, Richard J., and W. Kip Viscusi. "The Role of Social Security in Income Maintenance." In The Crisis in Social Security, edited by Michael J. Boskin, pp. 41-64. San Francisco: Institute for Contemporary Studies, 1977.

Zimbalist, Sidney E. "Recent British and American Poverty Trends: Conceptual and Policy Contrasts." Social Service Review 51 (September 1977): 419-33.

INDEX

275

Uruguay, children's allowances based on age, 215

Veblen, Thorstein, 10
Vermont, dependent benefits in, 196
Veterans Administration, Department of Veterans Benefits of, 27, 35
Veterans' compensation programs, 27-28

Wages and family needs, gap between, 129-130
Ways and Means, House Committee on, 101
War on poverty, 18, 64, 67, 96
WC. See Worker's compensation
Wealth of Nations, The, 10
Webb, Beatrice, 216
Webb, Sidney, 216
Weisbrod, Burton, 55
Welfare
  Aid to Families with Dependent Children (AFDC), 30-32
  food stamps, 37-38
  income and asset-testing for, 37
  work requirement for, 37-38
  general assistance, 34-35
  housing assistance, 38
  eligibility for, 38
  Medicaid, 35-37
  public's stereotyped attitudes toward, 120
  Supplemental Security Income (SSI), 32-34
  veterans' pensions, 35
Welfare mess, development of, 96-100

Welfare programs
  and classic liberalism, 5
  disincentive effect of, 100
  income-tested, 16
  residual, 16
  results of including working poor families, 116-119
  three basic features of, 108
Welfare reform
  benefit-loss rates, cumulative, 110-111
  Carter's attempt at, 105-107
  income provision, 106-107
  major features of, 105-106
  work requirements, 107
  equity and, 114-119
  horizontal, 114
  vertical, 114
  past attempts at, 127-130
  welfare in context, 127-129
  policy issues in, 96-134
  problems in, 107-126
  program costs and target efficiency, concern for, 112-113
  SSI and social security, linkage between, 123-126
  stigma and, 119-123
  work incentive, 108-110
Welfare and Social Insurance Programs, distinguishing between, 39-40
Wheeler vs. Montgomery (1969), 98
Widow(er)s, recommendations about, 184
Wilensky, Harold, 19
Wiley, George, 102
Williams, John J., 102-103
WIN. See Work Incentive program
Wohlenberg, Ernest, 121
Women
  alternative government plans on social security and, 160-175
  work at home as paid work, 168

ABOUT THE AUTHOR

Born in Ashikaga City, Japan, Martha N. Ozawa obtained a B.A. in Economics from Aoyama Gakuin University in Tokyo in 1956, and her M.S.S.W. and Ph.D. in Social Welfare from the University of Wisconsin in 1956 and 1969, respectively.

Past research and writings were concentrated in welfare, social security, and other governmental programs. In recent years, though, she has expanded her interest into industrial social services.

Dr. Ozawa has published numerous articles in social work journals, including "Development of Social Services in Industry: Why and How?" Social Work (November 1980); "An Analysis of HEW's Proposals on Social Security," Social Service Review (March 1980); "Distribution of Social Service Expenditures: A Study," Social Work Research and Abstracts (Spring 1980); and "The Earnings Test in Social Security," Social Welfare Forum, 1978 (New York: Columbia University Press, 1979).

Her contributions toward books include "Work and Social Policy," in Sheila H. Akabas and Paul A. Kurzman, eds., Work, Workers and Work Organizations: A View from Social Work (Englewood Cliffs, N.J.: Prentice-Hall, expected to come out in print in 1981); "Income Maintenance Programs," in Neil Gilbert and Harry Specht, eds., Handbook of the Social Services (Englewood Cliffs, N.J.: Prentice-Hall, 1981); and "Social Insurance and Redistribution," in Alvin L. Schorr, ed., Jubilee for Our Times (New York: Columbia University Press, 1977).

Before joining the faculty of George Warren Brown School of Social Work, Washington University, St. Louis, in 1976, she taught for 4 years at Portland State University School of Social Work and for 3 years conducted research on social security at the Center for Studies in Income Maintenance Policy, New York University.

Dr. Ozawa is mentioned in: Who's Who of American Women, American Men and Women of Science, The World Who's Who of Women in Education, and International Who's Who in Education.